PRAEGER LIBRARY OF U.S. GOVERNMENT DEPARTMENTS
AND AGENCIES

The Library of Congress

The Library of Congress

Charles A. Goodrum

PRAEGER PUBLISHERS
New York • Washington

Published in the United States of America in 1974
by Praeger Publishers, Inc.
111 Fourth Avenue, New York, N.Y. 10003

Library of Congress Cataloging in Publication Data

Goodrum, Charles A
  The Library of Congress.

  (Praeger library of U.S. Government departments and agencies, no. 38)
  Bibliography: p. 285.
  1. United States.   Library of Congress.
Z733.U6G66   027.573   72–189909

This book is No. 38 in the series
Praeger Library of U.S. Government Departments and Agencies

Printed in the United States of America

To
LESTER S. JAYSON,
respected colleague and friend

Preface

It is only fair to clarify the viewpoint from which this book was written, right at the outset. Is it the official position of Library of Congress management? Not in the least. Has it been "approved" by the Librarian's Office? No.

The book was built on interviews with the Library's middle managers, on discussions with working specialists in the various divisions, on conversations with and questionnaires sent to out-of-Library users, and from my own observations through almost twenty-five years in the Library's Congressional Research Service. After the text was completed, it was read by appropriate people in each department for factual content and ultimately by the staff in the Librarian's Office for their comment. At no point was there pressure to change text or conclusions—although there were plenty of good-natured suggestions on details, and nearly everyone urged a fuller description of his own particular specialty!

There are several areas where the emphasis or prognosis differs from the official Library position on the subject. After considering the frequently conflicting perceptions of an issue as seen at the division, department, and Librarian levels, I tried to select the one that appeared most convincing to *me*. The result should not be held against top management, and no endorsement should be assumed.

Although I endeavored to maintain an Olympian detachment throughout, it is only fair to admit that I have been trained as a *reference* librarian (we will find there are cataloging librarians, electronic data librarians, legal librarians, acquisition librarians, et cetera), and I was at least granted a degree in American history and political science. I have thus viewed the Library from the legislative reference corner for nearly a quarter of a century, and, while I am convinced the volume is totally objective and without prejudice (!), it seems only just to "let the record show ..."

Item: Whenever a statistic is cited in the book and tied to a specific year (as, "in 1971, 2,372,000 pieces were discarded and reduced to pulp"), the date will always refer to a government fiscal year. The fiscal year runs from July to June, and the number refers to the calendar year in which the June falls.

I want to thank the dozens of people who patiently explained their particular specialty to me—and who still speak to me in the halls after having seen a service that could justify a whole book in itself reduced to three paragraphs. My special thanks to John Y. Cole of the Reference Department for his chronology and reading list printed in the appendix. And let me assure my Kansas in-laws that nothing in this volume was prepared on government time. Annual leave was taken for all interviews, and the text was written at home.

I hope you find the great, gray institution even a fraction as intriguing as I do.

CHARLES A. GOODRUM

Alexandria, Virginia
October, 1973

Contents

A section of photographs follows page 86.

The Library of Congress

Introduction

Without really trying, the Library of Congress manages to project two quite different images of itself. In the eyes of the scholar, the foreign visitor, and the taxpayer, it is an almost incredible collection of books. From this picture comes the "Treasure House of the World's Knowledge," which attaches itself to the Library like fell goes with swoop and damn with Yankee. But the cliché is quite appropriate. The Library of Congress is almost certainly the largest library in the world, with over 64 million pieces on its shelves and in its vaults. (We have to say "almost certainly" since we've never been able to get a firm figure for the Lenin State Library in Moscow. The Bibliothèque Nationale in Paris reports 13 million pieces of all kinds, and the British Museum notes 7 million books and manuscripts—to give you some idea of the scale we're dealing with here. Harvard is runner-up in the U.S. with some 8.5 million volumes.)

The Library of Congress's collections are incredibly diverse. It has 16 million books, two-thirds of which are in foreign languages. It has 30 million manuscripts revealing the most historic and creative thoughts of our political and cultural leaders. It has a quarter of a million phonograph records, a hundred thousand reels of motion pictures, and endless cases of maps, photographs, volumes in Braille, rolls of microfilm, papyri, magnetic tape, and every other form of preserved thought.

But this Treasure House image is rarely the one held by the Library's staff or by the people who deal with it every day. To the 4,000 people it employs and the million-plus who use it each year, its image is one of action ... programs ... demand and response. They see the Congressional Research Service answering 1,500 inquiries a day from the senators and congressmen across the street. They see folk music being recorded in the sound laboratories, talking book cassettes being prepared for the blind, a mail-order house producing computer tapes and printed cards for other libraries to the extent of $7 million cash receipts each year. Their picture is of staff selecting illustrations for publishers, searching newsreels for television documentaries, identifying and translating court cases from iron curtain countries to be used as precedents at the next international conference.

In short, up close, the Library of Congress is people doing things. You can make a case that picturing it as a mass of books is no more appropriate than picturing a life insurance company as typewriters and filing cabinets or a newspaper as telephones and delivery trucks. The books are simply the tools with which the Library does its job. It is what is in the books that justifies the Library, and it is the securing of their contents, organizing them so they can be found, and then providing the answers to the specialists who need them that is the sole reason for its being.

The Library, which might be expected to serve as a haven for calm and reflective scholarship, finds itself at ground zero of the information explosion. As we will see, it has indeed, almost by accident, managed to accumulate almost all of man's recorded knowledge in one place, and it is thus under harsh pressure from a wide range of audiences to make this information available. Gross volume coupled with increasing—and often conflicting—demands are threatening to wrench the Library from its traditional course. It cannot stand still, but how it is to satisfy these demands and yet move forward is far from clear.

We will examine this unlikely institution in four steps. First, there will be a short statement of how it came to be what it is today, and then an examination of what its job is and how it is organized to do that job. Next, we will look at the various audiences and clienteles it serves, what they demand of it, and how well it is satisfying these demands. Finally, we will try to describe what its really fundamental problems are and what legitimate choices it has available to solve them.

I

The History Through Spofford

We begin our look at what the Library of Congress is today with a hasty—almost headlong—look at what it has been. The Library's major strengths and its biggest troubles are mostly the result of decisions made generations ago—decisions, as we shall see, which were about equally divided between careful thought and casual actions. Some were recognized at the time as affecting the institution for decades to come, while others slipped through unnoticed and have since cost taxpayers and scholars vast quantities of money and man-hours.

What started it all? It seems to have been the direct product of the work habits of the Founding Fathers. They were book-oriented from the beginning. Most were lawyers with their profession's traditional respect for the printed word in codes and precedents, and most of the few who were not were philosophers and pamphleteers, nourished on the literature of the European Enlightenment. For them, thinking meant, first, to read and then, as a rule, to write more themselves!

When the delegates convened the Continental Congress in Philadelphia in 1774, almost their first act was to secure borrowing privileges from the Library Company of Philadelphia. This book collection was already one of the strongest thus far assembled in the colonies, and with rare good fortune it was housed at the other end of Carpenters' Hall, where the delegates were to meet. The Library Company graciously resolved "to furnish the Gentlemen ... with the use of such Books as they may have occasion for during their sitting, taking a Receipt for them."

Thirteen years and a revolution later, when many of the same delegates met again in that incredible summer of 1787, they again relied on the Library Company's collection, and in 1789 with the Constitution written and passed and the new government formed, they reassembled as the National Legislature in New York's City Hall—which, conveniently, held four thousand volumes of the New York Society Library, thoughtfully chartered by George III sometime before. The legislators promptly secured access to these volumes, but there followed a trivial argument which came to absolutely nothing at the time but which presaged endless debates on the same subject ever since.

It was precipitated by Elbridge Gerry, distinguished signer of the Declaration of Independence and delegate to the Constitutional Convention. On August 16, 1789, he moved "that a committee be appointed to report a catalogue of books necessary for the use of Congress, with an estimate of the expense, and the best mode of procuring them." Acting with precedential dispatch, eight months later such a committee was indeed formed and in only seven weeks delivered itself of a report to the House. After commenting on the difficulty of the delegates being "obliged at every session to transport to the seat of the general government a considerable part of their libraries," and "having due regard to the state of the treasury," it recommended

that a sum not exceeding 1,000 dollars be appropriated in the present session, and that the sum of 500 dollars be hereafter annually appropriated to the purchase of books for a public library, and applied to the purpose by the Vice President, Chief Justice and Secretary of State of the United

States, without confining them to the catalogue reported until in the opinion of Congress, the books provided shall be adequate to the purpose.

Except for the implication that the collection was to be a finite, closed-end set of books once they should be "adequate" (and that they were to be selected by representatives from all three branches of the government), the motion was routine. What is noteworthy is the reception it got: It generated vast apathy on the part of Congress but splendid outrage from the taxpayers. A typical demur is the following from the *Independent Chronicle* of Boston, May 13, 1790:

The late motion respecting the "Library" for Congress is truly novel— could it be supposed that a measure so distant from any thing which can effect the general purposes of government, could be introduced at this important period? ... How absurd to squander away money for a parcel of Books, when every shilling of the Revenue is wanted for supporting our government and paying our debts?

... It is supposed that the Members of Congress are acquainted with history; the laws of nations; and possess such political information as is necessary for the management of the affairs of the government. If they are *not*, we have been unfortunate in our choice.... It is supposed that the members are fully competent for these purposes, without being at the expence of furnishing them with Books for their improvement.

... The people look for *practical politicks*, as they presume the *Theory* is obtained previous to the members taking their seats in Congress.

This was the last anyone ever heard of the committee or its recommendations, but the position of "the people" was to reappear.

By 1791 the government had returned to Philadelphia, and although the Library Company had moved into its own quarters, Congress recovered access to the Company's volumes. In this manner, for nearly twenty years the Founding Fathers managed to keep a broad information base easily accessible, and it was used daily as an integral part of their legislative activities—without having to "squander money" or further distress the treasury.

In 1794, however, the need for some in-house, arm's-reach volumes finally pressed upon them, and the Secretary of State was instructed to purchase copies of Blackstone's *Commentaries*, and Vattel's *Law of Nature and Nations*. Before too long, the House also began to buy, and soon some fifty-odd titles were on the congressional shelves. Without laboring the implications of these early selections, it is still intriguing to read those first order lists and note what Congress thought that it needed to know to govern. They bought laws and precedents as would be expected: Reeves and Wooddeson on English jurisprudence and Chalmer's *Collection of Treaties*. They had some works on elections and Hume's *History of England*. They ordered maps in Morse's *American Geography* (published in England), some science in Dr. Rush's *Yellow Fever* and Varlo's *Husbandry*, and literature in the poems of Robert Burns. And they started the first magazine subscriptions (which have grown to the 150,000 titles now received).

By the Spring of 1800, we come to the formal founding of the Library and the first attempts to decide whose library it was and what kind of a library it was to be. The decisions were forced upon the members of Congress by Hamilton's and Jefferson's compromise, which placed the new capital and District of Columbia-to-be in a marshy area just south of the Great Falls of the Potomac. The time had come to found a permanent seat of government, and funds were appropriated to move the personnel of all three branches from Philadelphia to the Federal City. On April 24, President John Adams signed the transfer bill, the fifth section of which legislated the Library of Congress into being. It called for the purchase of $5,000 worth of books and the "fitting up of a suitable apartment for containing them." The purchase was to be made by the secretary of the Senate and the clerk of the House; the books were to be used by both houses of Congress. A Joint Committee on the Library was established to assist in the selection of volumes and the establishment of rules. Neither the executive branch nor the judiciary was to be given access. It was strictly Congress's library.

There is considerable significance in the contents of this act and one passed shortly after Congress actually moved into the building, because the original concepts of "what the Library of Congress is supposed to be" appear here. This would seem to be a fairly self-evident question, but it is still unresolved and has been preoccupying librarians, patrons, and congressional oversight committees ever since.

The original joint committee appears to have felt it had three choices before it. First, as the committee saw it, the Library could simply be a small collection of working tools to assist the legislators with their legislative duties. This was the kind of collection they had already started—books of the kind to be found in their own law offices back home.

Secondly, the new collection could be a "public library" for the members. The concept of a public library at that time meant a private, usually subscription collection which was available either to the mercantile community in a city, to the social elite, or to a college community. Again, in terms of their experience in the towns from which they came, it would have been quite appropriate to build a broader, more balanced collection for the members of the legislature or even the leaders of the whole government, which would provide cultural and recreational content as well as working books.

Finally, the committee could have decided on a national library that would serve the federal government but also act as a cultural and historical archive for the young country. Several of the European nations had such, and the early leaders of the nation were both proud of the new government's achievements and eager to take on the ornaments of the older, established nations.

The committee opted for the first choice—a simple, functional collection of working tools. This choice was evident in the initial order for books sent off to London in June, 1800, while the legislature was still in Philadelphia. When the order was delivered, carefully filled and shipped in eleven hair trunks, it amounted to 152 titles in 740 volumes. (The trunks, according to the British bookseller, who was conscious of the needs of an underdeveloped country, had been selected because he "judged it best to send trunks instead of boxes, which after their arrival would have been of little or no value." When they arrived, Congress converted them to cash, having instructed the secretary of the Senate "to make sale of the trunks in which the books lately purchased were imported.") The books were strictly a working library. They emphasized law, political science, economics, and history, with a special case tightly packed with rolled maps. The need for maps recurs repeatedly throughout the early years.

Once moved to Washington—with the books housed in an upper room of the new Capitol building—Congress passed a second library law in January of 1802, which has been called a charter of governance for the new library. It called for the appointment of a Librarian to be made "by the President of the United States solely," not by the legislature whose books they were. Possibly because this step had already created a breach in the separation of powers, the President and the Vice-President were granted borrowing privileges, which had originally been limited to members of Congress. The Librarian was to be paid at a rate not to exceed $2 a day, and all monies spent on the Library were to be under the review of a joint committee made up of three members of the Senate and three of the House.

President Thomas Jefferson promptly appointed a close personal friend, one John James Beckley, as the first Librarian of Congress. The new Librarian and the new Joint Committee proceeded to carry out the instructions they had received and in the course of their search for purchase suggestions turned to Jefferson himself.

Jefferson replied in a detailed letter of April 14, 1802, in which he sent them a long list of recommendations "for the Library of Congress in conformity with your ideas that books of entertainment are not within the scope of it, and that books in other languages, where there are no translations of them, are not to be admitted freely." The letter continued:

> I have confined the catalogue to those branches of science which belong to the deliberations of the members as statesmen, and in these have omitted those classical books, ancient and modern, which gentlemen generally have in their private libraries, but which can not properly claim a place in a collection made merely for the purpose of reference.

Jefferson then described the volumes in detail. He listed historical texts, materials on diplomacy, much law and parliamentary practice, and everything he knew of that related to the history of the United States. Significantly, he pictured the Library of Congress at the outset as the depository of the nations's chronology:

> The travels, histories [and] accounts of America previous to the Revolution should be obtained. It is already become all but impossible to make a collection of these things. Standing orders should be lodged with our ministers in Spain, France and England and our Consul at Amsterdam to procure everything within that description which can be hunted up in those countries.

It is interesting to note that through all these early years, all of the books had been purchased from abroad. Not until 1806 was a conscious policy followed to query booksellers in New York, Philadelphia, and Boston before ordering from Europe. During the period, large shipments continued to be purchased in Paris and London, but the first volumes printed in the United States began to appear as gifts from proud congressmen, each book identified as having been published in the congressman's home district.

Thus through Jefferson's Presidency, and then James Madison's, the Library grew steadily if undramatically. Little notice of it was taken outside of Washington, and it was moved from room to room within the Capitol as its quarters were wanted for one purpose after another. Its total collection was approaching 3,000 volumes when John Beckley died in 1807 and Patrick Magruder was appointed clerk of the House and Librarian of Congress.

In the spring of 1813, a major event occurred that had a profound effect on the Library. An American force fought its way into the capital of Upper Canada (then called York, now Toronto) and set fire to the Parliament Buildings. The troops destroyed the archives, burned the parliamentary library, and carried off the plate from the church. On August 24, 1814, British soldiers marched into Washington, and the first thing they did was set fire to the Capitol, promptly destroying the nation's archives and the Library of Congress. Fifteen years of careful labor gone up in smoke, literally. But in one of the classic ironies of the nation's heritage, a small working library, which had scarcely been heard of before, suddenly became a lost national treasure. The press took up the cry, and Congress, supported by an outraged public, set about replacing the volumes on a scale far grander than it had attempted in setting up the original collection.

Congress wanted a library—a good library—and it wanted it fast. There was just such a library available, and the timing for its purchase was sublimely appropriate.

On September 2, 1814, ex-President Jefferson wrote a letter to his friend Harrison Smith, a newspaper publisher in private life and, in public life, Commissioner of the Revenue. Jefferson remarked to Smith that it was going to be exceedingly difficult to replace the congressional library "while the war continues, and intercourse with Europe is attended with so much risk." He described his own collection of "between nine and ten thousand volumes," which he had acquired while living in Europe and subsequently when he was President. The contents, he noted, mainly "related to the duties of those in the high concerns of the nation."

He explained that it had been his intention to give to Congress "first refusal" of his library at its own price on his death, but in view of present difficulties, this might be "the proper moment for its accommodation." He offered to sell the library in annual installments but was ready to make it available at once: "Eighteen or twenty wagons could place it in Washington in a single trip of a fortnight."

He appended a detailed catalog of its contents and declared, "I do not know that it contains any branch of science which Congress would wish to exclude from their collection; there is, in fact, no subject to which a Member of Congress may not have occasion to refer."

Commissioner Smith quickly brought the offer to Congress, where the joint committee promptly recommended its acceptance. The collection was counted and found to contain 6,487 volumes. The appraisers allocated $3.00 apiece for the common-sized books, $1.00 for the very small ones, and $10.00 for the full-scale folios. The total came to $23,950, and the Senate promptly passed a bill to buy the collection. But the House balked. The bill's supporters pointed out what an appropriate, economic, almost providential solution was available to them to replace the entire library in one sweep. The critics objected to "the cost of the purchase, the nature of the selection, embracing too many works in foreign languages, some of too philosophical character, and some otherwise objectionable." Note was taken of "books of an atheistical, irreligious, and immoral tendency."

The final vote was very close. The library was acquired by the narrow margin of ten votes, and the roll call went straight by party. Federalist New England was against it (the roll call included a nay from Representative Daniel Webster); the Middle Atlantic was for it by two votes; the West, by eight; and the South produced the rest of the votes needed for passage.

The books arrived at the capital in long pine boxes, which Jefferson had designed as tiered bookcases for his study back at Monticello. When the face-boards were pried off and the shelves restacked, the Library of Congress was a reality again—but it was a very different library from the one that had burned the previous summer.

Suddenly the volumes had changed from crisp, factual reference works to a broad-ranging collection reflecting the interests of one of the leading humanists of the age—philosopher, historian, and practical politician. The Librarian of Congress, fully supported by the joint committee and by Congress itself, set out to build on the foundation so skillfully set, and from this point on the collections of the Library have grown in the most comprehensive frame of reference.

Mr. Jefferson makes one more impact on the ultimate personality of the Library, and then he and his books merge into the helical stream of the institution. He had organized his collection around a rather philosophical division of the world's knowledge devised by Sir Francis Bacon. Bacon had identified three kinds of science: Memory, Reason, and Imagination. Jefferson developed these three into forty-four subject divisions and arranged his books within these clusters. The Librarian refined the forty-four somewhat, locked them into a printed book catalog, and froze the Library of Congress's classification scheme for a hundred years. As late as Theodore Roosevelt's time, the Library's catalogers were dutifully sorting hundreds of thousands of volumes into the same forty-four compartments in which the earliest titles had sat on the shelves at Monticello.

From 1815 we can move fairly quickly through fifty years to

the close of the Civil War. We are searching here only for those precedents that explain the Library of Congress as we find it today, and through these antebellum decades only a half-dozen events need be noted for our purpose.

Librarian of Congress Patrick Magruder overstayed his welcome, and he was urged to resign with the coming of Jefferson's books. President Madison then appointed George Watterston, a "local man of letters," to take his place. Three things happened to Mr. Watterston that interest us.

First, in 1816 the use of the Library was expanded to the Attorney General of the United States, the Justices of the Supreme Court, and the members of the diplomatic corps.

Second, just before Christmas in 1825, Watterston suffered a traumatic night when a menacing glow was observed in the windows of the Library in the Capitol. The guards broke down the door and sounded the alarm, and the occupants of the neighborhood rooming houses rushed in to extinguish the blaze. (Daniel Webster carried a bucket in the melee and made amends for his earlier vote against the purchase of Jefferson's library.) The fire was quickly controlled and only a few sets of duplicate government documents were lost, but it was a close call and should have made the custodians more careful than it did.

Finally, in terms of the long view, Watterston's most telling contribution to his post was the manner of his leaving it. He was fired. President Andrew Jackson was inaugurated on March 4, 1829, and Watterston was relieved on May 28. His sin had been too overt a commitment to the Whig Party. He had been active in political affairs and was known to be a supporter of Henry Clay, but most of all, as David Mearns, the leading historian of today's institution, has gracefully put it, "He had been Librarian of one side of the aisle rather than Librarian of Congress." His experience was not lost on his successors, and without exception since that time the Librarians of Congress have been as dispassionate and detached in their political careers as the speaker of the House of Commons.

Jackson appointed John Silva Meehan to the position, and he proceeded to hold it for thirty-two years. His contributions were unspectacular, but he has come down to us as a conscientious, able administrator.

Like his predecessor, Meehan, in one of his first acts, liberalized access to the collections: Under him, ex-Presidents, the secretaries of State, Treasury, War, and Navy, and the Postmaster General were permitted to use the books. The real point of interest here is in how literally the rules were applied. Only these half-dozen individuals were to be admitted to the Library—not their staffs or representatives of their departments. It was still a legislative library, not an executive one (much less a public or national library).

However, in 1832 Congress passed a law that began to open the collections, genuinely, for the first time. The statute instructed the Librarian to remove all the law books from his shelves and set them apart as an independent law library to be housed in a "nearby apartment." The Justices of the Supreme Court were to recommend continuing purchases to the Librarian, who was to buy the books with congressional funds, but the new Law Library was to be open to the use of the Justices "and the attorneys and counsellors, during the sittings of the said Court." Members of the two houses were still to have unrestricted access, but the "congressional" library was broadening its statutory clientele.

By 1836, the Library of Congress had grown to 24,000 volumes. At that time the British Museum had 180,000, the Imperial Library at St. Petersburg 300,000, the Vatican 400,000, and the Royal Library in Paris almost half a million.

The Library of Congress was about to start its plunge into mass acquisition. In 1840, under Meehan, it became the first agency of the federal government to participate in a program of "international intellectual cooperation." Congress passed a law that permitted the Librarian to exchange duplicate books and documents for other needed works and, more importantly, decreed that "hereafter 50 additional copies of each volume of documents printed by order of either House be printed and bound, for the purpose of exchange in foreign countries." With this began the broad programs of international exchange that have brought to the Library the governmental publications of the major nations of the world and, of nearly equal importance, have placed the record of our own government in the collections of the world's libraries. With this act, the acquisitions began to increase not by hundreds but by thousands of volumes. Most appropriately, too, it placed the first area of subject strength in the holdings on *government* itself.

Early in the morning of December 24, 1851, a passerby noticed another threatening glow through the window of the Library, and once again the guards broke down the door to find one end of the room in flames. Fire companies, neighbors, and sailors and marines from nearby barracks rushed to the scene, but by the time this blaze was put out 35,000 volumes had been destroyed. With them went almost all of the Library's map collection, Gilbert Stuart portraits of Washington, Adams, and Jefferson, and many lesser works of art. The Library had never had an open fire in its rooms. No light had ever been lit in the Library (it was locked when Congress met at night to prevent anyone carrying in a lamp or candle), but the flues from committee rooms on the floor below ran under the Library's floor and through its walls. One of these chimney flues had caught fire, and the result was the destruction of two-thirds of the collection.

This loss was a bitter one, and about the only positive note that could be struck was rejoicing over the safety of the Law Library, saved by its move to an adjacent room. Congress promptly passed substantial sums for the replacement of the book collection and the repair of the quarters. A minor footnote appeared in the floor debate over one of these restorative pieces of legislation. The chairman of Public Buildings and Grounds, in reading the bill, referred to "the fire by which the National Library was consumed" and then later apologized and asked that these words be changed to "the Congressional Library" or "the Library of Congress."

President Lincoln relieved Librarian Meehan from office in May, 1861, so he could install in his place a physician from Terre Haute, Indiana, John G. Stephenson.

By 1863 the Library held 79,214 volumes and was the fourth largest in the country. By the end of 1864, Dr. Stephenson was forced to resign because of "speculations created by war." Among these was a sum of $1,480, which a later law directed be paid an English bookseller who had been "unjustly defrauded by the conduct of the librarian in the year 1863." And thus ended the first portion of the Library's history.

During the first sixty-five years three things were established: (1) The Library was to be a broad, comprehensive collection, not a simple legislative one; (2) to survive, the Librarian must be firmly nonpartisan; and (3) the executive's power to remove a legislative employee had been repeatedly demonstrated.

THE FIRST GIANT: AINSWORTH RAND SPOFFORD

With Lincoln's appointment of Stephenson's successor begins the Library as we know it today. Ainsworth Rand Spofford, sixth Librarian of Congress, was the Cecil Rhodes of the institution, an empire builder in the finest Victorian tradition.

Before we examine Spofford's impact on the Library, let us recall again the major issue he represents. What was the Library of Congress to be: Congress's library or the nation's library? Since we have lived with it for more than 150 years, it seems self-evident that it was always "our" government's library; it was early one of the largest libraries in the country

—naturally it was the nation's library! Not so. This was not evident at the time and could easily have been otherwise. Recall, there is still no national university. There was no national art gallery until 1941, no national opera house or concert hall until 1971. There was no conspicuous need for a central, federal library for the people and no self-evident truth proclaiming that there must be one. The only obvious and immediate need was for a reference collection to support the legislative work of the two houses.

There was a European tradition for a national collection, but here again the institution should have developed down a different path. The European libraries had each started as the Sovereign's Library. The American analogy would then have been the President's Library, and the first copyright law of 1790 had indeed decreed that the record copy of all copyrighted works be deposited with the library of the Department of State. State's library was from the first the President's reference collection and for many years was the central collection for the whole executive branch.

When the first attempt was made to refine the copyright law in 1846, the new version contained an even more likely candidate for the "national library"—the newly founded Smithsonian Institution. Here was a tax-supported center, dedicated to scholarship and the advancement of research, ideal for housing a central collection. The Copyright Act of 1846 was therefore broadened to require deposit of three copies: one to go to the State Department, one to the Smithsonian, and one to the Library of Congress. Thus, an accumulation of any one of the three might well have become the national collection, if there was to be one, but the one that did was the copyright collection of the Library of Congress, and the reason was probably Ainsworth Rand Spofford. There was never a question in his mind. The Library of Congress was to be the National Library, and he dedicated forty-three years to bringing this about.

He began as the very model of a proper librarian. He had two rooms, a staff of seven, and 80,000 books. In 1864 he produced the first catalog of the Library of Congress to be arranged alphabetically by author. Previous catalogs, as he explained, had titles "distributed through a series of 179 distinct alphabets, arranged in an arbitrary sequence, and without an index."

He quickly secured the confidence and active support of the Joint Committee on the Library. And then he began to build.

He started with the Copyright Law. When he found it, it was in a state of near paralysis, at the exhausted end of a long, confused, and disheartening struggle. Ignoring its corrosive effect on authors, publishers, and the literary world in general, simply from the Library's point of view it was enough to make a bureaucrat despair.

There had been copyright legislation in 1790, 1846, 1859, 1865, and 1867, during which years the place of deposit was shifted from one agency to another; the method of securing protection was repeatedly changed, and what was copyrightable at all had been constantly amended. Throughout the period compliance was mainly an act of faith, and penalties for failure nonexistent. From the close of the Civil War, the situation had been as follows:

In order to get a work copyrighted, an author went to the clerk of his nearest district court, filed a copy of the title page of his work, and gave the clerk a dollar. Once the book was actually published, he sent the printed volume to the same clerk, who then forwarded it to the Patent Office in the Department of the Interior. (The books had previously gone to the Department of State, but the material was taking up so much room State had gotten the law changed to read Interior. There the Patent Office was putting the deposits in its basement—uncataloged and unarranged—and by 1870 had thirty to forty thousand volumes in dark storage and was as repelled by the whole thing as State had been.) The district

clerks were supposed to send the dollars they had collected to
the Treasury, but most district judges let the clerks keep the
money for their trouble. There were still no penalties for
noncompliance, so vast quantities of books were printed with
"Deposited for copyright ..." on the backs of title pages
that had never been registered, paid for, or deposited anywhere. Everyone was dissatisfied; nobody wanted to take
over the mess—except Spofford, who saw the copyright
collection as the base for the national library.

To skip all the lobbying, successive amendments, and
general legislative exercises—when "the great copyright law
of 1870" was finally passed it declared that "all records and
other things relating to copyrights and required by law to be
preserved, shall be under the control of the librarian of
Congress" and that anyone claiming a copyright on any book,
map, chart, dramatic or musical composition, engraving, cut,
print, or photograph or negative thereof must send two
copies to the Librarian within ten days of its publication.
Penalties for failure to comply were spelled out, and the
Librarian was given authority to demand the receipt of
anything that carried the copyright statement but had not
been filed.

It worked beyond Spofford's wildest hopes. In the next
twenty-five years the Library received 371,636 books,
257,153 magazines, 289,617 pieces of music, 73,817 photographs, 95,249 prints, and 48,048 maps. Each one had to be
acknowledged, recorded, and preserved somehow and somewhere, but the Librarian was at least consistent. In the midst
of the deluge he turned to the Departments of State and
Interior and carried off their previous deposits, so the Library
of Congress recovered most of what had slipped away before
his time.

State and Interior thus abandoned without apparent regret
their chance to be the national library. The Smithsonian
Institution yielded its opportunity with like eagerness.

The founders of the Smithsonian had almost certainly

pictured it as becoming *a* if not *the* national library. The Smithsonian dialogue, charter, and laws contain phrases like "for the purchase of a great national library," "for the gradual formation of a library composed of valuable works pertaining to all departments of human knowledge," and "a great national library, worthy of the country and the donor," but when the first Secretary of the Smithsonian was hired, he had a different image in mind. Joseph Henry came from Princeton with an international reputation as a physicist. He had accepted the new responsibility reluctantly, but once aboard he had very clear ideas of how the Institution was to act: It was to pour its energies into scientific research and pursue a vigorous publication program to disseminate the results of that research. The charter required him to operate a museum and a library, but these distractions were to be repressed as much as he dared.

The law did direct him to spend $25,000 a year on a library, so he hired Charles Coffin Jewett from Brown University to run it. In spite of the fact that Jewett was probably the leading librarian in the nation at the time, six years later he was relieved of his duties. He had been determined to build a great reference library, and Henry resented the money he spent and the space he absorbed. (Jewett went on to become the director of the Boston Public Library, where he made a major impact on both that institution and on librarianship in general.)

What interests us in respect to the Library of Congress is not so much Henry's library as his publications, which were eminently successful. The Smithsonian's *Contributions to Knowledge* began publication in 1848, its *Reports* in 1850, and its *Miscellaneous Collections* in 1862. Literally tens of thousands of volumes from all parts of the world were received in exchange for these widely distributed series. By 1865 Henry was becoming engulfed and repelled by the sheer bulk of the exchange publications—which Spofford saw and coveted, picturing them as filling the scientific gaps in his own collections. An exchange, satisfying to both parties, was worked out, and by the close of the year 1866 Spofford was able to report the transfer of "this large accession ... especially valuable in the range of scientific books, comprising by far the largest collection of the journals and transactions of learned societies, foreign and domestic, which exists in America."

The collection itself was spectacular, but the precedent it set was more so. First, from this point on, the Library of Congress was to be the recipient of the exchange material generated by the Smithsonian publications and agreements, which has since brought to the Library of Congress over two million pieces in the Smithsonian Deposit. Second, the law that made the exchange possible provided that "the Smithsonian Institution shall have the use thereof, in like manner as it is now used, and the public shall have access thereto for purposes of consultation." The legislature's library, first opened to Cabinet officers, then lawyers using the Supreme Court, was now to be available to the public in general. Amusingly, not only did the law permit access to the Library; it required the Library to remain open nights and weekends to keep faith with the scholars who had enjoyed such privileges when the books were in Mr. Henry's care.

Spofford thus had the Copyright Law and the Smithsonian Exchange working for him, automatically funneling into the Library of Congress almost limitless quantities of free, generalized material. Simultaneously, he was pursuing specific collections.

The most embarrassing gap in his catalogs lay in the one area that should have been the strongest: the history of America. Sixty years before, Jefferson had said that a national library should be the repository of the nation's traditions, but almost all of Jefferson's contributions had been lost in the ensuing fires. Spofford solved this as he had solved the problem of his scientific lacunae—by buying a library complete. The finest collection of Americana had been privately assembled by the publisher of the *American Archives*, one Peter Force. The historian Francis Parkman had been trying to raise money to secure the collection for the New York Historical Society, but Spofford swept in, convinced his joint committee that the expense was justified, and in 1867 Congress voted $100,000 to purchase all the Force holdings. When they were moved to the Library of Congress, they proved to contain 22,529 volumes of Americana, nearly 1,000 volumes of bound newspapers (a fourth from the 1700's), 40,000 pamphlets, 1,000 early maps, and 429 volumes of manuscripts, many from the Revolutionary period. Similar collections (the great Toner library of medical history and American biography is a pre-eminent example) were sought and acquired, while increasingly Spofford was able to get what he wanted as outright gifts to the nation, no money involved.

The outcome of all these labors was not hard to predict. In no time at all, Spofford ran out of room. He was inundated with paper and the printed word. Bulk. Sheer, remorseless mass. The struggle for space began to dominate his life and all his energies. He had barely taken his job when the room on his original shelves had been exhausted. He persuaded Congress to convert two nearby "wings" to stacks and he filled these. He put up wooden shelves in the corridors and filled them. He filled the Capitol attics. He filled the crypt under the Capitol dome. Material was piled in the halls between committee rooms and through the working space of both houses.

As early as 1872 Spofford admits that the reading room is "an unfit place for students" and complains that "masses of books, pamphlets, newspapers, engravings, &c., in the course of collation, cataloguing, labeling, and stamping, in preparation for their proper location in the Library, are necessarily always under the eye and almost under the feet of members of

Congress and other visitors." Pictures from *Harper's Weekly*
of the time show the reading room with books stacked on
tables and chairs in piles six and eight feet high.

By 1880 the Joint Committee on the Library was beginning
to worry about fire again. While the Library rooms were
fireproof, the collection was spread so widely through the
Capitol "that a fire once communicated would sweep shelving,
periodicals, maps, and all before it." "Fire may break out
at any moment in that dark upper loft, where gas has to be
lit.... The very dust of decomposing paper, and of the
friction induced by constant handling may become inflam-
mable."

The usual obligations of librarianship were abandoned one
by one. Periodicals could no longer be stored in series. Printed
catalogs fell further and further behind and were ultimately
abandoned. Complaints were increasingly heard about the
outmoded classification scheme, about the absence of updating of the manuscript catalog books, about the refusal to
consider inter-filable cards. As the century neared its close,
the energies of the Librarian and all his staff were devoted
desperately to copyright matters, acquisitions, legislative
reference—and getting themselves out of the Capitol's walls.

We need not go into the details of Spofford's struggles to
create the great, gray building which we now think of as *the*
Library of Congress. It took him a full fifteen years to get
a law passed and an appropriation for its construction, and
eleven more to build it. In many respects, however, it is some
kind of a wonder the work went as quickly as it did. Although
Spofford promised to leave a "legislative library" behind in
the Capitol, the members of Congress understood that they
were now abandoning even the appearance of an in-house,
at-hand congressional library and, instead, housing a library
for the nation.

Spofford's library clearly became a personal monument
to his singleness of purpose, and, as it happened, it became a

greater monument to its time—the end of the Gilded Age in which America had become rich and artistically sensitive.

Two city blocks were cleared of homes and churches, and then granite began to rise across the park from the Capitol. The building was magnificent (and eclectic) Italian Renaissance, but the floor plan was Spofford, who had given it long thought. (In 1872: The building must hold at least three million volumes. "The Library will reach 700,000 volumes by the year 1900; one million and a quarter by 1925; 1,750,000 by 1950; and 2,500,000 by the year 1975, or about a century hence." What design? It should be circular so that books could easily flow to and from the center for use and service, and as collections are added to be inserted in the middle of present arrangements, "only a single spoke need be shifted, rather than great masses of books as is required if books are in rectangular ranks"—and so forth through masses of detail.)

The building was immense for its day and decorated beyond anything the Medici had ever dreamed. Marble was brought from Verona and Siena, from France, and from Tennessee. Details from a hundred European buildings were incorporated, but each was re-expressed in American terms. Every wall, mural, fresco, and mosaic is drenched in allegory. The frieze above the Visitor's Gallery is typical: Here twelve figures symbolize the "Evolution of Civilization." Starting with Egypt, typifying "Written Records" it circles around to the United States as "Science"—represented by a picture of Abraham Lincoln seated by an electric motor and dressed "as an engineer, in the garb of the machineshop." The tenth figure gives us "England as Literature" with the actress Ellen Terry in an Elizabethan costume, and the eighth is "Germany and Printing." The Reformation figure standing by his printing press is that of General Thomas Casey, Chief of the Army Corps of Engineers, who built the building for Mr. Spofford.

No one knows how many craftsmen were involved, but a recent, rather casual examination of the more obvious walls, ceilings, and fireplace mantels revealed the signatures of thirty artists and twenty-three sculptors, not including the creators of literally hundreds of square yards of scrolls and birds and plants and cupids. While in detail much of the building's decoration no longer speaks to us, in the mass the building, even after seventy-five years, is a splendid success. It is still graceful, inspiring, and efficient, bearing with ease the almost monthly shifts of this department or that collection. The present occupants are as much in debt to Spofford for having the foresight to provide them with a working library as is the nation for his having provided it with its national library.

By the spring of 1897—after thirty years of dedicated labor—Ainsworth Spofford had led his library to the heights overlooking the promised land. The long wooden trays were being readied to move the books. The last fresco was drying. On March 4, 1897, William McKinley was inaugurated as President, and on June 30, he replaced Mr. Spofford with a new Librarian of Congress.

On July 31, the "Old Library" in the Capitol closed, and on November 1, Mr. John Russell Young reopened the Library of Congress in its own building, with a new life and a new role before it.

II

The History:
Putnam and MacLeish

While the injustice to Mr. Spofford was outrageous, it was also understandable. He had indeed stayed too long. His error in retrospect was an overpreoccupation with a single facet of the librarian's three-sided responsibility. Librarians are expected to acquire materials, organize them for use, and then use them—acquisition, cataloging, and reference. Mr. Spofford had fulfilled the requirements of acquisition beyond possibility of cavil, but his cataloging was in an unforgivable shape, and since he had such limited knowledge of what was in his own collections, his reference service was equally impaired.

Mr. Spofford's misfortunes, moreover, were as much those of poor timing as poor judgment. He had lived beyond the age of the amateur bookman into the time of the professional. By the close of his career, a librarians' association had been organized, standards of techniques and skills had been established, and the science of organizing material for use (nowadays we call it retrieval) had come to pass.

Librarianship had come into its own as the result of a confluence of forces. The nineteenth century closed with a surge of professionalism in education, the proliferation of free public libraries, the establishment and growth of colleges and universities throughout the country, and the simple combination of affluence plus popular, cheap publishing. The resultant creation of libraries in every town and on every campus called for organization and agreement on the science of librarianship. The result was the establishment of the American Library Association (A.L.A.) in 1876 and the coming to prominence of the Great Names of Librarianship: Melvil Dewey of the Dewey Decimal System. George H. Baker of Columbia University. John Cotton Dana from Newark. William I. Fletcher of Amherst. Herbert Putnam from Boston. These men were the very antithesis of the popular image of the timid bookman. They were zealots, dogmatic and doctrinaire, for whom all bibliothecal matters were either jet black or lily white.

Poor Mr. Spofford symbolized all the things that distressed the new men most. They believed in rational order so that any scholar or any man in the street could enter their libraries and quickly find precisely what he sought and take it with him. Mr. Spofford was so casual about order that when his 740,000 volumes were moved into the new building, barely one-third had been cataloged.

They believed in uniformity. They were trying to work out a basic set of rules by which all books would be identified and all classified in a similar way. Mr. Spofford felt no such obligation, and, as he shuffled his volumes into the forty-four classifications he had inherited, literally floors of volumes were mixed together in whatever organization he found most congenial at the time.

The new professionals were outraged at the duplication within their trade. A new book would be published. A thousand libraries would each buy a copy. A thousand librarians would each spend time reading the same volume to discover its subject, and each would prepare cards to describe it. Each would identify it in his catalogs by appropriate subjects and on his shelves by an appropriate call number. The new men could see no reason why a single superlibrary should not do all this well and do it once—and let everyone else copy the result. They felt, of course, that the Library of Congress was the appropriate place for such activity, but Mr. Spofford was so preoccupied with getting and housing that he had no time for the niceties of shared or centralized cataloging.

Finally, they felt the need for a system of interlibrary loans by which all their book collections could be mutually shared through a network of records and holdings so the sum would be vastly greater than the parts. Poor Mr. Spofford was having enough trouble finding the books he needed to keep Congress happy without concerning himself with the waiting world without.

For all these reasons, the American Library Association was not sorry to see him go and assumed that his successor would be one of the professionals. The *Library Journal*, the official organ of the A.L.A., declared in January, 1897:

> Mr. Spofford has been so busy with the mass of detail which he has undertaken to handle that he has not trained himself as an executive for this kind of work, nor been able to keep in touch with the modern developments of library organization and practice.

They assumed that his successor would be properly qualified, for

> that this library will ultimately become in name as it is in fact the national library is beyond doubt, and the failure to recognize now this manifest destiny and to provide now on the large scale which this implies will be nothing short of a national misfortune.

So President McKinley appointed John Russell Young, a newspaperman, Librarian of Congress. Young had been the managing editor of Horace Greeley's *Tribune*, had gone around the world with President Grant in 1877, and in the course of the trip so impressed the former President that Grant persuaded his successor to appoint Young minister to China in 1882. We are told that he won the confidence of the Chinese to an extent seldom achieved by Western representatives, settling long-standing U.S. claims against the Chinese Government and being instrumental in a peace agreement between China and France. In 1885 he returned to join the *New York Herald* and shuttled back and forth between Paris and London until the 1890's. He was in Philadelphia when McKinley called upon him to take over the Library of Congress.

The outrage of the professional librarians could scarcely be contained. In no time the outcry became so acrimonious, so personal, and so virulent that Melvil Dewey himself felt compelled to write the new appointee, trying to smooth things over. Whenever Dewey picked up a pen, he wrote as the Director of the New York State Library, the President of the Library Department of the National Education Association, and the Secretary and Executive Officer of the American Library Association. After the usual amenities, he declared:

> Many librarians have expressed themselves strongly against any appointment except of an experienced technical librarian. I have said from the first that I could easily conceive of a strong administrative man being put at the head, who might be better for the country than any of the professional librarians. I profoundly hope that you are the man needed for the wonderful work that is possible.

He elaborated this theme at some length (the letter was written on board an ocean liner and sent back by pilot boat, while Dewey proceeded to an international congress) and closed by saying:

> You can understand how deeply I am interested in having the whole body of librarians in cordial sympathy with the national library. I am sure that a

cable from you, followed by a letter which would reach me before we separate, if sent at once, would do much good.

John Russell Young was an unusually able man, so it is impossible to know whether he was intimidated by the initial torrent of criticism, but the fact is that in the next two years he initiated some of the most progressive programs of any comparable period in the Library's history.

He opened the new building on November 1, 1897. When the Library had closed in the Capitol, Congress had supported 42 positions. When it reopened, Congress permitted 108 for initial staffing, and Young decided to organize them according to a plan Spofford had recommended several years before. The personnel were therefore divided among a central reading room, a periodical department, the Law Library, and a copyright office, the latter to be presided over by a "register." In addition, there was to be an art gallery, a hall of maps and charts, a manuscript department, a music department, and a cataloging department that would serve all the units, regardless of the purpose or format of their materials.

The wide publicity about the new building, which appeared in almost all the popular magazines of the time, generated literally thousands of applicants. From these Young took the best for the junior positions (at $720 a year), but he personally sought out the men he wanted for the administrative roles. His first appointment, to the continued distress of the profession, was Ainsworth Rand Spofford as Chief Assistant Librarian. Spofford accepted the position without apparent resentment and worked diligently to make the public services a success. Young proceeded to fill the other roles with some of the leading figures in bookmanship. He brought in James Christian Hanson, then in charge of cataloging at the University of Wisconsin Library, to head the new Cataloging Department. Arthur R. Kimball, state librarian of New Hampshire, was placed in charge of the Order Unit. Appleton P. C.

Griffin of the Boston Public Library and the Boston Atheneum was made principal assistant in the Reading Room. Dr. Herbert Friedenwald, specialist in the records of the Continental Congress and Revolutionary War archives, became head of the Manuscripts Department. There were many others. The *Library Journal* relented and declared, "the new librarian of Congress continues to give the best of evidence of his intention to make the library worthy of its opportunities, by appointing skilled and fit men in the leading positions."

While Young built up his staff, he continued to build the collections. His ambassadorial experience had convinced him of the importance of foreign learning, and he planned to employ the worldwide network of foreign service officers as acquisition agents. With the help of the Secretary of State, he sent out five hundred instruction circulars to U.S. embassies and consulates, describing what the Library needed and how it was to be sent. His one-sentence list of specifics was imaginative:

> Public documents, newspapers, serials, pamphlets, manuscripts, broadsides, chapbooks, ballads, records of original research, publications illustrative of the manners, customs, resources and traditions of communities to which our foreign representatives are accredited, the proceedings of learned, scientific or religious bodies, the reports of corporations such as railways, canals, or industrial companies, legislative records and debates, public decrees, church registers, genealogy, family and local histories, chronicles of county and parish life, folklore, fashions, domestic annals, documents illustrative of the history of those various nationalities now coming to our shores, to blend into our national life, and which as a part of our library archives would be inestimable to their descendants— whatever, in a word, would add to the sum of human knowledge, would be gratefully received and have due and permanent acknowledgement.

Shades of Jefferson!

In October, 1898, Young extended the Library's Reading Room hours from nine o'clock in the morning until ten at night, adding an hour to his predecessors' most generous service. He requested Congress's permission to lend books

from the Library's collection to adult borrowers within the
District of Columbia and explored the possibilities of an interlibrary loan system to support scholarship throughout the
nation. He developed the details of a system of trust funds
with which to secure rare or large holdings inappropriate for
tax-supported, congressionally appropriated book budgets.

While organizing, acquiring, and extending services, he was
struggling to overtake the enormous cataloging arrearage he
had inherited. A half-million unprocessed volumes would tax
the resources of a present-day librarian. Young was bravely
trying to pull his shelved collections into a usable whole, pick
up his past receipts, create a "scientific classification scheme,"
and cope with daily acquisitions arriving in every mail—when
his health began to fail. In 1898 he suffered a fall on Christmas
Eve, and on January 17, 1899, he died. He had been Librarian
of Congress only nineteen months, but his impact on the
Library was many times greater than the span would imply.

Young's passing was followed by a rush of interest in who
his successor would be. The new Library building and the role
the institution was assuming in the national intellectual scene
had in a very brief time made the position widely known and
fashionably desirable. Candidates from the political world,
publishers, educators, Civil War heroes were suggested to
President McKinley by various groups representing either
a man or an interested elite. Contemporary news reports
identified over fifty leading candidates for the job. Nicholas
Murray Butler of Columbia was lobbying for James H.
Canfield, President of Ohio State. Henry Adams and Secretary of State Hay were pressing for William Woodville
Rockhill, the minister to Greece. William Coolidge Lane,
President of the American Library Association and Li-
brarian of Harvard, worked the White House and Capitol
Hill in support of Herbert Putnam, then head of the Boston
Public Library.

Apparently McKinley was leaning toward Putnam when he

was caught in a political crossfire over a Boston churchman who had been a congressman but who was now newly retired by his constituents. The pressures built swiftly, and McKinley nominated the Reverend Representative Samuel June Barrows to be the eighth Librarian of Congress, February 15, 1899. On February 28 the Joint Committee on the Library recommended against the nomination. On March 4 Congress adjourned without having considered the matter, so McKinley offered Barrows a recess appointment. Barrows refused, and on March 13 McKinley appointed Herbert Putnam, the library profession's candidate, as Librarian. Congress confirmed the appointment with apparent enthusiasm when it reconvened.

THE SECOND GIANT: HERBERT PUTNAM

With Herbert Putnam, we come to the second great figure in the development of the Library, and like Spofford he swung the entire institution in the direction which he, personally, felt appropriate. Putnam ruled for forty years, and again as with Spofford, when the power was transferred to his successor, the Library was in many ways vastly different from the form in which he found it. Spofford built it, Young housed it, and Putnam *used* it.

Putnam was the son of the founder of the publishing house which still bears the family name. He had been graduated from Harvard *magna cum laude*, had made Phi Beta Kappa, had studied law at Columbia, and was admitted to the Minnesota and Massachusetts bars. He had served as Librarian of the Minneapolis Public Library from 1884 to 1891, had returned to Massachusetts for reasons relating to his wife's family, and there practiced law until 1895. In that year, at the age of thirty-three, he was made Librarian of Boston Public on the strength of his nationally recognized innovations at Minneapolis. He was in the process of innovating at Boston when the American Library Association selected him as their prime candidate for the newly available position at the Library of Congress.

Putnam was a small, vital, red-haired man, with a bristling mustache, who is repeatedly referred to by his contemporaries as a patrician. His personality seems to have significance to our understanding of the Library because it appeared to have been the agent with which he steam-rollered his way through staff, Congress, and his intellectual peers. He was rarely blocked or even resisted, and, on the few occasions when this occurred, his ability to outflank the opposition was impressive. We are asked to picture a man "aloof, remote, detached, [with] impenetrable dignity." His associates describe him as "formal" (no one could ever recall his having been addressed by his first name, no subordinate was permitted to sit or take notes in his presence; orders were to be memorized as they were delivered).

His relations with his staff were particularly intriguing. On the occasion of his retirement—having taken the Library from the Gay Nineties, through World War I, the Roaring Twenties, and the Depression, to the threshold of World War II—he was repeatedly lauded as "venerated." This in spite of the fact that for much of his career he paid his employees less than a dollar a day, that his salaries were dramatically lower than those for similar employees in Washington or in the library profession, and that he had resisted any form of civil service, job classification, or merit increases for years. Instead, we hear how he was able to infuse his staff "with a sense of mission, dedication, and their almost limitless opportunities for patriotic endeavor." Throughout his forty Library of Congress years, professionals begged to work for him for nothing in exchange for training and experience.

He was a thoroughgoing bureaucrat but of a peculiarly perverse variety. On the one hand, while he hired, fired and paid each individual as he saw fit, on the other he was passionately fond of formal organization. He would create departments and divisions and units endlessly. When he arrived, he inherited nine administrative elements. In the first year he increased these to eighteen: an Executive Department, a Mail and Supply Department, a Packing and Stamping Department, an Order Department, a Catalog and Shelf Department, a Binding Department, a Bibliography Department, a Reading Room Department, a Periodical Department, a Documents and Exchanges Department, a Manuscript Department, a Maps and Charts Department, a Music Department, a Prints Department, a Smithsonian Department, a Congressional Reference Library at the Capitol, a Law Library, and a Copyright Department. By the time he retired he had increased these to thirty-four, all directly responsible to himself alone.

He had the good bureaucrat's ability to paint a proposed program in the most dramatic and appealing terms, but an even greater ability to implement it beyond the limits of the original proposal. He drove the institution into a frenzy of activity and seemed to be personally distressed at the sight of any parts of the collection simply sitting there.

He started with the cataloging arrearage. Young had managed to sort it according to a rational program of attack. Putnam promptly requested funds from Congress to carry out Young's program. He pointed out that in addition to working on the unprocessed materials (hundreds of thousands of untouched volumes in storage, 59,589 prints to be classified, over 50,000 government documents, 50,000 maps, 230,000 pieces of music, and "many tons of periodicals and newspapers"), he had decided to *re*-catalog every volume that was already on the shelves. Simultaneously, it was his intention to pursue Young's program of converting the book catalogs to cards and applying new subject headings and a "scientific format" to each revised entry. Until this was done, he complained, normal service would be impossible.

Faced with such righteous demands, Congress gave Putnam what he asked for, whereupon he instructed his staff that it would not do to be enthusiastic as to the amount of the Appropriation, as if it were a matter of surprise. The Committee must not be made to feel that they have been lavish. They have only done what an expert would say, I think, was necessary; but they have done no more, and ought not to be made to feel that they have done more, for it is their duty not to be lavish. So that the gratification should not be that Congress has been generous to the Library, but only that Congress has been able to take an intelligent view of the real needs, and to grant what was reasonable and necessary to meet them.

While Putnam was getting control of the processing problems within the Library, he threw himself into the task of resolving those of the profession at large. For thirty years they had talked about single-point preparation and distribution of catalog cards. In October, 1901, he circularized four hundred libraries and seventeen state library commissions to find out what their responses would be if the Library of Congress were not only to catalog and print cards for its own use of the books it received—but were also to make additional copies of these cards and sell them for the cost of printing plus 10 per cent? The question, of course, was rhetorical, and the response was immediate and as predicted. Within two years, he was producing cards at the rate of 225 titles a day, and in a short time it could be said that "libraries the country over have come to depend absolutely on the Library of Congress for the greater part of their cataloguing." (By our own time, the printed "LC card" has become so common to catalogs throughout the world that the Library is frequently credited with the invention of card catalogs in general. In point of fact, thanks to Spofford's preoccupation with other matters, the Library of Congress was one of the last libraries to use them. Putnam grew up with such a tool—Boston Public put its catalog on cards in 1853, Harvard in 1856, and these two libraries had been *printing* their cards since 1879 and 1884, respectively. The Library of Congress's records were still in manuscript, in book form, as late as 1900, and when Putnam came aboard he found what few cards the Library owned were handwritten and housed in a few drawers behind and below the issue desk.)

Putnam believed the libraries and scholars of the country had a right to know what was in the national library, and therefore, in the midst of his other accelerated programs, he began a series of published booklists of "books about ..." By the end of his second year, he had printed eight such bibliographies, containing over 2,300 pages; the idea snowballed as the years passed.

Recognizing that, as more and more libraries came to rely on the Library's cards, the Library's cataloging techniques would become the standard of the profession, he joined with committees and representatives of the American Library Association to systematize the rules by which books would be described and identified. The *numbers* by which they would be classified and shelved, however, had to be done for the Library of Congress alone.

Young's catalogers had rejected the forty-four categories of Bacon and Jefferson as hopelessly restrictive and had turned to the Dewey Decimal System as the proposed basis for an enlarged Library of Congress classification scheme. After extensive study and long discussions with Dewey himself they came to the disappointing discovery that the Dewey system was inappropriate for a collection the size of the Library of Congress. Elaborate as the system was, the Library's holdings were already so vast that many single numbers in the Dewey tables would represent complete floors of books in the Library of Congress. The purpose of a classification scheme—to pull together volumes of similar contents and similar treatment on shelves, properly adjacent to correlative subjects but in themselves separate and distinct—broke down under such volume.

The catalogers therefore embraced a plan for an "expansive collection" invented by Charles A. Cutter of the Brooklyn Public Library and, using his principles, built their own classification scheme from the ground up. By Putnam's twenty-fifth anniversary in the Library, he could point with pride to the Library of Congress Classification Schedules containing over 5,000 printed pages of specific subjects, each with its matching call number. By the same time, eighty-some major libraries had abandoned Dewey to convert their collections to the Library of Congress classification scheme, and Putnam was selling over seven million LC cards a year.

Putnam was obviously pulling the national library system toward the Library of Congress and doing it deliberately. There had never been any doubt in his mind as to the answer to the traditional question: Is it Congress's library or the nation's? In October, 1900, he said:

> It is the National Library of the United States. It is thus a bureau of information for the entire country; and as to Americana for the entire world, for of all American libraries it will sustain the most active and intimate relations with libraries abroad; and through the Smithsonian with all learned societies abroad. It will maintain a corps of highly trained experts who will make known its resources and will aid in research. It will undoubtedly become the most active center of research, for the largest area, of any library in America. It will not merely draw students to Washington; it will by correspondence stimulate research all over the United States.

With such an attitude on the part of the Librarian, it is little wonder that he began to hear murmurings from Congress about the Library's role in the legislative process. Except for a small room containing some reference books and a book delivery station, the Library's presence had disappeared from congressional halls, and its attention seemed to be distracted as well. A special room for senators and another for representatives had been built into the new building, but they were seldom used. By 1912, when a congressional committee queried Putnam on congressional use of the Library, he could point to an average of only "three or four" telephone calls a day from congressmen during the session. Only 93 members out of 490 had used the Library in any way the previous year, and this included all requests for novels and magazines as well as official business.

The increasing detachment from the parent organization might have gone unnoticed had it not been for an invention of the Wisconsin State Government in 1901. The Progressives were in power in Madison, and in the process of challenging the Establishment of the day, they found themselves blocked from access to the information and data needed to build the new legislation they were pressing through the state legislature. They solved their problem by combining the resources of the Wisconsin State Library with the expertise of the University of Wisconsin faculty, and came up with a device which became known as a Legislative Reference Bureau. It searched for areas of potential government improvement, brought together the data, the solutions and experience of other states with similar problems, and then drafted potential legislation for correcting the matter. The device worked so well that within ten years over two dozen other states had copied it, and it soon became an accepted fixture tied to state legislatures.

As time passed, members of these legislatures climbed the political ladder and arrived in Washington as senators and congressmen, expecting to find similar support available from Congress's library. The comparison between what they had known at home and what they found was distressing, and various members began introducing legislation to correct the situation.

By 1911, when seven such bills appeared, Putnam had resigned himself to the inevitability of the added service and reacted characteristically. He wasted no time on apologies but did a detailed analysis of the work and organization of all the known state bureaus and of what European experience there had been thus far. He described what would be required to set up a similar service in the Library and sent the completed report of over 20,000 words to Congress.

In 1912, Representative John M. Nelson of Madison pressed his bill, which would duplicate the Wisconsin idea on a considerably grander scale at the national level, and hearings were held. Representatives from various state legislative reference bureaus described their experiences, and Lord James Bryce, British Ambassador to the United States, testified about the equivalent services in the House of Commons. Representative Swagar Sherley of Kentucky, like other congressmen, felt that the bill-drafting should be left with the two Houses of Congress, but

> as to the reference bureau, there should be no great difficulty. You simply want here a corps of men sufficiently trained to give to Congress, or to a proper number of Members on request, data touching any particular question. In a sense the Library of Congress is supposed to supply that thing now. Practically it does not supply it at all. It may be somewhat the fault of Congress and the Members of Congress, but by having a small corps of men, whose duties pertain only to the demands of Congress, I think you could create a body that could gather together data—could be not the mind of Congress, but, so to speak, the hands and the eyes and the ears of Congress, because all of us, as our work increases with longer tenure, realize the impossibility of making the investigation that we would like to do before coming to a conclusion. No one desires to have Congress have some other body doing its thinking, but all of us would like to have the data collected that would enable us to arrive at better conclusions.

In 1913, six more bills were introduced, and under Senator Robert LaFollette's urging (he had been Governor of Wisconsin when the prototype reference bureau was created), the Senate held hearings, again with the Wisconsin model in mind. In 1914, the idea of setting up a bureau by formal statute was finessed through a Senate floor amendment to the Library's budget for fiscal 1915. Quickly accepted by the House, the amendment read: "Legislative reference: To enable the Librarian of Congress to employ competent persons to prepare such indexes, digests, and compilations of law as may be required for Congress and other official use."

Thus the Legislative Reference Service was founded. Today, under the name of the Congressional Research Service, it receives well over 1,500 congressional inquiries each day—rather than the "three or four" that had embarrassed Mr. Putnam.

The experience clearly impressed itself on Putnam's mind, and he never again slighted his legislative ties. From this point on, his congressional relations were flawless, so much so that by the 1920's a conservative legislature was appropriating $1.5 million to buy the Vollbehr collection of 3,000 rare books, and by the 1930's his appropriation requests were being passed exactly as he requested them, frequently with only the most cursory review.

With the close of World War I, Putnam had overcome his processing problems and firmed up his congressional support. From then on, he concentrated on building and using his collections. His library was to be "universal in scope; national in service," and, as he said when someone remonstrated that his expanding interlibrary loan program ran the risk of losing material from the permanent collections, "Some volumes might be lost to posterity. But after all we are ourselves a posterity. Some respect is due to the ancestors who have saved for *our* use."

He pursued every avenue to make the Library pre-eminent in Americana. Early in his tenure, Theodore Roosevelt had transferred all the so-called "Revolutionary archives" from the Department of State to the Library. These comprised the records and papers of the Continental Congress and the papers of Washington, Madison, Monroe, Hamilton, and Benjamin Franklin. In 1921, the Librarian of the Department of State suggested that the engrossed parchment copies of the Declaration of Independence and the Constitution also be transferred to the Library of Congress so the general public could see these fundamental documents. Putnam brought them to Capitol Hill and personally placed them in a special shrine in the Library's Great Hall.

A law was passed that authorized all federal departments to transfer to the Library all duplicate or superseded material, and this greatly strengthened the collections in documents of the executive departments and records of ongoing federal programs. There were limits, however, to what Putnam believed was appropriate to the Library's holdings, and he refused the records of the American military occupation of Cuba on the grounds that they belonged more properly to a "national archives depository," which he recommended be established elsewhere.

While Putnam emphasized Americana, he sought foreign material as well. He bought a complete library of Russian history and culture, 80,000 volumes (for a fourth of their true value), which was brought from Siberia across Europe in 500 specially built packing cases; he acquired 9,000 "carefully selected works" in Japanese and 5,041 volumes of the famous Chinese encyclopedia, *Tu Shu Tsi Cheng*. By World War II he had assembled the largest collections of Russian, Chinese, Hebraic, Judaic, and Semitic materials existing outside their parent country (a standing which still obtains today).

In 1925, he created a dramatic precedent by changing the Library's role from that of merely servicing the materials it had to one of producing new works for the nation. In that year, he accepted the offer of Mrs. Elizabeth Sprague Coolidge, the nationally known patroness of the Berkshire Music Festivals, to build a 500-seat auditorium in the northwest court of the building. With this as a showcase, Mrs. Coolidge established a generous endowment, with which to pay for free concerts by outstanding chamber music ensembles and to commission new compositions by famous (as well as unknown) composers. In 1935, the tradition was further strengthened by Mrs. Matthew Whittall's gift of her collection of five Stradivari stringed instruments and Tourte bows. She too paid for the construction of a separate pavilion to be built within the courtyard so the Strads could be properly housed and played. Whittall funds were similarly used to acquire such rare music manuscripts as Brahms's original score for his Third Symphony, Beethoven's final draft of the E Major Sonata, and the complete holograph of Mozart's Violin Concerto in A Major.

In like manner, Putnam brought in money with which to endow chairs of American history, fine arts, aeronautics, and poetry. As he explained them, these were neither teaching chairs nor research chairs, but each was to be an "interpretive" chair, "whose incumbent will combine with administrative duties an active aid and counsel to those pursuing research in the Library and general promotion of research within his field."

He was highly conscious of the Library's role in the intellectual life of the nation. He lectured widely before both the library and the scholarly professions, and he created an interesting device which frequently appears in the biographies of the period: the Librarian's Round Table. In those days the Library's dining room was located on the top floor of the building overlooking the Capitol (it is now buried beneath the street in the old boiler and generator room!). There was a private dining room off the public one, and here Putnam would preside over daily luncheons of writers, government officials, visiting intellectuals, diplomats, and his favorite library staff. The phrase "had a fascinating ... stimulating ... interesting luncheon at the Librarian's Round Table" appears in such diverse memoirs as those of H. G. Wells, Henry Adams, and the Supreme Court Justices of the day.

Throughout the period Putnam continued to divide and establish new divisions with a lavish hand—making each directly responsible to himself. In 1915 the Semitic Division appeared; in 1917 a Division of Classification was broken out of the original Catalogue Division. In 1922 a Binding Division was split off from the Printing Division; a Building and Grounds Division appeared, as well as the Slavic Division; 1928 brought the appearance of the Division of Chinese Literature, 1929 a Division of Fine Arts and a new Disbursing

Office (which also handled the funds for the Botanical Garden). In 1930 the Rare Book Room appeared, as well as the new Division of Aeronautics. The Division of Orientalia came in 1932; another fragmentation of cataloging came with the 1934 Division of Cooperative Cataloging and Classification, and in 1936 the Division of the Union Catalog. As late as 1938 the Librarian created a Photoduplication Service (with Rocke-feller Foundation funds) and a Publication Section.

Like Spofford, Putnam first filled then exceeded the space he had inherited and closed his career by creating a new build-ing for his successor. In 1928 he got land purchased behind the great gray building for an "annex." In 1930 the new building was begun, and Putnam opened it in April, 1939. It was solid, businesslike, and functional, holding twice as many books and twice as large a working staff in a third less space but with little style and less grace.

On June 7, 1939, after serving for forty years, Herbert Putnam retired to become Librarian Emeritus and was given an office "down the hall." Here he held formal state for fifteen more years while his successors struggled with first World War II and then the information explosion. At the age of ninety-two, according to a local reporter, he still "gets up at 6 A.M., prepares his own breakfast, takes a trolley to Capitol Hill, maintains regular office hours, handles his mail, receives numerous visitors and is available for consultation." In 1955, at ninety-three, he passed away, vigorous, respected, and viewing the activities of his successors with stern, de-tached disapproval.

ARCHIBALD MACLEISH

But the Librarian's position had become available in 1939. Who was to be the successor? It had been forty years since the argument over newspaperman Young. The few professionals who gave it any thought assumed that of course it would be a professional librarian. They assumed the issue had been settled and that hereafter the problem would simply be to decide who was currently the nation's leading librarian. Franklin D. Roosevelt, who had to make the choice, was unfortunately unaware of the tradition. On June 7, 1939, Roosevelt nominated the poet Archibald MacLeish to be the ninth Librarian of Congress. The scholarly world seems to have been surprised but noncommittal. The library profession was completely taken aback, at first irritated, then vocationally furious. The President of the American Library Association, Milton J. Ferguson, sent the President a letter which began, "We think that the confirmation of Mr. Archibald MacLeish as librarian of Congress would be a calamity," and pressed his point with such phrases as "Mr. MacLeish could not qualify for the librarianship of any college or public library in America which attempts to maintain professional standards," and "The appointment of a man as a figure-head would do no honor to the appointee." The letter concluded with the wet ink signatures of 1,400 librarians (who were attending the A.L.A. Convention in San Francisco at the time).

Confirmed by the Senate, Mr. MacLeish took office on October 2, barely four weeks after the outbreak of World War II and the invasion of Poland. Within a remarkably short time, he had endeared himself to the Library's staff, earned their warm loyalty, and been so forgiven by the profession at large that he was accorded a standing ovation at a subsequent A.L.A. convention where he was introduced as the best friend American libraries had. Anywhere.

He is remembered for two things. He reorganized the Library from top to bottom, and he faced up to a rationalized order of not only what materials the Library should seek and keep, but—possibly more important from a working librarian's point of view—what it could throw away. As a corollary, he attempted to describe where the Library should invest its energies and what its priorities of effort should be.

If you can't keep everything, what should you keep first? If you can't do everything, what should you do now?

The reorganization followed the course of events rather than design. As MacLeish wrote:

> What actually happened in 1939 and 1940 and thereafter was merely this: that one problem or another would demand action; that to take action it would become necessary to consider the effect of the proposed action on related situations; that related situations had, in turn, their related situations; and that eventually it would prove simpler to change several things than to change one.
>
> At the beginning ... there was no question in my mind of a "considered program for the institution as a whole." There was merely the question of survival.

As soon as he sensed the magnitude of the problems he faced, MacLeish set out to see what was causing them. For this he created, begged, and borrowed committees of every variety to study first one area and then another throughout the Library's system. Each committee was asked for an account of the status quo and an enumeration of the changes which would be required to bring it to top efficiency in its field. When the studies were completed, he had reports from eighteen examining groups, which included the leading names in librarianship of the day, federal agencies, professional associations, and the District of Columbia Fire Department. (An *obiter dictum* was also received from the CIO on the "underpaid and misclassified" status of the librarians.)

Astonishingly, these reports revealed a situation as bad as if not worse than when Putnam had taken over from Young. The Library now had an arrearage of 1,670,161 volumes (exclusive of maps, music, and manuscripts), and the arrearage was growing at the rate of 30,000 books a year. In one area alone, the Bindery Department, there were 373,721 volumes waiting to be processed, lying in bins and lost to use and circulation.

Considering the known skills and awesome reputation of MacLeish's predecessor, the obvious question was how could this have happened? The answer appeared to be that at least three things had occurred so imperceptibly that Putnam had not noticed them. First, the Library had become big business, a major bureau of government. Second, Putnam's attention was distracted; like Spofford, he failed to keep the three responsibilities in balance. And third, the mass of material pouring into the Library, the result of all the copyright, gift, exchange, and bulk purchase agreements of nearly a century's accumulation, had built into an avalanche. There seems no doubt that the work of the Library had indeed been current in the early 1900's, but as Putnam's efforts turned to the reference and cultural activities of the institution, he simply lost track of—or did not care—what was happening on the processing side. According to a distinguished committee of librarians from Harvard, New York, and Chicago:

> The great complexity of the Library machine had prevented effective control of technical operations and had permitted great variations in the quantity, quality, and uniformity of work done in the various divisions and sections. It had been impossible to maintain qualitative standards of performance because of the enormous increase in accessions. The quality of administration had also declined to such a degree that administrators had been unable or unwilling to find solutions for the resulting difficulties.... [There was] in all probability the largest and most diffused span of control to be found in any American library.

Putnam had carried the principle of unity of command to its farthest limit. When he had inherited the Library from John Russell Young, he had 850,000 volumes and a staff of 134. When he passed it to MacLeish, it contained 6,375,000 volumes and 1,300 employees, all depending (in the words of the poet-administrator) "from the Librarian as the miraculous architecture of the paper wasp hangs from a single anchor." Every decision of any significance in any unit had to be individually approved by Herbert Putnam. He hired, fired, promoted, maintained public relations, secured funds, controlled expenditures, detailed programs, determined policy, and kept personal tabs on the most routine items. We are told by public administrators that the highest degree of coordination takes place within departments when they are broadly structured, and the greatest frictions occur between departments or at points where they overlap. If this is so, Putnam had built in thirty-five lines of friction, and MacLeish began by reducing them as quickly as possible.

In 1940, he sorted thirty-six units into five groups; a Processing Department with five divisions (Accessions, Descriptive Cataloging, Subject Cataloging, Catalog Preparation, and Cards); a Reference Department with twenty-one divisions (with staffs ranging in size from the hundreds of employees in "Reading Rooms" to the handful in "Project F Indic Study"); an Administrative Department with six divisions; the Law Library; and the Copyright Office.

While this reduced the Librarian's own span of control to five, it left the department heads with more than they could cope with, so in 1944 MacLeish did some readjusting, splitting off parts of the Processing Department into an Acquisitions Department and breaking the huge Reference Department into three large, internal units: the Legislative Reference Service, the Public Reference Service (with nine "type" divisions, such as Maps, Rare Books, Manuscripts), and a Circulation Service with three divisions. His own Administrative Department grew to nine divisions. This gave him six departments with thirty-two divisions distributed among them, and this worked well. With only minor modifications—the Legislative Reference Service has taken on departmental status, and Acquisitions has been reabsorbed into Processing—this structure exists today. When we come to see how the Library actually works in our own time, we will examine its present organization in detail.

Of equal importance to his reorganization plans was Mac-Leish's rationalization of the Library's mission. The purpose was stated in his "Objectives of the Library of Congress." The character of the collections, he declared, was defined by the fact that they were

> available for the use of three categories of users: first, the members of the Congress; second, officers of the Federal Government and the staffs of various government departments and agencies including the Supreme Court and its Bar; and, third, the general public—all comers from all places. Since it is impossible for the Library to "collect everything," selection of books must be made upon the basis of the anticipated needs of these three classes of users in the order given. To this end the Library adopts three Canons of Selection.

The Canons were as follows:

1. The Library of Congress should possess in some useful form all bibliothecal materials necessary to the Congress and to the officers of government of the United States in the performance of their duties.
2. The Library of Congress should possess all books and other materials (whether in original or copy), which express and record the life and achievements of the people of the United States.
3. [It] should possess, in some useful form, the material parts of the records of other societies, past and present, and should accumulate, in original or in copy, full and representative collections of the written records of those societies and peoples whose experience is of most immediate concern to the people of the United States.

These generalities were then applied to the thousands of specific subjects covered by the Library of Congress classification scheme, and specific categories were assigned. Some topics were to be collected comprehensively, others on a research level. Still others were limited to major works alone—and two areas, medicine and agriculture, were abandoned to the other national libraries. These priorities, further elaborated and continually revised, are still an integral part of the acquisition policies of the Library.

Such rethinking of traditional procedures appeared in every department, division, and section. MacLeish brought a revitalization to the institution that generated its own momentum. Every element seemed to come alive. He achieved his hope that he had given "an increasing number of men and women the sense of participating creatively and responsibly in a work which all of them may well feel proud to share."

He served for barely five years. They were the World War II years, and not only was the Library of Congress itself swept into the war effort, but Franklin Roosevelt increasingly used MacLeish as a personal representative in affairs of state. While serving as Librarian of Congress, he was made the first director of the Office of Facts and Figures, then assistant director of the Office of War Information. This was followed by a period as representative to the founding meetings of what became UNESCO, and finally he was made Assistant Secretary of State, and for this he resigned his Librarianship, December 19, 1944. The employees he left behind compared the experience of having worked with him to having lived in the tail of a comet, but there was no question of their enthusiasm for MacLeish and for the adventure they had shared. In retrospect, there is similarly no question that he pulled the institution into the twentieth century (albeit belatedly) and prepared it for the demands which would be laid upon it in our own time of accelerated information transfer.

With Archibald MacLeish's departure, we will conclude this skeleton history of the Library. The purpose of this book is to show how the Library functions today and what its problems are for tomorrow. MacLeish was followed by Luther Harris Evans, whom MacLeish had brought into the Library to serve as head of the Legislative Reference Service and then had made Chief Assistant Librarian. President Truman appointed Evans tenth Librarian of Congress and, although he was a political scientist by training and experience, the library profession appeared still so embarrassed by their recent challenge to MacLeish that they accepted him with minimal comment. He served from June 29, 1945, to July 3, 1953, and was followed by the present Librarian, L. Quincy Mumford. Mumford was the nationally known Librarian of the Cleveland Public Library and president-elect of the American Library Association, so his credentials satisfied all concerned when he was appointed by President Dwight D. Eisenhower on September 1, 1954.

Today's Library is the working tool of Luther Evans and Quincy Mumford. We will therefore see their contributions not as "history" but as part of the explanation of "what is happening now."

III

The Organization of
the Library

I do not wish to hesitate too long over the formal organization of the Library. We will see it most clearly as we examine its functions. However, a general road map of who does what may be helpful at this point.

There are three ways, traditionally, by which libraries can be organized. They can be structured by activity (what is done to the material that they preserve); they can be structured by audience (who uses the material); or by the kinds of material they contain. If the library is organized by activity, you will find a series of units that follow the steps between getting the material and using it: acquisition, cataloging, binding and labeling, reference, and circulation. If the library is organized by user, you get such elements as a Children's Department, a Graduate Library, a Business and Technical Department, or a Fine Arts Division. If it is structured by material, you find a Government Documents Section, a Serials Unit, or a Map Division. It will come as no surprise, considering how the Library of Congress was put together, that the Library combines all three types of structures in every possible permutation.

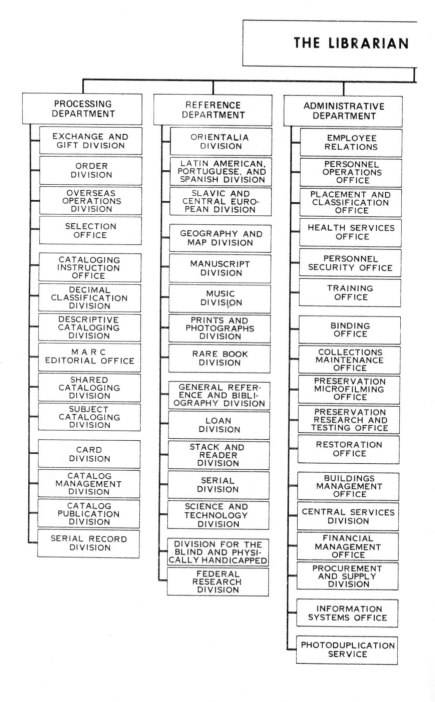

THE LIBRARIAN

PROCESSING DEPARTMENT

- EXCHANGE AND GIFT DIVISION
- ORDER DIVISION
- OVERSEAS OPERATIONS DIVISION
- SELECTION OFFICE
- CATALOGING INSTRUCTION OFFICE
- DECIMAL CLASSIFICATION DIVISION
- DESCRIPTIVE CATALOGING DIVISION
- M A R C EDITORIAL OFFICE
- SHARED CATALOGING DIVISION
- SUBJECT CATALOGING DIVISION
- CARD DIVISION
- CATALOG MANAGEMENT DIVISION
- CATALOG PUBLICATION DIVISION
- SERIAL RECORD DIVISION

REFERENCE DEPARTMENT

- ORIENTALIA DIVISION
- LATIN AMERICAN, PORTUGUESE, AND SPANISH DIVISION
- SLAVIC AND CENTRAL EUROPEAN DIVISION
- GEOGRAPHY AND MAP DIVISION
- MANUSCRIPT DIVISION
- MUSIC DIVISION
- PRINTS AND PHOTOGRAPHS DIVISION
- RARE BOOK DIVISION
- GENERAL REFERENCE AND BIBLIOGRAPHY DIVISION
- LOAN DIVISION
- STACK AND READER DIVISION
- SERIAL DIVISION
- SCIENCE AND TECHNOLOGY DIVISION
- DIVISION FOR THE BLIND AND PHYSICALLY HANDICAPPED
- FEDERAL RESEARCH DIVISION

ADMINISTRATIVE DEPARTMENT

- EMPLOYEE RELATIONS
- PERSONNEL OPERATIONS OFFICE
- PLACEMENT AND CLASSIFICATION OFFICE
- HEALTH SERVICES OFFICE
- PERSONNEL SECURITY OFFICE
- TRAINING OFFICE
- BINDING OFFICE
- COLLECTIONS MAINTENANCE OFFICE
- PRESERVATION MICROFILMING OFFICE
- PRESERVATION RESEARCH AND TESTING OFFICE
- RESTORATION OFFICE
- BUILDINGS MANAGEMENT OFFICE
- CENTRAL SERVICES DIVISION
- FINANCIAL MANAGEMENT OFFICE
- PROCUREMENT AND SUPPLY DIVISION
- INFORMATION SYSTEMS OFFICE
- PHOTODUPLICATION SERVICE

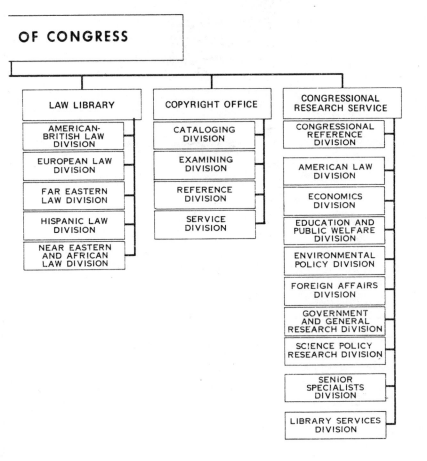

At its highest level, it is divided into an Office of the Librarian and six major departments. (See the chart on page 56 and page 57.) Three of these departments conform to the first concept of organization; they are structured in terms of activities surrounding the materials preserved in the collections. The first of these is the Processing Department of 1,700 employees, which combines all the skills of acquisition and cataloging. The second is the Reference Department of 850 employees, which provides most of the service that brings the reader and the material together; and the third is the Administrative Department of 746 employees, which concerns itself with the housekeeping for the entire institution.

In addition to these three are three departments that are separate partly by logic but mostly by statute—the departments which have over the years been created by laws of their own. These are, first, the Law Library of 83 employees, which services the legal collections of the Library. It has a double unity: a single kind of material and essentially a unified audience. Next is the Copyright Office of 450 employees, which first serves the creative elite of the country by registering and protecting their copy right and then serves as a primary source of the collections themselves when it transfers many of its deposited items to the Library's shelves. Finally there is the Congressional Research Service (known as the Legislative Reference Service from 1914 to 1970), which has a unity of audience. It has a staff of 438 employees and serves a single client, the Congress of the United States. The Office of the Librarian, of course, supervises all of the departments of the Library, which, indeed, are extensions of the Librarian himself.

Within each of the six departments there are a multitude of combinations of the three (activity–audience–material) kinds of organizational units. As suggested by the dangling dependencies on the aforementioned chart, the Processing Department is grouped into three major blocs by the process performed: The first involves the various activities concerned with acquiring material; the second pulls together the techniques concerned with cataloging the material for use; and the third unites the skills involved with recording the actual location of the material within the collections.

The Reference Department is divided into fifteen divisions, which fall into four general groups but less formally than the Processing Department's clusters. Here you will find three Divisions based on geographic/cultural unities: the Orientalia Division, the Latin American, Portuguese, and Spanish Division (understandably referred to as LAPS!), and the Slavic and Central European Division; five more are tied to the specific format of the material which they serve—maps, manuscripts, music, prints and photographs, and rare books; five units provide general services to the public in the form of reference work, the loan of material, the maintenance of the stacks, and the care of the Library's serials and scientific volumes. Finally, there are two units which specialize in work for the blind and physically handicapped and in special research for federal agencies.

The Administrative Department is divided by the services it performs into four broad areas of purpose. The personnel activities of employment, security, placement, classification, and training form one area; the preservation of the collections occupies units of binding, microfilming, restoration, and general maintenance of the Library's holdings; there is a generalized management area and an automatic data process unit; and the 160-man Photoduplication Service falls within this department's responsibilities.

The Congressional Research Service claims a unity of expertise. It is structured by the subjects with which its specialists deal: American Law, Economics, Education and Public Welfare, Foreign Affairs, Environmental Policy, Government, Science Policy, and general Congressional Reference.

The Copyright Office has four units divided by activity into divisions of examining, cataloging, reference, and general service. And the Law Library is divided by materials from geographic areas such as American-British law, European law, Far Eastern law, and Near-Eastern-and-African law.

Altogether there are almost one hundred of these departments and divisions, with three times that many "sections" and "units" at the supporting levels. Thus, the accompanying chart is necessarily skeletal.

Organization implies "span of control" and the "transmission of directives," and this brings to mind the carrying out of decisions needed to get the job done. Where the decisions came from in the first place is an even prior thought, and we might at least frame the proper question at this point, although we will be looking for the answer to it all along the way:

HOW DO DECISIONS GET MADE IN THIS LIBRARY?

As might be expected, the Library's decision chain has been more a reflection of the personality and the interests of the incumbent Librarian than it has of the organization chart. Under Herbert Putnam, the chain seems to have extended rigorously from the top down. Most innovations came from Putnam's own office, and when conflicts arose over the commitment of resources, they were usually resolved in favor of enriching the collections and gaining favor with the research community. With Archibald MacLeish, the chain became something of a horizontal loop. He spread the word among his professional peers that he wanted innovation and efficiency from all departments, and it was up to the department heads and the *ad hoc* committees to come up with the ideas. These flowed to the Librarian, and if they appeared to be appropriate, he supported them. MacLeish was open and eager for suggestions, and he attempted a deliberate democratization of the staff to counter the autocracy of Putnam. Given conflicts and limited resources, MacLeish tended to embrace anything that improved the Library as an institution, and, if he favored an elite, it was the cultural elite and the press.

With Luther Evans, the chain became vertical again. His interests were research oriented (politics and history in particular), and his innovations began in the area of service to the scholarly world. The majority of these innovations originated with himself and were sent "down" to the departments and divisions as directives from on high. He relied as much on outside suggestions from the public as he did on his own staff. "Decision-making" frequently amounted to getting his attention and making a colorful or convincing case. Once he had embraced the idea, he galvanized the appropriate division into frightened energy. Formal decision patterns were limited in spite of the fact that he organized the most complicated lattice of employee suggestion schemes and interunit communication of any Librarian before or since. Evans' ties were originally with the academic profession so he first committed funds to support the services that pleased the scholars, but as his tour of office developed, he moved toward internationalism and concentrated his energy (and the Library's) on reciprocal cultural relationships with like organizations around the world.

With L. Quincy Mumford the chain of decision-making reversed direction again. He has played the role of the arbiter and tends to stimulate innovation in his department heads. His style is to give these six administrators maximum independence and to urge them to improve their own areas of responsibility; then he chooses from among their competing demands those he wishes to back with the weight of his office. Having selected the areas he wishes to support, he begs the necessary funds from Congress and underwrites the innovation with the power of his position.

Under Mumford, the mechanics of the decision flow are formal and controlled. Dialogue goes up and down with great sensitivity to the pecking order. (Evans would burst into the system at any level, any time, unannounced and explosive; Mumford deals quietly through department heads.) Most innovations start with the division chiefs. Their innovations are born of their own skills and experience, mixed with the daily interplay with their staffs. Once coalesced, however, the ideas then start toward the top for conversion to action. Division chiefs have easy access to department heads on request, but all departments have frequent, formal meetings of all chiefs in concert so the advocacy process can be stirred when necessary. Since the Library's department heads have great freedom of action within their own spheres, the majority of changes are implemented at this point, but those that require staffing, resources, and "change of Library policy" must go higher. The six department heads then have access to the Librarian through three devices: individual consultation by request (used sparingly); a regularly scheduled, weekly, private "reporting and consultation" session; and the formal Librarian's Conference of all department heads plus the Librarian's personal officers (the deputy and assistant librarians, and the personnel director).

The Librarian's Conference is the principal policy-making device in the Library and is usually an evenly divided mixture of reporting—so all departments can have a feel of what is happening elsewhere in the system—and decision-making, where major programs are thrashed out through free debate. The sessions follow a formal, pre-announced agenda, and the Librarian tends to conclude each topic either with an acquiescence to the consensus or by delivering an apposite fiat to indicate where he stands on the matter—and therefore what the policy now is.

Without further elaboration at this point, let us see how all the organizational elements fit together to make a research library work.

IV

Acquiring the Collections

Where does it all come from? Six million pieces a year; twenty-four thousand pieces a day—the equivalent of a complete public library arriving to be processed every working morning. It pours into the Library in endless, undifferentiated streams. As it builds up in canvas tubs, on rolling trucks, in bins, in shopping carts, along decks of cluttered, ragged shelves, it gives the appearance of undisciplined, random confusion. At the arrested moment between receipt and processing, that is exactly what it is. Its presence in the Library, however, is intentional; the mass of material comes from four rather clear-cut sources.

THE COPYRIGHT OFFICE

The first source is the transfer of material to the Library from the Copyright Office of the United States—itself a part of the Library of Congress but a discrete, independent unit within the institution. In 1971, the Copyright Office received 530,933 articles deposited for copyright, and 316,972 of these were transferred to the Library for its own use.

Oddly enough, although this material is pushed and rolled

into the Library on the same vehicles as the other 5.5 million items, copyright material is easily identifiable. It actually looks different from the rest. For our purposes, the copyright materials can be divided into three roughly equal portions. The first third is simply books. These are bright, colorful, mostly in English, and have the appealing look of the contents of a lively new bookstore. The second third is composed of periodicals and is not quite so colorful, for, while it includes all the popular magazines from the newsstands, it also contains even more professional and trade journals, which somewhat dignify the mix. The final third looks even less appealing, being tens of thousands of pieces of sheet music. Very little of this music will have been published, so the majority consists of handwritten sheets on all sizes and kinds of paper. In addition to these three thirds (just to keep this from being too precise), there are three or four percentage parts of rather unlikely miscellany: maps, motion picture cannisters, mounds of telephone directories, photographs, some computer tapes, and various odds and ends.

As we have seen, all of this comes as a product of the American method for protecting the ownership of creative works. Securing copyright involves two activities: registering the work and depositing two copies with the Library of Congress. Contrary to what one might expect, the primary purpose of the deposit element is to get free books for the Library. The deposits have no archival role in subsequent litigation, the Library can keep or discard what it pleases, and this somewhat cavalier method of creating a national library has existed for well over a century. (The British have exploited the idea even further. They require copies to be deposited with the British Museum, the Bodleian Library at Oxford, the University Library at Cambridge, Trinity College in Dublin, and the National Libraries of Scotland and Wales.)

In order to receive a copyright, an author, composer, or

artist fills out certain forms, which he forwards with the creative work and $6.00 to the Register of Copyrights. The Register checks the forms to see that they meet the legal requirements, and if so, the $6.00 are transferred to the U.S. Treasury, and a certificate of registration goes back to the "claimant." The Library keeps none of the money, not even to pay the staff of the Copyright Office, and, as registrations rise, the Library must beg appropriated funds from the Congress to service the money it receives and hands on. Record cards are made under author, title, and claimant, and the books themselves are passed to the Library's selection officers to determine which of the volumes are to be retained. The paper work up to this point can take from two to six weeks, depending on the backlog at the time of receipt.

There are a few rather unusual aspects of the copyright process. Books must be printed before they can be copyrighted. The courts have held that books still in manuscript do not meet the requirements of "having been published." On the other hand, music and theatrical works *can* be copyrighted in manuscript and usually are. The courts have held that this is appropriate since the theft and use of performable works is evanescent and much harder to prove than the production of a pirated volume.

Some unlikely things can be copyrighted. You can copyright maps prepared for sale, drawings, magazine advertisements, comic strips, billboards, and phonograph record jackets. "Useful designs" are patented (by the Commerce Department), but works of art are copyrightable and thus, each year, the Copyright Office receives literally thousands of plaster statues, carnival dolls, designs for lingerie lace, choreographic diagrams, place mats, and Charlie Brown or Snoopy in a bewildering variety of beach balls, night lights, door stops, and what-have-you.

The Copyright Office offers all its receipts to the Library. As a rule, the Library selects a bit over half, and what it does acquire can be generalized fairly simply. It takes the majority of the hardback books, but only a sampling of the paperbacks. It takes many college textbooks, but almost no texts at the elementary or high school level. It takes all of the published music and most of the unpublished. It retains most of the maps it is offered and all of the prints and photographs.

Motion pictures are an exception to every rule. From the time of their invention, two copies of each reel have been deposited with the Library to secure copyright protection, and from the beginning the Library has not quite known what to do with them. In the early Edison days, individual paper prints were made of each frame of the film and deposited for record. This was soon recognized as cumbersome and expensive, but the film itself could not be easily stored. From the 1890's to World War II, it was made of a nitrate compound which became violently flammable and ultimately explosive with age. Further, it had to be rewound regularly to keep the surface from fusing together. Even after the industry adopted safety film in 1950, the huge bulk of a year's film production exceeded the kind of storage the Library had available. Various solutions were tried, but in the mid-1950's an agreement was worked out with the motion picture companies under which all films—feature, educational, and television—would be deposited for copyright, examined, and then returned to the producer with the understanding that, if the Library later wished to acquire a copy, it could do so. Under this arrangement, the Library surveys motion picture activities in general and selects titles falling into a number of categories. It calls back the films which win the major prizes, the several dozen that appear on the "ten best" lists each year, the significant documentaries, films that represent the work of outstanding directors or involve innovative techniques, and a representative sample of "run of the mill" productions. Under these criteria, in 1969 the Library recalled some 1,200 films for inclusion in its permanent collections.

Any material rejected by the Library (other than motion pictures) is held in the Copyright Office for approximately five years. Although the deposit copies are rarely requested for legal purposes, what few calls are received are almost all satisfied within this period, and the items are then destroyed. The five-year retention is simply a courtesy; it is not legally required.

The records of the Copyright receipt are kept on the three types of cards mentioned earlier, but cataloging at this point is strictly for record purposes. The works are completely redescribed by the catalogers in the Processing Department before they are added to the Library's collections and catalogs.

The Copyright receipt contributes roughly 300,000 items to the Library each year, barely 4 per cent of the total. In terms of later use, however, the books secured by copyright are probably pulled from the shelves more frequently than those from any other single source of material, while the deposit device saves the taxpayer literally hundreds of thousands of dollars annually.

GOVERNMENT EXCHANGE

The next area of receipt is "government documents." They sound dull and may look dull, but from the point of view of original research, they are the lifeblood of a contemporary library. "Government document" once implied a yellowing, thin paper report of some obscure bureau, filled with production statistics of some unlikely—and probably unwanted—commodity. This image is no longer appropriate. With the government involved in practically every aspect of the national life, documents have become startlingly relevant. With most of the nation's universities and art museums supported by some form of taxation, scholarship and culture appear as government documents. With great quantities of the nation's medical and scientific research supported by government, reports of such research are government documents. Every aspect of social issues and ills—drugs, urban blight, environmental pollution, housing, integration, the energy crisis—is analyzed, and the ameliorative successes and failures are duly described in government documents.

The copyright receipt brings in the commercial publishing of the nation; the government exchange programs bring in the records of all governmental affairs. And note especially: *all* governmental affairs. The Library must have not only the federal record but the activities of the states, the major cities of the nation, all governments abroad, and all supranational creations. This adds up to a vast operation, highly organized, which handles nearly four million publications a year.

Documents of the Federal Government

Obviously, the Library's first obligation is to have at least one copy of every significant publication of the U.S. Government. In point of fact, it attempts to get and keep at least two. Traditionally, this has been done by assigning to the Library a quantity of all publications printed by the Government Printing Office (GPO) at the time of publication. Laws to this end have been in effect for a hundred years. In 1971 the GPO sent the Library 988,794 items. At one time this enormous receipt would have meant that the Library had thus, automatically, received all the publications of all the federal agencies. This no longer follows.

With the invention of the mimeograph and multilith machines, more and more government studies and reports are being duplicated "in-house," or are being printed under contract by private printers at the instigation of the agency. The result is that, in order to secure any degree of totality in its federal collections, a constant program of begging must go on by letter, telephone, and Office of Management and Budget directive to secure documents issued (from a librarian's point of view) through the back door of the agency.

Notwithstanding the problems that "non-GPO" publications present, between the automatic transfer from the Government Printing Office and item request from individual agencies, the Library manages to secure a substantial proportion of the documents of the federal government.

Documents of the State Governments

State government documents are considerably harder to acquire. In the past, their primary importance to the Library was for historical purposes—a means to the preservation of the American experience. Now, with the federal government deeply involved in grants-in-aid, shared funding, and interstate and intranational activities, state documents are required as daily working papers for the use of the Congress. State documents are principally received through agreements negotiated between the Library and whatever agency in a state is most likely to know about and have access to all its publications. In some cases this is the secretary of state, in some cases the state printer, but oddly enough, in most cases it is the state librarian himself. The other officers come and go, parties and personnel change, agreements evaporate, but the state librarian tends to endure and seems to know whom to call. As an acquisitions librarian will point out, he also recognizes the absolute importance of unbroken serial sets and the need for prompt receipt of unemployment statistics, highway outlays, and welfare totals when an importunate legislator is pressing for materials.

Ironically, one of the chief motivations behind the acquisition of state documents is the very confusion and isolation of the publications and publishing sources in the field. State governments are eager to find out what other state governments are doing, and the primary source for this information is a publication prepared by the Library's Exchange and Gift Division, entitled *Monthly Checklist of State Publications.* This catalog (itself a serial government document published by GPO) is now in its sixty-third year and goes out to over 4,400 subscribers. In order to be listed, a copy of a state publication must be received by the Library of Congress. Thus, in this case, an unusual form of exchange appears: trading a publication for a service.

In 1971, the above arrangements together brought in 176,452 state documents, but this figure, *mirabile dictu*, has been shrinking in the past few years. Peaking in the mid-1960's, as federal grant money diminished through the Nixon years, state documents evaporated from research programs and demonstration projects and, at least for the present, appear to be less numerous each year than the year before.

City and County Materials

There has been no diminution in the numbers of city and county documents, and as might be expected, local government documents are even more difficult to identify and acquire than state documents. It is reasonably simple to work out agreements with the major departments in New York and Chicago, but trying to get a complete set of pollution reports from each of the Los Angeles communities or crime figures from all the fragments of East Coast megalopolis becomes an increasing challenge. Here the work is shared between the acquisition librarians of the Exchange and Gift Division and the subject specialists of the Congressional Research Service (CRS). Within the latter, each of its analysts is obligated to oversee the documentary intake generated in his assigned fields. He is required to make a continuing examination of what is secured and to make recommendations to keep the intake current and reflective of present congressional concerns. In this manner, a CRS welfare specialist may be providing addresses of county commissions on migratory labor, while a CRS civil engineer is identifying sources of irrigation reports or nuclear power statistics. In 1971, 6,305 items were secured from city and county governments.

Documents of Foreign Governments

In most of the above instances, the Library's position is one of a supplicant, appealing to an organization for its materials for the use of the federal government or as a contribution to a central depository of American history. The Library has little to offer in return except its own annual reports and some bibliographic publications, but when it turns to acquiring documents from foreign governments, it can deal from strength.

First, under terms going as far back as the Brussels Conventions of 1886, the major nations of the world have exchanged copies of their laws, their administrative directives, and their official journals under long-time formal agreements. One hundred twenty-five copies of the *Congressional Record*, the *Federal Register*, and *Presidential Publications* are made available to the Library for this purpose. Library publications go out, other nations' publications flow back and are bound, classified, and added to the collections. To all intents, the Library thus has complete collections of the laws and legislative journals of all the nations of the world, received and continued with a minimum of effort.

Next, a series of statutes going back as far as 1840 have given the Library a steadily increasing number of copies of all GPO publications to be used as items of exchange in broad trading programs with foreign governments. This device has grown to a point where the Library is now conducting wide-ranging exchange programs with sixty-one nations and selective programs (limited to specific subjects or to the publications of specific agencies) with forty-six more.

In the case of the sixty-one larger nations, a "full-set" agreement is common, under which the Library chooses the most significant publications of the U.S. Government, draws copies of these from its allotments, and sends them off at convenient intervals to the exchange partner. A "full set" usually involves about 12,000 pieces a year.

The developing countries are particularly eager to keep abreast of U.S. solutions to modern governmental problems, but they simply cannot cope physically with receipts of this magnitude (12,000 pieces would frequently fill the complete storage space of a young library, not to mention the manpower required to sort and identify the material so it could be of any use.) To meet situations of this kind, the Government Printing Office selects a partial set of approximately 2,000 pieces, containing the kinds of material that would appear to be the most useful to the particular exchange partner involved.

The purpose of any kind of exchange—full or partial—is to get the publications of the exchange partner into the Library of Congress. The actual process is quite formal. The Library first approaches a nation through the State Department, then continues through the Washington embassy of the country involved. Working with embassy officials, it selects the most appropriate agency with which to carry on negotiations. In larger countries this is usually the equivalent of a national printing office. In smaller or newer countries such an agency seldom exists, and the Library will deal with the Ministry of Education or a cultural officer. In such cases, its representatives work out an arrangement by which some officer of the government agrees to keep track of new publications from all its agencies—someone who will pull the materials together, and see they are shipped to the Library. Once an agreement is reached about the precise agency that is to receive and house the U.S. documents (this is usually the largest university, occasionally a national library), the Library of Congress goes back to the State Department to request that a formal, international agreement be drawn up and signed by both parties.

The exchange programs are no respecters of ideologies. American scholarship seeks "everything," (and so do its foreign counterparts). The State Public Library at Ulan-Bator in the Mongolian People's Republic submits its nation's documents in return for a selected group of U.S. publications. The National Library of Albania operates a smoothly running exchange operation, as do most of the Balkan governments. The Library of Congress's receipts do reflect difficult times, however. Nigeria's usual contribution of over 2,000 documents a year dropped to 750 during the civil war, while Egypt's contribution seems to rise and fall with the mood of its leadership.

Scholarly and Cultural Exchange

The formal products of the foreign governments merge into the last form of government documents—those of private sector (but tax-supported) cultural and think-tank type materials. In this category there are over 22,000 individual agreements worked out with such dignified centers as Heidelberg University (*Sitzungsberichte der Heidelberger Akademie der Wissenschaften*) and the Louvre (*La Revue du Louvre*). To such institutions as these, the Library offers limited lists of U.S. federal documents, from which the organizations can choose the U.S. publications in their own fields of interest—in exchange for sending the Library their own publications.

These bibliographic "deals" cover the globe, and in 1971 brought in some 400,000 pieces of such glamorous or unlikely series as *The Warunda Review* (from the Warracknabeal and District Historical Society of Warracknabeal, Victoria, Australia), *The Adelphi Papers* (from the Institute for Strategic Studies, London), *Acta Naturalia Islandica* (from Reykjavik), and *Poirieria* (from the Conchology Section of the Auckland Institute and Museum in New Zealand).

GIFTS

With gifts, the third source of the Library's materials, we come to the glamour part. We need only scan the recent accession sheets to sense the importance of this port of entry.

In just three recent years the records show the receipt of personal papers from Wernher von Braun, Truman Capote, J. Robert Oppenheimer, Clare Boothe Luce, James Michener, Vannevar Bush, Felix Frankfurter, Philip Roth, Hume Cronyn and Jessica Tandy, and Catherine Drinker Bowen. Records for the same period show handwritten musical scores, sketches, and working pages from Leonard Bernstein, Walter Piston, Igor Stravinsky, and Aaron Copland. More holograph notes and scores were given by friends and heirs of Sergei Rachmaninoff, Richard Strauss, and Samuel Barber. A publishing firm deposited its holograph manuscripts of Maurice Ravel's orchestration of Musorgski's *Pictures at an Exhibition*, Prokofiev's Classical Symphony, and the full score and piano reduction of his First Violin Concerto. These are rare single items; the same thirty-six months saw gifts in bulk: all the letterbooks of Samuel Gompers, the tapes of the speeches delivered by world leaders at the National Press Club for the past seventeen years, 400,000 pieces from the records of the National Association for the Advancement of Colored People, the complete picture files of the New York *World-Telegram* (over 1.25 million photographs), all the radio scripts of "Amos and Andy," and the W. C. Fields collection of vaudeville sketches.

It is obvious that the two great strengths of the Library of Congress are its size, which gives it the quality of comprehensiveness, and the glories of its unique collections—the only-one-of-its-kind manuscript, historical record, or creative work. The great majority of the latter are received through the Library's "gift source."

Most gifts are of the most deeply personal nature. They are given to the Library for a variety of reasons: the recognition by the owner that he has something of value the nation's scholars will find useful, or the feeling that something will be left behind by which his life's contributions will be remembered. Many come as the result of long pleading by specialists on the Library staff, who finally convince the donor he should part with his treasures for the nation's good; and some came because of the tax benefits that could be reaped in exchange.

Gifts to the Library are acquired or held through a spectrum of arrangements. Most personal papers, for example, are given outright for the benefit of scholarship. Others are "deposited," which means that the donor continues to own them but is making them available for immediate use by the public. The deposit device is frequently used to insure the papers' preservation when a celebrity retires or breaks up housekeeping. It is also employed while litigation is being resolved between heirs and there are counterclaims to ownership—and in cases where the donor simply cannot bring himself to give away his life's work and wishes to "try out" living without his personal files. Traditionally, they are thus deposited for ten years or so and then donated at the end of that period. In some cases they are placed on deposit through the donor's lifetime and given outright at his death through instructions in his will. In cases connected with the papers of national figures, reservations can be placed to avoid embarrassing private individuals who are discussed in the letters—or who actually wrote them in the first place. In these instances, the collection can be closed to public use until the death of the donor, or even for his lifetime plus a given number of years. Notwithstanding its attempts to be equitable, the Library tries to discourage any limitations on access, and such restrictions remain the exception with most gifts.

The tax-benefit aspect has recently passed through a change for the first time in a century. Traditionally, as in the donation of paintings to public galleries, the government has permitted an individual to deduct from his taxable income the fair cost of his papers—what they would have realized if they had been sold on the open market rather than given to the nation. In 1969 Congress changed the law so that, while the old arrangement is still true for heirs or private purchasers, the individual whose papers they actually are cannot claim tax compensation if he is in the kind of work where he produces words or music for a living—such as an author, a composer, or statesman. Their donations are now limited to the cost of the materials involved: the ink and paper. The result is that some collections are now being sold on the open market in order to secure their cash value or, in the case of large or especially valuable units, are being broken up. Dealers are buying one letter at a time out of the whole, or research institutions are buying portions covering special time periods or subjects so the papers, as a collection, are fragmented. This practice of splintering collections has not yet become common, but it is increasing at a rate that gives the Library concern for scholars yet unborn. Many donors cannot believe that the law will stand in its present form and so are "depositing" their collections for the moment, waiting to see how the situation will resolve itself before offering the papers for sale in fragments to individual bidders.

Gifts are an extraordinarily valuable source of the Library's materials and are in no way limited to individual donors. Some of the most useful, unique, and significant materials come from scientific societies, labor unions, church denominations, industrial corporations, and utility companies, from groups like the Rotary and Kiwanis clubs or the Red Cross, from symphony and opera societies, and from the national political parties. Altogether, their contributions add up to the rarest portions of the Library's record of the national experience.

Over a million pieces are received as gifts each year in this fashion.

PURCHASED MATERIALS

What could possibly be left? With the copyright deposit bringing in the books other libraries have to buy, with exchange agreements bringing in the world's documents, and gift arrangements gathering the rarities for preservation, what could be left over? The answer (in 1971): 976,671 items that could be secured in no other way but by paying for them!

The missing pieces fall into three rather clearly defined categories. The first is newspapers. Less than a dozen newspapers in the world are copyrighted, and being in business for a profit, they are not likely to be donated as gifts. So the Library buys them. In the United States, it subscribes to some 700, which add up to all the major communities in the nation; abroad, it pays for more than a thousand subscriptions to newspapers in all the national capitals and in the remaining largest cities around the globe.

The second category of purchase is foreign magazines in general. There is no shortcut to acquiring these, and the Library of Congress subscribes to them in the same way any citizen would, the only difference being the quantity. It pays for approximately 20,000 continuing, foreign periodicals.

The third category is foreign books. In many respects, this is one of the most interesting sources of all the Library's receipts. As we have seen, Librarians of Congress have been trying to get the books of foreign countries for the past 150 years. They first sought the publications of the nations from which our people came, then Western Europe and China in general, and gradually, since World War I, the publications of all the nations of the world. To put it somewhat differently, for the past sixty years the Library has deliberately sought *all* the significant nonfiction and representative literature of *all* the countries of the world.

If you consider the challenge of this, it poses an intriguing problem. Suppose you, as a librarian, wished to be certain that you were getting everything of significance published each day in Argentina, Poland, or Indonesia, how would you go about it? Long trial and error has proved that the most efficient way in terms of proper coverage—and the cheapest way in terms of getting only what you want and that at the lowest possible price—is to go to a single bookseller in a country and give him what amounts to a blank check.

This rather frightening device is called a blanket order agreement, and the Library has over a hundred of them. They involve the following procedure. Most of the industrialized countries of the world publish a list of all books available for sale in each nation. In some cases this "national bibliography" is little more than a collection of catalogs in which an individual bookseller can find where to order a book he wishes to secure. In other countries, they are carefully prepared indexes. In either event, the Library goes to a leading bookseller and signs an agreement with him that he will search his national bibliography and purchase for the Library of Congress all volumes that meet certain Library guidelines. These the bookseller will secure and ship at frequent intervals to the Library, which will then pay for them at wholesale prices plus a minimal profit. No returns. The books are sent with copies of the national bibliography, so the Library can see not only what it did get but what it failed to receive, so instructions can be sent to make future shipments more precise. Foreign books are published frequently in small lots and rarely held in storage for any length of time. For this reason, it is more efficient for an on-site purchaser to get a volume at the time of publication than for the Library to search the lists and order the material subsequently—when much of it will have disappeared. The potential dangers of putting a blank check in the hands of some far-off entrepreneur, remarkably, have rarely materialized. Within a few years, a bookseller becomes astonishingly skilled at knowing what the Library wants and what it will discard, and the majority take great pride in responding appropriately.

Trust Funds

One final area of purchase should be noted: trust funds. Like the gift receipt, the items purchased with these moneys are relatively few in number but of extraordinary value in terms of their significance to the Library and to scholarship. Through the years it has become traditional that when a particularly valuable collection of material is deposited with the Library, the donor places funds in trust to continue purchases in the same subject area so his special collection remains comprehensive and current. An example of this is the Stern Fund to continue the purchase of manuscripts and memorabilia relating to Abraham Lincoln. Thus when the original Stern deposits were made, it was probably the finest private collection of Lincolnia in existence. With the Stern Trust Fund, the collection continues to be added to and strengthened. Other examples of the same device are represented by the Pennell Fund for the purchase of the best of each year's etchings, lithographs, and block prints; by the Babine Fund for rare Russian books; by the Huntington Fund for Hispanic materials; by the Gulbenkian Fund for Armenian material; and by the very large Wilbur Fund for the purchase of microfilms of material in foreign archives pertaining to American history.

All told, from all sources of purchase funds, in 1971 the Library spent $2,158,204 for the purchase of 976,671 pieces of material.

ORGANIZATION TO ACHIEVE THE PURPOSE

All the above devices add up to the total intake of the Library each year. Nothing happens by itself. Each source has to be pursued, developed, and watched over; materials must be checked in and checked off. Organizationally, this work is done in one department and two divisions.

The department is the Copyright Office, which in turn is divided into four divisions: one for Cataloging, one for Examining, a Reference Division, and a Service Division. It employs 308 staff members.

The other two divisions are part of the Processing Department. The first is the Exchange and Gift Division, which is divided into eight sections. Four relate to areas of receipt: the American and British Exchange Section, the European Exchange Section, the Hispanic Exchange Section, and the African-Asian Exchange Section. There is a Federal Documents Section and a State Documents Section. There is a separate Gift Section; and all seven sections are served by a Receiving and Routing Section. The combined Exchange and Gift Division employs a total of 58 staff members.

The Order Division is also part of the Processing Department and has nine sections. Five are administrative: Fiscal, Customer Services, Publishers' Liaison, Administrative Services, and Documents; four are operational: Automation, Bibliographic Inquiries, Inventory, and Shipping. They add up to 61 employees.

These 427 people brought in 6,656,086 pieces of material in 1971. Of these, 1,828,390 items were selected for the collections. Having been sought vigorously, they have now been checked in and lie in a great undifferentiated mass. Let us now see how the Library gets them under control for use by its ultimate customers.

V

Controlling the Collections

Let us first consider the problem of bulk. When a research library decides to add a volume to its permanent collections, in effect it contracts to house that book, keep it appropriately warmed and cooled, provide it with light, with dry, dust-free air, and in general care for it ... *forever*. This sounds moot, but in fact it poses a very genuine problem. If you were to give up a bedroom in your home just to house books, you would have in effect built a room costing roughly $4,000, which would hold (even if stored on floor-to-ceiling shelves set so close together you could barely pass through) scarcely seven thousand books. The Library of Congress adds this many volumes to its collections every working day. Four thousand dollars to store seven thousand books—and, once on those shelves, there they would stand for generations to come until their paper turned to dust.

The same amount of space is much more expensive in a fireproof library building. The Library is now erecting a second annex, the largest, hopefully most economic and efficient building ever designed for library storage and use, but it will cost close to $40 a square foot (compared to the $26 per square foot for that converted bedroom above).

The point is that not only is the myth that "the Library of Congress has one copy of every book ever printed" demonstrably untrue, but it signifies a luxury the Library dare not even approach. In point of fact a great deal of the Library's energies are spent in throwing away as much material as it dares, while still struggling to achieve the mission articulated by Archibald MacLeish a quarter of a century ago. You will recall he set the Library the task of securing the materials that Congress and the federal government need to govern, of preserving the materials which express the life and achievements of the people of the United States, and of acquiring the record of "those societies and people whose experience is of most immediate concern to the people of the United States."

The responsibility for choosing what is worth keeping and for throwing out what cannot be justifiably kept falls to a remarkable unit of the Library known as the Selection Officer.

THE SELECTION OFFICER

The Selection Officer, at the present time, is in fact three persons who do indeed see every book and pamphlet received by the Library of Congress. They examine the first copies of every magazine and government document series—all the vast tonnage generated by the exchange programs and blanket orders—and they decide what shall be kept and what discarded. They cover all languages except the Oriental, and they work their way through mounds of material with awesome speed. They determine not only which items shall be retained but which shall be cataloged first and how each shall be treated in the processing sequence. Their decisions—from which there is next to no appeal—are based on the following criteria.

First, through many years of debate and refinement, each major subject area of the Library has been examined and a judgment made concerning the degree of its retention. These selection standards are carefully recorded in a 200-page manual which amounts to the "Canons of Selection" reduced to reality. Distributed through its thousands of individual subjects are four levels of retention: "comprehensive," "research," "reference," and "minimal."

"Comprehensive" obviously means that the Library will attempt to secure, catalog, and retain *any* material in all editions and languages that contributes to the understanding and history of that topic. Examples of fields in which the Library collects comprehensively are law, American music, and aeronautics. "Research" means that the Library will limit its acquisitions to the major works, the major primary resource material, and the significant documentation of the assigned field. In practice this tends to mean mostly books and documents but comparatively few pamphlets and next to no "near-print" materials such as mimeographed and multilithed reports. (Great quantities of the latter will be used as working data in such units as the Federal Research Division or the Congressional Research Service, but there they will be employed for possibly three to five years and then pulped. They will not be added to the permanent collections of the Library.) Examples of subjects that are retained at the "research" level are politics and government, economics, and American history.

The "reference" category retains only the most important single volumes—often simply a representative sample of commercial publishing—in subjects in which the Library feels no obligation to provide research depth. Subjects collected at this level include religious sermons, military manuals, and histories of fraternities and sororities. The "minimal" collection is obvious and embraces such categories as insurance company annual statements, books on real estate, and fortune telling.

These four levels of selection determine how much material in each subject should be kept and how much thrown away.

84   THE LIBRARY OF CONGRESS

Some materials can be eliminated simply by category. As we saw in relation to the copyright receipt, the Library keeps very few textbooks (next to none below the college level), few paperbacks, and even fewer reprints. It keeps almost nothing in the medical or agricultural fields, sending materials in these areas to the National Library of Medicine in the Public Health Service or to the National Agricultural Library in the Department of Agriculture. It keeps American doctoral dissertations only on microfilm, few master's papers, and foreign dissertations only in the field of law. It rarely keeps translations from English into a foreign language (although if it cannot secure a piece in English, it will take translations from a "difficult" language into an "easier" one—Hindu into French, or Russian into German), and except for family genealogies, it rarely keeps publications from vanity presses or privately published works.

The Selection Officers do not examine every magazine or document in a series once they have determined that the series will be retained, but they must examine the first issues to make the initial decision. This judgment is chancy in the extreme. With only one or two issues in hand of a new teen-age periodical or "Occasional Study Number One of the Citizens' Land Use Committee of Montana," they must decide whether to keep, collate, bind, and preserve each successive issue as long as the series with that title shall last. Once a library commits itself to a periodical, it rarely abandons it in midstream, and, conversely, it is almost impossible to buy a periodical backward. A publication which looked fairly ephemeral in its early issues, like the *Village Voice* or *Playboy*, can take on unusual social significance as it ages, and failing to save the title from the beginning can leave a library with a frustratingly broken set. The problem is equally irritating with the product of small-town junior colleges. Departmental series that looked highly questionable when the school was one year old with a class of thirty freshman may later mature into major scholarly series when the school becomes a campus of the state university with an enrollment of 30,000. The selection of serial futures requires the prescience of a stockbroker.

Notwithstanding all these difficulties, the three Selection Officers reduced 1971's 6 million pieces acquired to a mere 2.5 million approved for retention in the permanent collections of the Library of Congress.

SEARCHING

The winnowing process has yet one more step to go. In spite of the Selection Officers' having approved a volume for retention, there is always the possibility that another copy of the same work may already have been received and processed by the Library and may now be sitting on a shelf. To test this, each selected volume is handed to a "searcher" who checks the piece in the Library's catalogs. Searching through every possible way in which the item might have been identified, he will discover, astonishingly, that *one-third* of the works approved for retention will already have been received and processed!

This will not mean that all of this third will then be discarded. On instructions from the Selection Officers, many of the duplicates will become second copies for the main collections or additional copies assigned to various specialized reference collections. This matter of duplicates does dramatize, however, the variety of ways that materials can be received. Duplicates can be generated by the combination of copyright deposit, publishers sending volumes for early cataloging and early preparation of printed cards, by the receipt of discards from other federal agencies, by the acquisition of complete collections donated to the Library, and so forth. In 1971, between the first round of elimination (by the Selection Officers) and the second round (by preliminary searching), the 6,000,000 items received were finally reduced to 1,828,390 actually processed and placed on the shelves for perpetual preservation. Hopefully they were the very best, for processing is expensive and space is dear.

PROCESSING

Processing is simply getting control of the material—by describing what it is about so the user may know what is available and by preserving it in some order so it can be found when it is needed. Processing is about one part for the benefit of the library and two for the reader who comes through the front door. The library must know what it owns, and the user must be able to find what the library has—either by an author or title he already knows or through a subject he seeks but whose authors or titles he has not yet learned. This adds up to bibliographic control, and it starts at the point where the Selection Officers have finally said, "This shall be preserved: describe it, identify it, and store it in a place where it will be of the greatest use."

In a small library the material would be processed by a single librarian who would do all these things himself. In a larger library, there would probably be a division of labor— English-language material would be handled by certain catalogers, foreign-language material by others. In a yet larger library, subject specialties would appear: A lawyer would be hired to do the law books and a scientist to handle physics and chemistry. In the fullness of time the lawyer becomes increasingly expensive, so someone else is assigned the "routine" parts of his work and he is saved for professional content analysis. The scientist grows increasingly restless, so he is removed from all descriptive activities. The end result is productive use of both brainpower and money—up to a point. The cost is that each person who deals with the book must start afresh. Even though each worker has only a small task to do, it always overlaps the task before and the one

The Main Building of the Library of Congress, opened in 1897, contains a third of the Library's collections and most of its public-service and administrative units.

Right: The Annex Building, opened in 1939, houses two-thirds of the collections and the processing personnel.

Below: This is a model of the James Madison Memorial Library, third building of the Library of Congress complex on Capitol Hill. Its occupation in 1976 will permit the reassembly of over a dozen Library units now scattered through three states and the District of Columbia.

The Library of Congress was housed in the U.S. Capitol from 1800 to 1897. Librarian Ainsworth Spofford's success in building the collections is shown in the above illustration from *Harper's Weekly* and in the photograph at the left, taken about 1890. It was said that Congress appropriated money for an independent library building as much for self-preservation as from sympathy for the scholarly public.

The Main Reading Room is the heart of the Library. Study facilities in each of the buildings are linked by pneumatic tubes so that books from any floor or building can be delivered to the requesting scholar, regardless of the study room in which he works.

In the Preservation Research Laboratory technicians race against time to solve the problems of accelerating deterioration of paper, vellum, scroll leather, and similar materials stored in the Library of Congress.

About 1,500 congressional inquiries a day are routed to subject specialists in the Congressional Research Service. Computer data banks are used to respond to inquiries. Here, an environmental specialist draws a printout from one of the Service's fifty computer terminals.

Three distinguished artist-judges select the winning prints from among 1,700 entries in the Library's biennial National Exhibition of Prints.

Playing on the Library's own Stradivari instruments, the Juilliard String Quartet gives free concerts in the Library's Coolidge Auditorium.

The Library owns two handwritten drafts of the Gettysburg Address. Contrary to legend, Lincoln wrote the one on the right before he left Washington; the differing draft on the left was written in Gettysburg at the time of the memorial celebration, November 19, 1863.

The Library's Archive of Folk Song has been capturing folk music on disc and tape since 1928. These recordings, as well as readings by eminent authors and poets of their own works, are sold at cost by the Library.

The Library employs 1,700 catalogers and support personnel to process nearly 2 million pieces a year into its collections.

Ainsworth R. Spofford, sixth Librarian of Congress (1864–97), broadened the Congressional Library into the national library.

Herbert Putnam, Librarian from 1899 to 1939, built the Library into the largest center of research in the world during his forty-year tenure.

L. Quincy Mumford has emphasized service to Congress and to the national library community since his appointment in 1954.

Above: The Hispanic Society Room is typical of the special facilities serving such area and language groupings as Slavic, Hebraic, Oriental, and African cultures.

Below: In the Great Hall of the Main Building, the Gutenberg Bible, Jefferson's handwritten draft of the Declaration of Independence, and other treasures of the Library of Congress are on permanent display.

behind, and each is doing something over again which, if the whole job had been given to a single person, would have proceeded with considerably less slippage and duplication.

The Library of Congress, whose holdings represent the ultimate in variety of material, has been driven to the ultimate in specialization. All its material is processed in a formal progression, each piece being passed from hand to hand along the way. A routine volume will normally be worked on by thirty different specialists. In fact (staggering statistic), if you include the people who sort the books by language or subject, the messengers who place them on trucks and move them between processing stops, and the technicians involved in the printing and filing of the appropriate cards, three-fourths of all books processed will be touched by over sixty different people—each making his contribution toward getting the record into the catalog and that *one* volume on the shelf!

The piece of material, be it book, magazine, phonodisc, or government document, is first *described*.

DESCRIPTIVE CATALOGING

The Descriptive Cataloging Division describes a book as an entity; it does not care what the book is about. It describes it precisely, so the resulting card matches this book and this book alone, carefully establishing who the author is, what the title is, what edition is represented, who was the publisher, where it was published, when this particular volume was published, and how many pages it has. Its height is given in centimeters, and any special parts are pointed up which might be useful to scholars, such as maps, bibliographies, or illustrations by noted artists. The result of this quite formal description is a single, complete catalog card which is known as the Main Entry. This card then becomes a module, which can be used in an endless number of ways. By simply writing additional information across its top, it may become a title card, a subject card, or an insurance record (to be stored in a fireproof vault), but all these manipulations are done with a single Main Entry. And the Main Entry is basically an author card.

This hardly seems worth noting. How else would you catalog a book except by setting up an author card? Oddly enough, many experts consider the author device to be an American invention. European libraries came to it very reluctantly, and the Orient still does not fully accept it. Foreign librarians would say a book has only one clear cut *title*, but its authors can be infinitely confusing. Rachel Carson was a civil servant in the Department of the Interior when she wrote the department's *Food From the Sea* document. Who is the author? Rachel Carson? The Fish and Wildlife Service? Or the U.S. Department of the Interior? The famous *Report of the President's Commission on the Assassination of President Kennedy* was actually written by a lawyer, J. Lee Rankin. Would you expect to find the report under the Commission's name or the man's? And so forth through nameless government reports and numberless symposia. (When the Japanese began to move toward author entries after World War II, they described the practice as "progressive" and "democratic," since it "recognizes the worth of an individual," but, they added, regrettably it is "not as logical as the single title" by which books are commonly known.)

The greatest value of the author entry is that it instantly brings together the works of a single author in a single place for a single look in a catalog tray. The difficulty is that there are now almost two million names already in the Library of Congress catalog, and without the catalogers' help it is almost impossible to tell which is the precise author the reader is seeking. If you look for a tract by the Abolitionist John Brown, you will find there are no less than 229 John Browns, 52 of them without a middle name or initial. There are nearly 1,400 books by or about the 229 John Browns. Unless the cataloger can sort out and distinguish which John Brown is which, the idea of bringing books together by the man's name is lost. (The problem is not limited to common American names, either; a chess enthusiast recently discovered 86 different Hans Müllers in the same catalog drawer.) The difficulty is resolved by "establishing" an author, which means ferreting out his birth date and the years of his creative work ("flourished 12th century," they say when the trail vanishes in the mists of time), and, when he dies, his death date is added and the entry is "closed."

Such is the flowering of the literary spirit that one out of every two books newly received in the Library of Congress is by an author as yet unknown to the catalog. And of these, nearly one half require some creative research to differentiate a particular author from others of the same name in the drawers. Each new author receives the same treatment. The book itself is scanned for internal evidence, and biographical directories are searched. In extreme cases the catalogers may be forced to query publishers or send letters to the authors themselves. This procedure is followed regardless of the fame or anonymity of the author and regardless of the language of his works or of his country of origin.

Interestingly enough, the major element used to organize the mechanics of descriptive cataloging is language. At the present time three-fourths of all the material received by the Library is in a foreign tongue, and the Library actually employs specialists to deal with some 125 living languages. Others are covered by specialists hired for *ad hoc* consultations. (At the time of this writing, the Library has accumulated twenty titles in Malagasi, and an African specialist will be employed for one day to prepare entries for these, working with one of the Library's own African specialists; there are also 450 Irish and Welsh titles awaiting the return to a local university of the Celtic specialist, who traditionally handles these on an occasional basis.)

Specific administrative sections are divided as follows: Germanic Languages, Romance Languages, Slavic, Far Eastern (including Chinese and Japanese), South Asian, English, and "Miscellaneous" (which includes Arabic and Hebraic).

In addition to the language units, there are three sections organized by the specialized materials they handle: Audio-visual, Manuscripts, and Music. Altogether, the Descriptive Cataloging Division employs 150 professional librarians and 50 subprofessionals and clerical staff.

It is the task of all these catalogers to create the Main Entry, which serves as the basic card. Regardless of what the thing described may be, the cards all come out looking pretty much alike. Films and filmstrips are established under their titles even if the scenarist is known, but all the other odd forms end up looking like the usual author card of any book in any public library. (Phonograph records are entered under the composer of the music, and the card comes out just like a book card except for the "imprint and collation" which instead of a line like New York, Praeger, 1974. 292p., one gets: Columbia MS 7169 2 s 12 in. 33 1/3 rpm. microgroove. stereophonic.)

The task of establishing an author is time-consuming and expensive, but the cataloger will pursue it until he has either satisfied all the questions or exhausted all the research sources. An average book will absorb anywhere from three to five hours of professional staff time as it moves through the complete cataloging sequence. When the expense of accessioning is added in, it costs between $25 and $30 to process a book from receipt to shelf. Descriptive cataloging accounts for a substantial share of this cost.

Once the author is established and the work described, the draft catalog card is inserted in the book. It is reviewed by a senior cataloger-librarian for accuracy and consistency with the Anglo-American rules for cataloging, and it then leaves the Descriptive Cataloging Division for the Subject Cataloging

Division. Here they establish not *which* book it is, but what it is *about*.

SUBJECT CATALOGING

If the reader seeks a book by its author or title, the work done by the Descriptive Cataloging Division will take him to the volume. But if he is seeking a book—any book—on a certain subject, he must rely on the Subject Cataloging Division, which will try to get the reader and his books together by two different devices: first, by arranging the volumes on the shelves so that books on a single subject will stand together (with related subjects on either side), and then by loading the card catalog with copies of Descriptive Cataloging's original author entry, now filed under the most appropriate subjects for the books' contents. These techniques are more difficult than they sound. They are employed as follows.

Each work day the Descriptive Cataloging Division hands on to Subject Cataloging an average of 950 books. Subject Cataloging sorts these into seven piles for distribution to its seven groupings of subject specialists. The first group is called "Humanities I," and it handles all works concerning history, plus whatever volumes on language and literature the Selection Officers have decided to keep. No distinctions are made regarding the language the book is written in so long as it is in a Roman alphabet. All subject specialists are expected to have a working knowledge of French, German, Italian, Spanish, English, Dutch, and the Scandinavian.

The second grouping of subject specialists, "Humanities II," handles books relating to philosophy, religion, education, fine arts, and library science. The third group is responsible for the social sciences.

The fourth group of specialists is concerned with law, the fifth with the life sciences and their related technologies. A sixth group covers the physical sciences, including geography, mathematics, and general technology; the final sort depends on the language of the text, that is, any material in a non-Roman alphabet such as Hebrew, Japanese, Thai, Greek, or Russian goes to this seventh unit, which catalogs its material independently when the subject is obvious and consults with the specialized subject experts when it is not. The seven groups add up to sixty catalogers.

Once the volumes are sorted and passed on to the appropriate unit, they are redistributed among its catalogers. The professional life of a subject cataloger is beset by frustration. He is cribbed and confined by the limits of mass, money, and time. As a subject specialist, he would love to read each book he handles and to explore its smallest detail. He cannot. Hundreds of books a day are remorselessly flowing into his unit, readers are waiting for the volumes to reach the shelves, libraries all over the world are waiting for the printed card. So he is instructed *not* to read the book! He must limit his analysis to the table of contents, the introduction, the preface, and the publisher's blurb on the dust jacket. He would love to put the book in a dozen places in the library so it will be a part of a dozen involved subjects. He cannot. He must select *one* subject, convert it to a numerical code, and give it the resulting *single* call number which will place it most appropriately on the shelves. He would love to spray subject cards all through the catalog, to lay a road map of headings so the reader would be led to the volume from a dozen points of access. He cannot. The catalogs are already groaning with 16 million cards, and the hand-filing is backing up everywhere. So he is limited to no more than three subject cards and urged to keep it to one or two.

In addition to these troubles, he is engaged in a philosophical tug of war with the user. For the past sixty years (ever since the principles for subject cataloging were made firm), readers have gone to card catalogs and looked up what they wanted by the broadest, most generalized term. And subject catalogers have entered it under the most *precise* term. The reader wants a book on canaries, so he looks up Birds. The cataloger puts the card in the catalog under Canaries. No place else. The reader wants something on the income tax, so he looks in the T's for Taxation. The cataloger puts all books on income tax in the I's under Income tax. The reader wants something on jukeboxes so he looks under Phonographs, Musical instruments, Coin machines, Record players. The cataloger puts jukeboxes in the J's under Jukeboxes.

This long-standing feud, now entering its seventh decade, merits a little elaboration. From the cataloger's point of view, almost any conceivable subject is part of a much larger frame of reference. The Pueblo incident is a part of the history of the United States, of North Korea, of the U.S. Navy, of the Vietnamese War in general. It concerns international law, maritime law, freedom of the seas, search and seizure, territorial waters, military intelligence, the Johnson Administration, etc., etc. The cataloger would say it is hopeless to try to draw a level of subject description so that each of the above subject headings in the catalog would include every book that dealt with all the ramifications of the topic. All the subject cataloger can hope to do is describe a particular volume precisely and rely on the reader to come to the topic in the course of his search.

The result of this decision is that subject headings in a catalog are always focused on the lowest point in a scale of correlations. For example, if you have a book on Erasmus, it is given a subject card under E for Erasmus. The book is at least half about his great friend, Sir Thomas More. It clearly involves British history, the Reformation, the history of the Catholic Church, and *In Praise of Folly*, but the book will not appear under any of these subjects. Conversely, if the reader is researching Sir Thomas More, even though our volume on Erasmus may have three or four hundred pages on More, it will not appear under More. The catalogers say it is up to the reader to know enough about More to know that if you really want to know all about More, you had better look in books about Erasmus (and about Catholic Church history, the Reformation ...). The librarian cannot and does not supply see-also references for every subject he deals with. He relies on the reader to do this for himself.

Attempts were once made to do this sort of thing by inverting the subject headings. (Backward ran descriptors till reeled the mind.) Thus, although the librarian insisted on having a specific heading for automobile insurance, life insurance, property insurance, to keep these very clear-cut subjects from being swallowed up in a morass of cards, he tried to link them together in his catalog trays, alphabetically, by inverting the heading. You would find Insurance, Automobile; Insurance, Life; Insurance, Property—to remind you that there are all sorts of *insurance* to be considered. The idea was tried for several decades (just long enough to get library users accustomed to thinking backwards when they confronted a card catalog) before it was abandoned. Why put property insurance in the I's under Insurance, Property, instead of in the P's with Property taxation, Property assessments, Property management? Why put Automobile insurance in the I's, when it clearly belongs in the A's along with Automobile accidents, Automobile repairs, Automobile design? Nowadays, subjects are entered under the most precise form possible, described by the phrase most commonly used. (Incidentally, if that reader who wanted a book on canaries had looked under Canaries he would have found canaries. However, if he had wanted a book on canaries, lovebirds, and parakeets, he would not have found that one under Birds, either. It goes under Cage-birds—the most specific subject possible!)

THE LIBRARY OF CONGRESS SUBJECT HEADING LIST AND CLASSIFICATION SCHEDULES

If the subject catalogers cannot run their headings in every direction, they are still sufficiently challenged simply by keeping up with their single, precise terms. Each day new books appear on their desks discussing new subjects—the discovery of a new insect, the development of a new tax, a new uprising in Africa—for which no subject heading yet exists. It is the cataloger's duty to research the topic to determine the importance of the new subject, its scope, its validity, and its relationship to other subjects already established. Once the cataloger is convinced the subject is a genuine expansion of man's experience, he determines the most appropriate words to be used in describing it and defends his recommended heading through various formal review procedures. If it is accepted, the heading eventually becomes a part of the 1,432-page *Library of Congress Subject Heading List*. Approximately 9,000 new subject headings are established each year.

The *List* is a basic tool of librarianship used throughout the Western world. It includes terms that can be used as subject headings in the Library's catalogs and, equally important, contains the terms that must not be used. (Is it to be Pornography or Obscenity? Is it Robbery or Larceny or Theft?) Subject headings can be established in all varieties of forms, but once determined must be used uniformly throughout the topic. They can be single nouns (for example, Radar, Contracts, Trade-unions), adjective plus noun (Agricultural credit, Irish literature), or complete phrases (Optometry as a profession, Radio in navigation). They can be compound headings to express a relationship (Church and education, Law and ethics), or paired terms (Strikes and lockouts). These last are specific terms individually, but when concepts are usually treated together by authors the catalogers feel no obligation to split them apart simply for the sake of consistency.

The *Subject Heading List* has its twin in a second cataloging tool of almost equal importance: the *Library of Congress Classification Schedules*. These contain the call numbers which go on the spines of the books to bring volumes on like subjects together on the shelves.

Most users of libraries are familiar with the Dewey Decimal System, which divides all the world's knowledge into ten major headings and uses numbers to divide and subdivide these into tens of thousands of increasingly detailed topics going from the broadest to the most specific. It was devised by Melvil Dewey, one of the founders of librarianship, and was developed, almost literally, while he sat in an armchair with his fingertips together, trying to figure out some way in which knowledge could be rationally organized. The Library of Congress classification scheme (which relies on numbers *and* letters) was created in a different manner. It was designed to organize the collection of almost a million volumes that Librarians Young and Putnam found already sitting on their shelves. It thus differs from Dewey's system in that his forms a logical progression from level to level of specificity. The Library of Congress's scheme is arbitrary and essentially one of convenience: If there were a lot of books on a lot of topics, they gave them a lot of numbers. If there were very few books on a lot of topics, they lumped them together so as not to use up numbers too fast.

After nearly seventy-five years of use, the *Library of Congress Classification Schedules* have grown pragmatically until they too are now a very complete statement of man's knowledge. They divide all experience into thirty-two volumes of descriptions and tables. The letter A covers general works (Polygraphy!), the letters B through P serve the Humanities and Social Sciences, Q through V cover Science and Technology, and Z is Bibliography and Library Science. By doubling letters and adding numbers, the system has become vastly detailed, and, where Dewey provides a number for a common subject and all works about it are so labeled, the Library often provides a separate number for every minor aspect or element. Thus the Social Sciences are given the single letter H; Economics is HB; Economic history is HC; Commerce is HF. Within Commerce you find Tariff policy (HF 1701 through all kinds of ramifications to HF 2701) and Advertising (HF 5801 through 390 steps to HF 6191).

Under the Dewey Decimal System, Economics and Commerce would be further and further subdivided under the same general numbers. In the Library of Congress system, when another substantial part of knowledge appears, numbering simply starts all over again. Finance, instead of being a small part of Commerce in the HF's, is HG. One might expect that *Public* finance would be a subdivision of Finance in the HG's, but not so. Public finance starts over again as HJ and has fractional topics; for example: Income and expenditure (Budgets) is HJ 2005 through 2199, and Taxation is HJ 2240 through 5957. This all adds up to thousands of specific numbers for thousands of specific topics. The result is that the Library's books are organized with great precision —but without any particularly logical progression. Under Dewey, once you know the general idea of his scheme, it is possible to guess fairly closely what the proper number will be. Under the Library of Congress classification scheme, there are no rational shortcuts; the cataloger and the user must "look it up" each time—once again, the price that must be paid for size. And like the subject headings, new classification numbers must be continually created to reflect a changing world. Each year some 3,000 new numbers are put together, described, and added to the classification schedules.

The Shelf List

Finally, the Subject Cataloging Division is responsible for what is called the Shelf List. This is a huge catalog of seven million catalog cards, each one of which is filed according to the classification number on each book's cover. It thus exactly represents all the books on all the shelves throughout the Library and becomes a complete inventory of the Library's holdings. Books on the shelves are checked against it regularly to be certain that all the volumes are in place and accounted for. The Shelf List serves one additional purpose beyond simple organization and inventory.

The subject call numbers will bring all books on the same topic together, but no matter how precisely the number can be focused—MT 68 is Improvisation, a fragment of the larger Musical composition, which in turn is an element of still larger Music instruction and study, which is but a sub-element of Music in general!—in a collection as large as the Library's there will still be dozens of volumes carrying the exact same classification number (there are 188 different titles under MT 68). To sort books within a subject, they are made separate and discrete from each other by the use of a "Cutter number," which is determined and assigned by the Shelf Listing Section of the Subject Cataloging Division. Cuttering is a complicated system by which letters and numbers—plus dates—sort out all the volumes, arrange them by author or place or industry or edition (whatever order seems most appropriate to the topic) and assign each book with a number like (in the case of books on music improvisation as an aspect of instruction and study!) MT 68. D2125 1954a—about par for length of an LC call number.

THE FINAL STEPS

We have thus taken a book from the mail bag, decided if we wanted it, checked to be sure we don't already have it, created a card for it to go in the catalog, given it a call number and left clues in the catalog as to where it can be found. We have entered it in the inventory, and from this point there is little left to be done before it is placed on a shelf. If it is unbound and paperbacked (half of everything received will be), it will go to the Binding Office for shipment to an out-of-city contractor. He will bind it in thick cardboards covered with heavy buckram cloth and return it to the Library. Records will be cleared, "secret" Library of Congress identification marks will be punched into an inside page, the classification letters and numbers will be labeled on the spine, and it will be trucked into the stacks for shelving. A new best-seller will take an average of three to four weeks from receipt to shelf. An unbound book or document will require many months. "Rush" material for congressional requests or Reference Department requirements can go through in as few as three or four days.

The Serial Record

All the things we have processed so far were single entities complete in themselves—books, phonograph records, government documents—each a single "it" which (in the case of printed material) a cataloger calls a monograph. We must also note the control exercised over an even more elusive form of material, the "serial," which is any publication issued in sequence in a series. The interval between issues does not matter. It can be the daily *Treasury Statistics*, the weekly *New Yorker*, the monthly *Bluebook of Used Car Values*, the quarterly *FBI Crime Statistics*, the annual *Report of the National Education Association*, or the biennial *Who's Who in America*. It can be federal bulletins that appear without any regularity at all, so long as they are numbered as a series and have a single point of issue.

The Library sorts this mass of sequential fragments in a unit called the Serial Record. This is housed in a block-long room of the Annex Building and presents one of the most chilling sights in the Library of Congress. Here row upon row of flat-drawered, steel cabinets are tended by a staff of 107 people who sort and record over 6,000 pieces of printed material every working day.

The trays are filled with check-in sheets showing the title, the source, the way each item is received (gift, purchase, exchange), and from where. It will tell which section of the Library has custody over the loose fragments while they are accumulating toward a complete volume and what call number the volume should be given when enough fragments have arrived to be bound.

The Serial Record itself is so vast that every two or three accessioners are assigned to a *single* letter of the alphabet, and they will check in publications whose titles begin with that one letter and only that letter every working day of the year. Some accessioners have spent a decade specializing in the letter G! Traditionally, the U's have the greatest status, being exceptionally complicated and encompassing both the United States and the United Nations.

It will be recalled that the Selection Officer decides whether a serial will be kept or discarded. Since publications pour in from so many sources, it is as important to keep track of which items it was decided to throw away as which items to retain. To this end the Serial Record carries entries for approximately 348,000 serials that are currently kept, checked in, and prepared for binding; but it also has cards for 142,000 serials that are to be discarded when received. An interesting footnote relates to the ever present problem of foreign languages. While 70 per cent of monographs are in foreign languages and 30 per cent in English, serials break down as 55 per cent in English, 9 per cent in Spanish, 8 per cent in German, 3 per cent in Russian, and 3 per cent in Italian.

THE CATALOGS

One final device must close our look at how the Library's material is controlled for use: the catalogs of the Library of

Congress. Probably nothing so typifies a library as its "card catalog." The Library's is almost certainly the largest in the world and, as we will see, the source of many of the Library's greatest problems for the future.

While there are literally dozens of small, specialized catalogs scattered through every research division of the Library (picture catalogs, pending legislation catalogs, genealogy catalogs), there are six basic catalogs of major size.

The Main Catalog. This is the one in the Main Reading Room that the public uses for looking up books in. It now has 16.5 million cards in 21,077 card drawers filling four large rooms in the Main Building. It contains cards filed by author, title, and subject in one great alphabet, and many believe it has become almost unmanageable. (There are 787 drawers which hold nothing but cards beginning with the two letters: U.S.).

The Official Catalog. Hidden away in windowless stacks in the Annex Building is an even larger catalog: the Official, or Catalogers', Catalog. It has the same 16.5 million cards as the Main Catalog, plus 2.5 million more "authority cards." These are yellow record cards which give the source of all the information accumulated in establishing authors. Each authority card tells where the descriptive cataloger found the information he used, as well as the places he tried and failed. For convenience' sake, the Official Catalog is divided into two parts: One part has all the authors and titles filed in one alphabet, and the other has all the subjects.

The Process Information File. This is a strange catalog filed in open trays on tables, and it is used to keep track of each book "in process" as it works its way through the processing sequence. If a second copy of a title arrives late, it can thus catch up with the original, or if a congressman wants an unprocessed volume, it can be located and converted to a "rush process" item.

Special Catalogs. The last three catalogs are highly specialized. Their titles are self-explanatory: the Law Library

Catalog, the Music Catalog, and the Far Eastern Languages Catalog (which is filed, not by the Chinese or Japanese characters in which the rest of the card is printed, but by a conversion into Roman letters printed across the top; the romanization is then filed alphabetically as if the book were in English).

All told, the six catalogs add up to an excess of 50 million catalog cards, each of which has been tediously slipped into its proper place by hand, one at a time.

This piece-by-piece filing is done at a sustained, almost frantic pace by roughly thirty filers, who set three million cards in place each year. That there must be a better way was recognized decades ago, and for this the computer, when it arrived on the scene, was welcomed in bibliographic circles with open arms. Its failure to provide the solution to the catalog problem has thus been doubly disappointing. We will examine this frustration at the proper time.

In Conclusion

In this chapter we have taken a superficial glance at how the Library's material is sought and acquired. We have noted how it is arranged for maximum use and recorded for later retrieval. These steps employ the "technical processing" skills of librarianship and involve what most people think a librarian does for a living. It is essential to recall that the acquiring and cataloging of a library is not done simply because it is the traditional thing for a librarian to do. It is pursued with the single justification of *use*. The librarian gets the material his particular library's clientele will need to use and arranges it and controls it so it can be found when its time for use arrives. *Use*. The cataloger is tied as tightly to use as is the reference librarian who will put the book in the requester's hands. The obligations of use are shared equally by all members of the staff of the Library of Congress. Keeping this in mind, we will now turn to the "reference" departments of the Library, where dwell the specialists who deal directly with the Library's users.

VI

The Reference Department

Back in the days when Jefferson's library was up for sale, one of his friends learned it had been offered to the Congress, and the friend was distressed. He knew it to be a splendid collection—he was particularly awed by its strength in the sciences—and the idea that it should be buried in a governmental library "where it cannot produce any benefit to them or to the World" gave him concern, for there in Washington it must "become motheaten upon the shelves" and lost to the world of knowledge. The library, of course, did go to the government, as did all its succeeding particles, and it is the responsibility of the three Library of Congress *reference* departments to see that it does not sit upon the shelves and turn to dust. The three departments serve three audiences: the Reference Department itself serves the general public and the scholarly world; the Law Library serves the legal world; and the Congressional Research Service serves the Congress.

Each element of the three departments has in turn three responsibilities. First and foremost, each must act as a bridge between the users and the collections—and be the "experts" who know what is where and put it into the hands of the requesters who need it. Second, the reference units must act as the custodians of the particular parts of the over-all collection that they serve. While the Processing Department has accumulated the material and organized it for use, once the material is passed on, it is the reference librarians' responsibility to care for it, preserve it, and keep it available for immediate delivery. Finally, the specialists in each subject area are required to act as recommending officers to see that the collections do in fact have what is needed by the users. It is their responsibility to request through the processors the further acquisitions needed to keep each collection balanced and complete. Use, preservation, and enrichment. The Manuscript Division demonstrates these elements especially well, so let's start with it.

THE MANUSCRIPT DIVISION

Here I must admit my own bias. Each person who knows the Library of Congress cherishes a portion of it that ceases to be simply a federal warehouse and becomes an area of pure emotion. Some find it when the Library's four Stradivari are lifted from their cases, and the Juilliard String ensemble begins a Beethoven quartet—playing from a Library score in Beethoven's own hand. I've seen the same sort of quiet tension in a visiting mapmaker when he carries a portolano of Vasco da Gama's to the light, knowing that this particular piece of parchment may have gone around the Horn with the great man. For me, the most moving portion of the Library is the Manuscript Division.

One can walk through rows of stacks and be surrounded by its names that read like an opening stanza of Benét. An alphabetical sample: Nicholas Biddle, the Breckinridges of Kentucky, Salmon P. Chase, Andrew Jackson, George B. McClellan, Robert Morris, Samuel F. B. Morse, James K. Polk, Edwin M. Stanton, Martin Van Buren. Women's Lib? Here are the most personal and private papers of Clara Barton,

Susan B. Anthony, Carrie Chapman Catt, Margaret Sanger, Clare Boothe Luce. The Wright brothers, Charles Evans Hughes, and Cordell Hull came in together. Another aisle: Frederick Lewis Allen, Tom Connally, Douglas Southall Freeman, Phil Sheridan, and Frederick Douglass. Twenty-eight thousand papers of Sigmund Freud. And of course the Founding Fathers: Franklin, Jefferson, Madison, Monroe (indeed, twenty-three of the presidents from Washington to Coolidge), plus long rows of the signers of the Declaration of Independence and the Constitution. As the leaflet at the front door explains, these shelves bear "the papers of those men and women who, throughout the centuries, have most profoundly influenced the lives and destinies of their countrymen." Notwithstanding my own awe of these particular decks, they are just another part of the operation to the Library as a whole, so let us examine them as such.

What are "personal papers"? David Mearns, one of the past chiefs of the Division, has described them as:

> an individual's or an organization's correspondence (both letters received and retained copies of letters sent), memoranda, notebooks, journals and diaries, logs, orderly books, commonplace books, drafts of speeches, articles and monographs, trial lines, scrapbooks, reports, press releases, ephemera; in short, writings (inherently unique) of whatsoever sort or kind that possess evidential value, illuminate a personality, or provide a basis for scholarly judgment on actions and events.

All such bits and pieces from, to, and about an individual are kept together and referred to as the Lincoln collection, the Oppenheimer collection, and so on. There are over 10,000 such individual collections housed in the division.

What do they look like? They stand on the shelves either in bound volumes or in vertical cardboard boxes. The George Washington papers, for example, are preserved in huge red-leather, tooled, and gold-stamped folios, each in its own slip case and each weighing 10 or 15 pounds. The volumes' pages are heavy rag paper on which the Washington material is mounted, one item to a page, each item hinged on the left side, so (in the case of a three- or four-page letter) each leaf can be turned and read in sequence, all on the same sheet. There are 163 linear feet of the George Washington papers.

There are, on the other hand, 443 feet of the Booker T. Washington papers. These, like all modern manuscripts, are packed in manuscript boxes, which are metal-edged and de-acidified so nothing touches the papers that would threaten their preservation. The manuscript stacks are themselves a huge vault, fireproof and humidity-controlled.

How are the manuscripts used? How would you yourself have access to them? First, you would have to have some serious purpose behind your request, such as the preparation of a book or some specific research quest. The materials are far too valuable to make them available for general browsing. A piece of paper with nothing but George Washington's signature on it is worth at least $400 in today's market; the Library's holograph draft of his First Inaugural Address is worth well over $25,000.

Assuming that you have a serious need to examine the material, you would present yourself at the register desk where you would be asked to sign in and identify yourself. After explaining what you sought, you would be introduced to a reference librarian who would discuss your project in terms of the Library's actual holdings, so you can know what papers are available for your purpose and how to ask for what you want.

Manuscripts are kept in one of two ways: either chronologically by date of creation, or alphabetically by the persons who wrote them or to whom the originals were sent. The materials are rarely accessible by subject, so if you are working on the driving of the Golden Spike in Utah, you must know beforehand who was there, who might have been involved, and when the event actually happened. If you are trying to trace the letters Hamilton wrote the afternoon before the duel, you must know not only when it happened in order to search his own files, but guess to whom he might have written in order to search *their* collections of the same date. (In this case, for example, you would come on the tragic, final letter to his wife in the Hamilton collection, but the other communications would have appeared among the papers of his contemporaries.)

All of the Library's papers are preserved in some logical order and indexed in an author catalog, but in addition the staff of the Manuscript Division has prepared some five hundred detailed, individual "registers." Each of these is a small book analyzing a single collection for the scholar. A typical one will first have a statement of "provenance" which tells how the Library came to get the collection. Some of these are straightforward records of the legal deposition by the owner, but others are dramatic stories of lost trunks found, of shattered collections laboriously reassembled over the years, and of similar treasure hunts.

A register will next describe the status of the literary rights to the materials. Manuscripts are not covered by copyright. Instead, the author's interest is protected by the common law rights of literary property. The man who wrote the manuscript (or his heirs) owns the literary property in his writing, even though the Library owns the manuscript itself. If the literary rights have been dedicated to the public, you can quote verbatim. If not, you will have to paraphrase or use the information for "background understanding." The register then tells how many pieces the collection contains, what kinds of materials are in it, and their over-all arrangement—down to the contents of each individual box, book, or filing folder.

With one of these registers in hand, the reference librarian can steer you very precisely to the parts or particles you need. If it turns out, however, that the object you are pursuing is a difficult one—some obscure premise you are trying to prove or possibly a hunch you are trying to substantiate—the reference librarian may well pass you on to one of the Division's resident historians. There are five of these, each responsible for a particular specialty: early American history to 1825, the National Period to 1861, Civil War and Reconstruction, the twentieth century, and cultural history. (Cultural history covers the papers of such figures as Walt Whitman, Robert Frost, and Edna St. Vincent Millay.)

Each of these historians is knowledgeable about his assigned period and the contents of the Library's papers which concern it. Thus, if you are trying to reconstruct an event or are challenging some piece of conventional wisdom, the resident historian can tell you quickly whose papers might discuss what you are seeking and how to search the specific areas he recommends.

While the Division's own collection of original manuscripts is comprehensive, its collection of *copies* of manuscripts from *other* institutions is equally broad. Since as far back as 1905, the Library has sent copiers (and now microfilm technicians) around the world to duplicate materials in foreign archives that bear on the development of American history. Great quantities of these have been reproduced and brought home from such depositories as the Archives of the Indies in Seville, which record the Spanish colonization of America, early British colonial reports preserved in the Public Record Office in London, and the records of the Society for the Propagation of the Gospel, which contain minutely detailed reports sent to England from individual parishes on the American frontier in the sixteen- and seventeen-hundreds. Other copied collections contain correspondence from foreign diplomats to their home governments during the Civil War, German records of the Hessian mercenaries in the Revolution, and the like. Remarkably enough, because of the general destruction in World War II, some of the duplicated European documents are now the only extant copies, and European scholars are coming to the

Library of Congress to use duplicates of their own papers, here.

Any of the above materials would be available to you as a researcher. You could bring your typewriter or tape recorder or camera into the reading room and, within the limits of the specific collection you are working with, copy away. The Library also maintains a Photoduplication Service which would reproduce whatever you wished as Dennison or Xerox hard copy, photostatic enlargements, glossy photographic prints, or microfilm and microfiche miniatures. Indeed, many of the most frequently used collections have already been microfilmed and are for sale to libraries and individuals by specific time periods or as complete collections. No matter when you might visit it, you would find the Manuscript Reading Room as crammed with readers as a high school library at term paper time. In 1971, 15,022 researchers used it, some for a single afternoon, others spending many months pursuing some specific research project. An additional 10,109 were served by correspondence or telephone. The division has forty regular staff members, including fourteen who organize and describe incoming materials. And to answer the most asked question: Yes, the scene is under continual surveillance to be certain nothing is stolen, nothing defaced—and that no one uses a wet-ink fountain pen. Ball points are welcome.

The Division's activities in "use" and "preservation" are obvious. Its obligations in "enrichment" might bear stating, because very little of the material simply comes to the door, begging to be admitted. The division's specialists and historians must constantly plow their respective fields, contacting rising authors, pursuing the current favorites of the stage and Neilsen ratings, or grimly reacting to the obituary notices of the great. Simple enrichment of the collections is secondary; enrichment of scholarly source material—so that users can enhance our understanding of national traditions, achievements, and, on occasion, failures—is paramount.

THE GEOGRAPHY AND MAP DIVISION

In many respects, the Map Division is similar to Manuscripts. While many of its materials are duplicated somewhere else and thus are not as unique as manuscripts, they are not duplicated in *many* other places, and some indeed are available nowhere but here.

The first catalog of the Library in 1802 listed seven maps and six atlases. By 1971, these had grown to 3.5 million maps and 32,000 atlases. The Map Division is omnivorous. There is none of the "just take the best representative samples." The division will take anything it does not already have and thus without doubt has the largest collection of cartographic material of any institution in the world.

When a map (land) or chart (water) is received, each one is mounted on broad sheets of muslin and then stored flat in huge steel cabinets with the maps laid out in drawers 4 feet wide and 3 feet deep. The cabinets themselves are housed in long warehouse-like rooms under closely controlled conditions of heat and humidity.

The maps cover the history of the art. The division has vellum charts drawn by Italian, Spanish, and Portuguese cartographers in the fifteenth and sixteenth centuries. It has Champlain's original map of Canada on parchment (1607) and an early map of Manhattan Island (1639). Sixty per cent of all its holdings relate to the Americas. It has literally thousands of individual maps of the Colonial and Revolutionary periods, both in manuscript and in print. Many of these came to the Library with intriguingly complicated pedigrees.

The so-called Faden collection (which, among other things, contains 101 maps of the Braddock Expedition and the French and Indian War) was first put together by William Faden, map publisher of the 1700's and geographer to the King of England. A Reverend Converse bought the collection from Faden's estate; Nathan Hale—the hero's nephew and father of Edward Everett Hale—bought it from Converse; and the Joint Committee on the Library of the U.S. Congress bought it from Hale for $1,000 in 1864.

Similarly, the Hummel collection was purchased by Andrew Mellon in 1930 from Arthur W. Hummel, who had collected the maps through many years in China. Mellon in turn gave them to the Library. They include two atlases of "all China," one containing twenty maps drawn in the Ming period (1368–1644), and another from 1662; a huge wall map of China drawn around 1673; and a vast and complicated road map of the "great and ancient highway from Sian in Shensi to Ch'engtu in Szechuan Province."

How do you find a map to use it? Oddly enough, in spite of the librarian's propensity for making catalog cards about anything with dried ink on it, there is no single catalog for maps. Instead there are endless published lists of special kinds of maps ("Catalogue of Insurance Maps . . .", "Descriptive List of Maps of the Spanish Possessions Within the Present Limits of the United States, 1502–1820," "A Descriptive List of Treasure Maps and Charts"); there are indexes of special publishers (the Army Map Service, the Coast and Geodetic Survey, British Ordnance Surveys), and "finding lists" like those generated from the annual record of all maps deposited for copyright ("Catalog of Copyright Entries, Third Series, Maps"). These compilations are known to, and used by, the reference librarians in the division, but by their very nature they require all access to the collections to be through verbal request and hand delivery.

The *modus operandi*, therefore, in this division is for the reader to describe to the librarian across a counter what he wants and how it is to be used. Then with astonishing speed he finds himself facing large sheets of paper depicting the area he is seeking. The "area," it should be noted, can be maps of the bottom of the sea, census tracts, logging trails, the incidence of cancer, mine fields, glacial moraines, annual income, skin pigment, or the back of the moon. The division has thirty-one staff members and served 11,906 researchers in 1971.

The Rare Book Division

Manuscripts, maps, and bibliophilia. The final member of the "treasure house triad" in the Reference Department is the Rare Book Division.

At the beginning of this book, we noted some of the early collections the Library acquired, which later became the base on which the rare book holdings were built. Prime examples were the Jefferson library itself (of which, in spite of two fires, some 2,400 volumes still remain), the Peter Force collection of early Americana, and the Joseph Meredith Toner collection of biography and medical history. Since then, rare books have been added by the tens of thousands, and they fall into two fairly clear-cut categories: They are either distinctive, unified collections of books and pamphlets about a single topic and accumulated by a single bibliophile, or individual books that were come by in the normal course of library business but that are of such value or form that they need special preservation techniques and protection.

The term "rare books" immediately suggests either pristine first editions in hand-tooled slipcases or huge volumes of vast age. There has been a years-old argument in the library profession over whether it is appropriate for a public institution to hoard volumes merely because of their publication date. (In point of fact, 95 per cent of *any* library is composed of first editions simply because libraries buy books when they appear and few books ever go beyond the first edition!) But there is seldom an argument over the appropriateness of an institution accumulating the earliest examples of printing and bookmanship because libraries are almost by definition museums of the printed word. Such early examples are costly and rare. The rarest of all are those printed between the invention of movable type around 1440 and the end of the fifteenth century. These are called incunabula, and the Library owns 5,600 of them. Of all the incunabula, none is quite so dramatic as the Gutenberg Bible.

The Vollbehr Collection

The Vollbehr collection was assembled by Dr. Otto H. F. Vollbehr in the early twentieth century and was purchased by the Congress in 1930 for $1.5 million. It contained some 3,000 incunabula, making it one of the richest collections of fine and early printing in the world. Among its treasures was the Library's Gutenberg Bible—one of the three perfect vellum copies in existence.

This splendid work is, of course, the earliest known volume to be produced by movable type. Its fame rests, however, not only on its age but equally on the fact that it would have been a masterpiece of bookmanship no matter when it was done. That it was cast so near perfection at the very birth of the art boggles the mind.

The Gutenberg Bible cost Dr. Vollbehr $350,000, the most money ever paid for a single volume up to that time. Oddly enough, considering its fame and the amount of scholarship lavished on it, there are many things about the Bible which are still lost in the haze of time. No one is absolutely certain, for example, that it was really produced by Gutenberg. It is known to have been printed in Mainz, where Gutenberg had only recently perfected his technique of printing from movable type, and he is known to have been personally interested in the project. Who actually designed and set it in type is anybody's guess. The precise date of the Bible's production is similarly blurred. The second perfect copy—in the Bibliothèque Nationale in Paris (the third is in the British Museum, London)—carries two scribbled dates, August 15 and August 24, 1456, but the Library's copy has no dates at all. Because of its size and the limitations of the equipment of the time, scholars assume it would have taken at least three to five years to complete.

The Library's copy originally belonged to the Benedictine monks at Saint Blasius in the Black Forest. During the Napoleonic Wars, their copy was moved from one house to another in Switzerland and Central Europe and finally to the Abbey of Saint Paul in Eastern Carinthia, Austria, where it remained until it was brought to the Library of Congress in 1930.

The Bible is bound in three volumes totaling 641 leaves, each leaf being about the size of a tabloid newspaper sheet. Most of the leaves carry 42 lines of type in double columns, and the text is in Latin from Saint Jerome's translation of the fourth century. In spite of its somewhat hazy origins, what is clear to anyone who looks at it is the majesty of the piece. Today, over five hundred years after its production, the vellum is still dazzling white, the ink rich black, the initial letters deep velvet red and gold. Each page is almost sublimely proportioned—margins, spacing, type size simply could not be improved by even the finest adjustments. The type itself, instead of being the primitive, chipped elements we are accustomed to in Colonial printing, is full-bodied and graceful with delicate serifs and uniform color. In sum, nothing symbolizes "rare books" quite so much as this single work, which seldom fails to awe both the sophisticated scholar and the visiting tourist.

The Lessing J. Rosenwald Collection

In our own generation the Library is receiving a collection of bibliophilic treasures similar to the Vollbehr through the gifts of Lessing J. Rosenwald of Jenkintown, Pennsylvania. Since 1943 Dr. Rosenwald has given the Library and the nation over 2,200 rare books and manuscripts. There are 567 from the fifteenth century (over 100 are the sole examples in the United States) and 638 from the sixteenth century.

The Rosenwald collection has been selected and shaped to

demonstrate the historical progress of fine printing and thus traces the development of the great printing houses of the Renaissance and Reformation. It contains superb examples of the binder's art and is probably the world's finest single collection showing the development of book illustration from the mid-1400's onward. Among its treasures are the *Catholicon* of Johannes Balbus, printed at Mainz in 1460, the 1462 Fust and Schoeffer Bible (the first dated edition of the Scriptures), and sixteen extremely rare works by William Caxton, the first English printer. The earliest printing of France, Spain, and the Low Countries is as fully developed as the more familiar German and English work.

Special Collections

In addition to the "treasure" rarities, the Rare Book Division services and preserves many individual collections assembled on a single topic or about a famous figure. It has a bloc of almost 14,000 children's books. It has 16,907 different early American volumes printed before 1800. It has 1,500 books, pamphlets, and broadsides produced in the Confederate States between 1861 and 1865.

It has a number of collections relating to individual authors. The William Montelle Carpenter collection of Rudyard Kipling contains manuscript copies of many Kipling stories and poems including "Mowgli's Brothers" (the first story in *The Jungle Book*), a long series of letters and photographs, and a complete set of his first editions.

The Jean Hersholt collection is a remarkable assemblage of Hans Christian Anderseniana, including the manuscripts of ten of the original fairy tales, an annotated transcript of Andersen's autobiography, and long runs of his first editions.

The Bitting collection contains 2,500 volumes on the "sources, preparation, and consumption of foods, and on their chemistry, bacteriology, and preservation from the earliest times to the present day"—a gastronomic library. Finally, we should note the unlikely library of Harry Houdini which contains 4,350 books and pamphlets on conjuring, magic, and spiritualism.

All of these literal treasures are housed in a huge, fireproof, multilevel vault, kept at 68 degrees Fahrenheit and 50 per cent humidity. The special Rare Book Reading Room is modeled after a room in Independence Hall in Philadelphia and is served by a staff of seven. Its collections currently contain some 300,000 books and pamphlets, and they were drawn upon by 14,605 scholars in 1971.

In addition to the codexes, broadsides, jeweled bindings, and blockbooks, the various collections have accumulated a strange assortment of memorabilia as well. As Frederick Goff, recent chief of the Rare Book Division, has said, how can you describe holdings which contain "Mrs. Lincoln's seed-pearl necklace and bracelets, Charles Dickens' fruit knife and walking stick, the death masks of Lord Lothian and James Joyce, and the six white china dessert plates upon which Rudyard Kipling painted rather entertaining verses about certain fruits"?

General Reference Services

The three divisions of rarities—Manuscripts, Maps, and Rare Books—are inherently dramatic and serve highly specialized audiences, but the Library also has a group of "plain, ordinary" library divisions similar to those in any large research library. They provide the basic operations that in fact serve *most* of the users of the institution.

Stack and Reader Division

The Stack and Reader Division of 143 positions shelves the books, brings them to the readers in the two large reading rooms (the "Main" in the Old Building and the "Thomas Jefferson" in the 1939 Annex across the street), and operates such special study facilities as reserved desks and carrels for scholars doing long-term projects. The general collections now contain over 8 million individual volumes of which roughly 1 million will be used each year by the 600,000 readers passing in call slips.

Who can use the Library's reading rooms? Any citizen above high school level. A reader simply comes through the door, looks up the books he wants in the card catalog, fills out a call slip, hands it in, and then waits at a desk for the books, exactly as he would in a home-town public library. The 8 million volumes are divided about equally between the two buildings, but despite the two-block distance, books are flashed back and forth between floors, decks, and buildings by a series of endless belt elevators and pneumatic tubes, so a reader sitting in either reading room can have any books he wishes brought to him from any deck anywhere in the system. Regrettably, the time between request and delivery has been growing longer and now approaches one hour per volume. This is a source of increasing distress to management and reader alike, and the knowledge that the equivalent time at the British Museum and Bibliothèque Nationale is roughly twice as long is small comfort to anyone.

In addition to the books, the Stack and Reader Division is also keeper of the microform collections of the Library, and many believe that in these lies the future of the great research collections of our time. At present the Library uses 520,000 reels of microfilm, 355,000 microcards, and 597,000 pieces of microfiche. Essentially all the Library's newspapers are kept solely on microfilm, and so are its doctoral dissertations. The greatest potential use of microforms, however, seems tied to a new problem which is taking on the proportion of a helical nightmare: the headlong deterioration of the book collection itself. From 1400 to 1850, ordinary paper (if kept from fire or water) was virtually indestructible. Then in the mid-nineteenth century the paper makers turned to wood pulp and alum rosin sizing, and the world's books began turning brown and brittle and are now falling apart before our eyes. In 1970 alone, the Library microfilmed 2,220,658 dying pages, yet this represents less than one-fourth of 1 per cent of its volumes known to be in a deteriorated condition with splintered pages falling out of bindings, sheets cracking down the middle, and in many cases literally turning to dust between their boards. Acid left in the wood pulp is eating up the paper of every twentieth-century page.

The library world hopes that long-lived plastic film will both save the text and solve the increasingly expensive costs of storage, but it has not yet settled on the proper format. Presently the race appears to be between microfilm reels, opaque cards with miniature pages printed on them (microcards), and transparent sheets of film with similar pages for enlarged projection (microfiche). Microfilm was the early favorite. In the 1960's microfiche seemed to have overtaken it, and then in the 1970's microfilm reassumed ascendency. Many feel that the future holds a combination of some form of miniaturized transparency for storage, plus computer coding for analysis and retrieval. Whatever the solution is, it cannot come too soon.

The Loan Division

All books requested from the shelves must be used within the reading rooms; the institution is not a lending library—with certain exceptions.

The Library, being Congress's library, loans practically anything in its stacks to Congress at the request of members and their staffs. Notwithstanding the occasional reader who complains, "But I thought Congress had its own library!" the Congress borrows some 90,000 volumes a year through the Loan Division.

Further, the *libraries* of the various federal agencies throughout the government have the right to borrow books (but not magazines or newspapers), and *libraries* throughout the world have the right to borrow materials from the Library of Congress's collections that are not available in their home communities. These so-called interlibrary loans amounted to 158,606 volumes in 1970 and may merit some elaboration.

Except for congressional staff, the Library does not lend directly to individuals. It does make its collections available for two-week periods to *libraries* both here and abroad, which are then responsible for the materials while they are being used by researchers in their own institutions. Although they are in the minority, there are a few kinds of materials the Library will *not* lend. It resists requests for materials which ought to be in a home-town library (it will not send out copies of the King James version of the Bible or the *World Almanac*); it limits loans of materials that a small library should be able to borrow from nearby state or college libraries; and it refuses requests for common federal documents which should be available in the 1,082 document depositories distributed throughout the country. Except for these limitations, it will loan almost anything in English that cannot be bought from a local bookstore and will loan pretty much anything in a foreign language, across the board. At the rate of 150,000 loans a year, the interlibrary loan service is one of the Library's greatest strengths— and one of its biggest problems.

By congressional instruction, many federal agencies have been urged to borrow from the Library of Congress rather than build duplicate collections under their own roofs— yet the books so borrowed are frequently the very volumes Congress itself needs to study the legislative aspects of the problem being explored by the executive agency that borrowed the books. Similarly, many scholars come to the Library expecting its collections to be comprehensive, only to learn that the books they were expecting to find are now on loan to a college library 3,000 miles away. The converse, of course, is that one of the major justifications for building a comprehensive national collection is to make it conveniently available to the nation's research community when and where it needs it. It makes for a dilemma.

General Reference and Bibliography Division

We come now to the question answerers. These are the reference librarians who meet the public in the two great reading rooms or who open the mail that has been inspired by the traditional, "I dunno, why don't y' write the Library of Congress?"

In the reading rooms, the twenty-four-man staff provides two services: It helps the visiting scholar use the catalog and reference tools so he can find his answers for himself, or it serves as a referral point to get the visitor into the appropriate specialty division (such as Manuscripts, Orientalia, or Law Library) where the proper specialist can serve him. A reference librarian is skilled at knowing short cuts to answers. He carries with him a vast memory of what is where, which books have what in them, and, in the absence of previous knowledge, how to find out what he didn't know before the question came up. (And once a fugitive fact is found, the model reference librarian never forgets where he located it!)

At the Library of Congress, the majority of the patrons are themselves skilled researchers, so much of the time of a reading room librarian is spent helping the scholar plot an efficient course through the literature he is searching. The librarian brings him in contact with the bibliographic tools he will need and tries to make his research time as short and as profitable as possible. How well he does this will be determined by the librarian's knowledge of the collections and the ways in which they are organized. Nevertheless, since the visitor can be anyone from Aunt Sarah working on her genealogy to the chancellor of the oldest university in Europe, each "May I help you, please?" starts a new story with a new challenge.

The Bibliography and Correspondence Section of this

division does the same thing for the written word that Public Reference does for the spoken. The Library receives roughly a hundred question letters a day. It invests skilled reference time on something better than half of these. The rest are returned to the sender with a recommendation that he consult his local librarian for the answer.

This superficially high-handed approach is the only realistic way the Library can operate. Since the Library of Congress comes close to having the world's greatest collection of information, it follows that it could theoretically come close to providing answers to most of the world's questions.

But it has to draw the line somewhere, and it does this under the banner: "The Library of Congress should be the point of last resort." By this it means, if a citizen or scholar is seeking a fact, he should first try his local library or his nearest university or his state or regional reference facility, since that is what they are there for. He can properly turn to the Library of Congress for those questions where *only* it—because of the breadth and uniqueness of its collections—would be likely to have the answer. There are still plenty of questions that meet these requirements. In 1970, the Bibliography and Correspondence Section wrote 9,100 replies to inquiries that could probably be answered only (at least in this country) at the Library of Congress.

The "Bibliography" part of the section's title refers to printed guides to Library materials the unit prepares for visitors and the general public. Recent examples (which are traditionally sold by the Government Printing Office) are: *Presidential Inaugurations, Carl Sandburg*, and *The Negro in the United States*.

General Reference and Bibliography also contains three smaller units: a three-woman Children's Book Section, which assists writers, illustrators, and students of children's literature; an Arms Control and Disarmament Section; and an African Section—of which more later.

AREA STUDIES

Three Reference divisions are identified by the *language* of the material they serve: the Orientalia Division; the Slavic and Central European Division; and the Latin American, Portuguese, and Spanish Division (LAPS). They are staffed with 41, 19, and 12 positions, respectively. Each of these divisions is peopled with specialists who have made a life's work out of the language and the literature of their subject area.

While the language groupings make some sense as they stand, in the Orientalia Division the coverage is so broad that the division is redivided internally to serve the greatly differing cultures covered. "Orientalia," in the Library's scheme of things, includes its holdings of Chinese, Hebraic, Korean, Arabic, Japanese, Hindu, Korean, and the Southeast Asian languages; it requires six sections to serve them all. "Slavic" is slightly more rational, covering the related languages from Russia and from the Baltic, Central, and Eastern European countries. LAPS—clumsy acronym—is the most homogeneous of the group, involving the Spanish, Portuguese, and Latin American world of books and culture.

Each of the three divisions maintains its own reading room, each has its own catalogs and reference tools, and all of their staffs are, by definition, multilingual. (The LAPS Reading Room is particularly dramatic, with enormous floor-to-ceiling murals, Moorish decor and furniture, a hammered silver chandelier from the Escorial, and a huge coat of arms of Ferdinand and Isabella spread across the far wall on a sheet of stainless steel.)

There are other parallels. Major portions of the collections of each of the three divisions are unique in the scholarly world. Each division prepares printed bibliographies (sold by the Government Printing Office) which have become basic tools of the research trade, and each is headed by internationally famous scholars. But there is a junior in their midst that might make what the Big Three do more understandable by showing the large in microcosm.

The African Section

The African Section is the Reference Department's youngest child. It has seven positions, and it relies on the Library's embryonic collection of some 80,000 volumes of Africana to do its work. (Orientalia is backed by over a million volumes in forty languages.)

The Library's interest in Africa began early but built slowly. It sought books from and about Africa as quickly as they appeared from the Victorian period onward, and in 1908 its Division of Bibliography put together a short list of "Books Relating to the West Coast of Africa (excepting Liberia & Nigeria) in the Library of Congress." In 1910 it prepared similar lists for German and British East Africa and Zanzibar. Then, except for some minor bibliographic projects on the Ethiopian War, nothing much was undertaken for the next thirty-five years. With the coming of World War II, the Library was asked to prepare a series of literary guides to all the African colonies, and it was thus at least partly prepared for the work explosion that struck it in the early 1950's.

The Library was first caught up in the near-frenzied African research pursued by the federal agencies in Washington; this was soon followed by the arrival of private scholars from everywhere. The General Reference and Bibliography Division began its response with two detailed and annotated surveys of the published work in the field: *Introduction to Africa; A Selective Guide to Background Readings*, which concentrated on politics, history, culture, and social conditions, and *Research and Information on Africa; Continuing Sources*, which identified the major scholarly journals (domestic and foreign) concerned with the area. The two guides were printed by the Government Printing Office and sold by the hundreds to the research community.

Publishing by and about Africa continued to grow so that, by the late 1950's, inquiries from outside the Library and swelling collections within called for a full-time African Section. This was established in 1960, and with a permanent, concentrated staff the unit began to provide the kind of service on which the three old-line area divisions had built their reputations: individual assistance to individual scholars. Now a researcher could sit down with a librarian who knew what materials the Library had, what they contained, and how they were organized, and help him chart an efficient, productive attack on his research problem. Use of the special collections by both federal officials and African area scholars accelerated. The publications of the unit grew with a new series of study guides and three general surveys: *United States and Canadian Publications on Africa*, *A List of American Doctoral Dissertations on Africa*, and *Serials for African Studies*.

The African Section is conscious of the fact that its main role is one of a cross-over and switching point for African bibliography and that it would be both impossible and inappropriate for the Library of Congress to try to build the sole, comprehensive collection of African materials in the United States. The staff therefore invests a good deal of its energy helping other groups in the field achieve their broader missions and purposes—such groups as the African Studies Association, the Association of Research Libraries' Farmington Plan Subcommittee on Africa, the Advisory Committee on Africa of the National Academy of Sciences–National Research Council, the Interagency Book Committee's Task Force on Africa, and the Subcommittee on Africa of the Foreign Area Research Coordination Group. Cooperation with *inter*national agencies is equally remarkable. The

African Section has participated in the International Congress of Africanists, the Standing Conference on Library Materials on Africa of Great Britain, meetings of the African Center for Training and Research in Administration for Development, and the International Conference on African Bibliography.

Such grim conference-going serves a double purpose. It makes more meaningful the appropriate division of labor between the staff of the Library's African Section and its fellow African specialists, and it serves as a sublime device for improving the Library of Congress's own African acquisitions. It is here (and in the resulting invitations to specific national capitals) that the exchange agreements are negotiated and the new deposit programs established.

Thus the unit duplicates in miniature the responsibilities of the over-all Reference Department—serving the public, improving the collections, and caring for the materials in its area of expertise.

SCIENCE AND TECHNOLOGY

Let us conclude our hurried glance at the Reference Department with a look at the chromium and glass world of the Science and Technology Division—brave but not new. The Library of Congress projects a baroque image of history, culture, and literature, but not only are its scientific holdings now extraordinarily strong, they have been so almost from the beginning. Only the Philadelphia community could challenge Thomas Jefferson's collection of eighteenth-century experimental records, and, with the addition of the Smithsonian collection, from 1866 onward there was no institution in America that could approach the Library of Congress when it came to scientific holdings. They started rich because of the interests of the founders. They got richer because of the way research has been funded in the United States. Somewhere along the line it became routine to write into federally financed projects, "Copies of the results from this experimentation shall be deposited with the Library of Congress," and thus there is almost no area of applied science in which the Library is not as current as yesterday's mail.

Science Is Different

A scientific library both looks and operates differently from one in the humanities. The Science and Technology Division relates to some 3 million books in the Library's collections, but it lives out of its 1.5 million technical reports and nearly 20,000 scientific journals.

In the *soft* sciences research goes forward; once a research project is concluded, the scholar puts it all together and interprets its meanings. He then attempts to prove that what he has learned is sufficiently important to justify its publication for the profession, hopefully as a book, if not, as a journal article. Either way it becomes a long drawn-out task of "selling" his product.

The *hard* sciences operate differently. As work progresses, a researcher is expected to share the results of his successes and failures with his fellow researchers at frequent intervals along the way; further, there is much less pressure to prove that what he has done is of towering significance, since any new data may be useful to someone, so his own profession supports him with its publication and dissemination. The product, however, appears in tiny transactions—multilithed and mimeographed documentation, microformed reports—all pouring out in great quantity and requiring immediate, uniform indexing so that they can be made quickly available to ongoing researchers in parallel fields. Thus life in the Science and Technology Division is unique.

Services to the Scientific Public

The Division operates with approximately sixty staff members, the majority of whom are professionals and, since

Russian, German, and Chinese experimentation is just as important to its customers as Anglo-American (if not considerably more so!), the staff is broadly multilingual.

The Division operates a Science Reading Room for in-house assistance. It operates a highly refined bibliographic search service for out-of-house help. Scientific projects, both in government and in the private sector, start with the question "What do we know so far?" Thus a search of the literature "as of today" is essential. The Science and Technology Division will provide such service either on a one-time-only basis or as a continuing reporting contract for a charge of $11 an hour.

The Division pursues its own publishing program so the various professions can know what is available in the Library of Congress as well as what is going on in appropriate fields. Recent examples are a 308-item bibliography on fish protein concentrate, *Nuclear Science in Mainland China*; *A Selected Bibliography*, and *Japanese Scientific and Technical Serial Publications in the Collections of the Library of Congress*.

The division frequently works jointly with federal scientific agencies on a contract basis to support some major area of government research. The products of these arrangements take such forms as *Bibliography on Cold Regions Science and Technology* and *UFO's and Related Subjects: An Annotated Bibliography*. (The latter runs to 401 printed pages and 2,400 items and, like most of the Division's studies, is available from the Government Printing Office.)

The Collection

Books are an obvious part of the science collection. Technical reports may not be. Nowadays a substantial proportion of these are received and kept *solely* as microfilm or microfiche, thus the literature search is mechanically different from the usual "look it up in the card catalog," and the use of the material itself involves row upon row of great, hulking micro-readers in a dimly lit room. The kinds of subjects they cover are revealed by their sources (scientific bibliography is strong on acronyms): 247,500 AEC, 195,700 AD, 190,000 NASA, 45,000 ERIC, 37,000 PB, and 1,500 TT reports.*

The National Referral Center for Science and Technology

The reading room and bibliographic staff try to bring the reader in contact with the proper printed material. The National Referral Center, another unit of the Science and Technology Division, tries to bring people seeking information in contact with people having that information—throughout the country.

The Center has queried over eight thousand institutions, departments, and individuals working in the major fields of the physical, biological, social, and engineering sciences to find out who knows what. The results of these surveys are loaded into the Library's computer, and the nation's scientific community is invited to use the service as a cross-over directory. When a researcher is pursuing a topic, he writes or phones the Center, stating his query as precisely as possible, and the Library then spins its tapes through various search programs. The reply comes out with names, addresses, telephone numbers, and brief descriptions of the sources shown. It tells the researcher about people and places, not books and articles in the usual library manner. Some examples of search requests: Who is working on He^3 neutron detectors and cross sections of He^3? Who keeps track of tide measurements in Boston Harbor? Who has test data on the vibration damping properties of thermoplastic materials with induced vibrations between 500 and 5,000 cycles per second? Who knows what attracts termites? Who has information on the effects of disarmament on innovation and invention?

The service is free for the asking, and the center currently handles more than 3,000 questions a year.

*A[tomic] E[nergy] C[ommission]; A[rmed Services Technical Information Agency] D[ocuments]; N[ational] A[eronautics and] S[pace] A[dministration]; E[ducational] R[esearch and] I[nformation] C[enter]; [the federal] P[ublication] B[oard]; [Commerce Department] T[echnical] T[ranslations].

VII

The Congressional
Research Service

With the Congressional Research Service we come full circle. The Library of Congress started as Congress's library entire, but, as we have seen with the growth of its responsibilities it broadened into the national library instead. The Congressional Research Service (CRS) continues to be that part of the Library which works exclusively for the Congress.

Like the portions of the Reference Department we looked at in the preceding chapter, the CRS also provides reference service, but it carries out its mission in a substantially different way. The Reference Department gives its patrons the materials they need to do their own research; the CRS actually does the research itself and gives its patron the finished product. Indeed, as the result of two relatively recent laws, the CRS now goes well beyond traditional research and in effect has become one of the nation's major "think tanks." Today it provides legislative policy analyses, cost analyses, and environmental impact projections—all in response to specific congressional requests.

The Congressional Way of Life

The way Congress requires its information affects the CRS in three rather dramatic ways. In the first place, Congress demands its facts in great quantity. At the peak of the congressional session it calls on the CRS at an average of 2,000 times a day. Even when the members of Congress "go home," leaving only committee staffs and reduced office personnel, the calls rarely drop below a thousand a day, with the requests running from as simple a query as "What is the current tariff rate on Japanese transistors?" to as extensive a request as "Give me the legislative history of the Higher Education Act and analyze what's been recommended to improve it since it was passed." These requests pour into the CRS, two-thirds by telephone, the other third by letter or personal visits of the members and their staffs.

A second element in Congress's demands for information is timing . . . speed. While the executive branch can enjoy the luxury of two-year studies of water resources and five-year studies of Indian affairs, congressional studies are tied to the legislative year. The session opens in January, and as many as 12,000 bills are written and dropped into the hopper in the first 90 days. The committees then gear up to process this glut of proposed legislation. Hearings are called. Witnesses are questioned and reports written. Legislation is modified, amended, and sent to the floor. Debate begins, and hundreds of bills are sorted, massaged, and amended with increasing speed as the session builds to adjournment in the fall. The result is a span of nine to twelve months in which the CRS cannot afford the luxury of leisurely research, developed to fit the temperament of the specialist; the legislation must be dealt with at once. The bill will either be voted up or voted down or changed, and the CRS must gear itself to provide what Congress needs at the time it needs it. One half of all the inquiries that come to the Service must be answered the same day they are received. These inquiries come off the floor of Congress, out of ongoing hearings, out of meetings with lobbyists, from constituents from home, and the CRS response must be measured accordingly. Conversely, of course, many of the studies are time-consuming and extensive. The Congressional Research Service is called on to provide thousand-page committee prints; it prepares over 14,000 reports and memoranda every year, and, while these take longer, time is still limited. Even in multivolume CRS studies, the product is not that of one researcher spending two years, but of six spending two months.

The third element that makes Congress's demands for data and analysis different is what might be called the Lighthouse Effect. Congress faces up to national issues like the circling beam of a lighthouse on a dark night. A topic will surface for congressional attention, and four or five hundred representatives of the people will focus their attention on it simultaneously. Everyone will want to know how much, how long, how else, why, and why not; a legislative decision will be reached—and then the subject will be all but abandoned for another year. The blinding light of congressional attention pours on to that single subject—be it foreign aid, Medicare, or meat prices—with each member needing briefings, alternative solutions, probable consequences through one year, five years, twenty years, and, once the subject is resolved, the light swings remorselessly to the next topic. The Congressional Research Service must be geared to respond accordingly. It must anticipate most of its work before it is needed and must have great quantities of data analyzed and stockpiled in a variety of forms for hasty assembly to fit just the point of view or the regional requirements of the inquiring member.

A word about the CRS's reason for being might be appropriate before we examine how it does its work. From its beginnings in 1914,* it was recognized that the Congressional Research Service was to be more than a mere transmitter of facts. It has had to go further and provide the legislative

*The Congressional Research Service was known as the Legislative Reference Service (LRS) from 1914 to 1970.

branch with much of the expertise it has to have to maintain some degree of parity with the executive branch. The executive departments have over 2.5 million civil servants at their beck and call while the Congress has barely five thousand, yet if it is to carry out its Constitutional role of initiating law or of challenging, testing, and refining the executive's demands, it must have access to a broad variety of independent knowledge that can match the executive's in quality if not in quantity. Congress needs its own specialists—men it can trust, who have no axes to grind or "official positions" to defend—to help it to ask the proper questions, whose answers point the way to proper decisions. More than anything else, the Congress wants to know *all* the possible solutions to the problems it faces, not simply the one pressed by the bureau or party with the most to gain. The CRS and the congressional committee staffs are supposed to provide this balance.

How the CRS Works

The Congressional Research Service has a staff of 438, of which two-thirds are professionals and the remainder administrative and support personnel. Of the 300 professionals, barely 50 are librarians; the remainder are civil engineers, Social Security analysts, atomic chemists, Asian experts, attorneys, environmentalists, and the like. These 300 have some 2,000 national issues divided among them, which they are required to "track." (Tracking involves keeping up with the past, present, and recommended legislation in a subject area. It requires the researcher to cover his subject literature in journals, newspapers, and governmental reports at all levels and obliges him to keep up with the lobby groups, professional associations, and involved elites in his fields.)

For some sixty years now, the CRS has found that its work load—what it does for a living—falls into two somewhat opposing activities. The result is that there is a sort of dumbbell shape to its product charts and a kind of tension in the devices and staffing developed to get the work out. Specifically: of two thousand calls received on any one day, it will develop that roughly half are informational. A member or a committee wants to know who, what, when, where, how, and which. These questions can be answered very quickly and accurately by someone who knows information literature —data and facts in print. Librarians. Thus the so-called reference questions are fed to the first of the CRS divisions, the Congressional Reference Division, made up of approximately fifty professional librarians and reference specialists. These handle vast quantities of queries on a quick turnaround basis. (Fortunately, experience has proved that librarians are endlessly turned on by a perpetual Twenty-Questions game. Thus end-to-end questions that can be answered out of previously prepared CRS reports, reference books, the vast CRS clipping files, and so on, give them considerable job satisfaction.)

The other half of the daily requests require not a simple identification and transmittal of a fact but some explication of the fact: an analysis, a synthesis, a comparison. It can be a legal analysis. ("Our Committee is considering a bill to withhold highway funds from any state failing to meet desegregation standards for schools. Would it be constitutional? Would the courts sustain it?") It can be cost impact and evaluations. ("If we limit payroll checkoffs to 10 per cent what effect would this have on the social security trust fund?") It can be a request for alternative solutions. ("Please give us a review of the Medicare program to date—be sure to include a comparison of its present cost with what was originally estimated and describe what's been suggested to bail the thing out.") It can be environmental impact projections. ("Our Committee has been told that if we underwrite development of electric cars, the electricity that's got to be generated to charge the batteries will cause more pollution than the gasoline used now. Is this true? What's the trade-off?")

To answer these types of questions requires not an informational specialist but a subject expert and analyst, preferably someone who has had experience in the field as well as on the campus. These specialists are organized among seven divisions, each clustered around the concept of like professional skills. What they do is obvious from their divisional titles: American Law, Economics, Education and Public Welfare, Environmental Policy, Foreign Affairs, Government and General Research, and Science Policy.

It bears noting that this division of labor was only one of three organizational choices considered in the mid-1940's. Ernest S. Griffith, the director who created the CRS in its present form to carry out the Congressional Reorganization Act of 1946, first considered two arrangements, one based on the then ten executive departments (a Justice unit, a State unit, an Agriculture unit) and one based on the congressional committee system (Ways and Means, Veterans, Education and Labor). He finally opted for a third arrangement, the present organization, which is essentially the university department idea. It has proved to be an inspired choice. In the intervening quarter century, numerous management studies have invariably arrived at the same solution. Since the 1946 Act, Congress and the executive have each fractionated so badly that no one is talking to anyone, while the CRS has become an agency for pulling the disparate pieces together at both ends of the Mall. As examples of the problem: Education is handled by no less than 26 committees of Congress, and educational programs appear in 23 agencies of the Executive; energy matters are under consideration by 24 congressional committees and are administered by 50 Presidential agencies.

The specialists that staff the seven subject divisions are professionals in research rather than professionals in reference skills. Experience has proved that they do not want to answer short, fast, and responsive inquiries but find more satisfaction in pursuing a subject, developing it, briefing a member on its legislative elements, and in general saturating themselves in limited professional areas. Finding personnel appropriate for CRS provides an unusual challenge. It is essential that the specialists represent the best in their respective fields because members of Congress consider them *their* man on space, *their* analyst on civil rights, *their* expert on gun control. The result is, hopefully, that CRS specialists are as good as the best in the executive branch, albeit they are fewer. Even more important, however, is the hairline distinction between being a leader in a field and being an advocate of a solution. In order for the CRS to survive, the congressional inquirer must never be able to guess where the researcher himself stands on any particular issue. The result is that if someone believes deeply that a particular solution is the only answer, that person is inappropriate for the CRS. He must go elsewhere to promote his cause. But the person who believes deeply in the importance of his subject field and who is eager for the Congress to have as many solutions available to it as possible and to have as great a knowledge of the impact of these alternatives, together with a sensitivity to what these solutions will cost this generation and five generations to come, and who yet recognizes that for the democratic system to survive the choice of a solution must be left to the elected representatives—that is the person the CRS seeks for its staff.

In any particular area—labor, public health, United Nations affairs—the Congressional Research Service will usually have four or five people in what is essentially a hierarchy. The senior person will be mature and nationally recognized; he will usually have published extensively; he will have had experience in the field, perhaps in state and local government or in the private or academic sector, and frequently will have a Ph.D. Beneath him will be two people with newly acquired doctorates or extensive graduate work who will be able to handle middle-level research, and, beneath them a pair of junior members with master's degrees and as yet limited experience in the gathering and analysis of information about their professional area.

One Question ... Four Answers

Congress can ask these people about many different things. Not only different *kinds* of queries, as mentioned above, but frequently the same question at many different levels. A simple question on how the salt water conversion program is going could take five minutes to answer if the congressman has a lobbyist waiting in his outer room to plead for water-research tax concessions. It could take two hours' work to pull together a hundred pages of clippings, reports, and documents if the congressman's office needs it for a constituent newsletter or a TV presentation. The same question could cost the CRS two days' work if the member wished it to apply to his home district and wanted to know what programs were available for his local university, how he should go about getting grants, and if there was anything developing that his local businessmen should know. And it could cost a month's time if the question "How is the salt water conversion program going?" is asked by a committee chairman about to start hearings that require legislative histories, suggested witnesses, presentation of the witnesses' known positions, and the preparation of questions to bring out the particular knowledge of each—plus time for a background committee print on all past activity in the federal agencies designed to brief the other committee members sharing in the investigation.

TOOLS FOR EFFICIENCY

The Congressional Research Service has developed a variety of special tools and devices that permit it to do a substantial amount of in-depth research and analysis with a

minimum amount of professional time and effort. The
specialists it hires are very expensive. To get the people
who are the best in their fields requires that the Library must
match their present salaries and their present career expectations. The result is that, once these specialists are aboard,
the CRS struggles to eliminate as much of the mechanics of
research—the look it up, copy it out, and put it together—as
possible. It does this through a battery of information assembly
and control devices. For example:

The Morgue

For twenty-five years the CRS has been building one of the
most complete "morgues" of clippings on public issues in
the country. It clips 9 daily newspapers, 350 magazines, the
Congressional Record, all the products of the Government
Printing Office, publications of the United Nations and the
Organization of American States, the products of hundreds
of state and local governments, university studies series,
and the output of some 1,500 lobby groups. It subscribes to
some 3,000 specialized journals, which it assigns to the
appropriate specialists on its staff. It indexes and codes the
contents of its own annual product of more than 14,000
reports and memoranda. Finally, it examines the daily input
into the Library's English-language collections, and the
cream of all the above is loaded into the computer to be
retrieved as weekly "current awareness" reports to individual
researchers, or as on-demand bibliographic searches in
response to specific research projects. All this selecting,
abstracting, and classifying is done by the CRS's Library
Services Division, a support unit of professional librarians
dedicated to having material found, sorted, and in place for
the analysts before they need it.

Prefabricated Parts

The Congressional Research Service has found that, since
so many of the same public problems affect so many different

constituencies, what is distressing one member is usually distressing ten or a hundred. Thus it has found that it is useful to prepare basic briefing papers in advance on many issues. Briefing papers are designed as prefabricated parts on which tailored responses can be built. Their basic format is therefore a statement of the history of the problem and a description of the present laws which attempt to deal with it. This is followed with an abstract of the major legislation pending before the session designed to cope with the difficulty and finally with an enumeration of the various solutions being pressed by the two parties, the academic community, business and labor, and any specific lobby groups and affected elites involved. When the rush call comes ("Come over right away and explain the problem of X"), the researcher can take the briefing paper with him and with that as a base concentrate on answering the question, "How will these solutions affect my own particular district?" The CRS keeps approximately 1,000 of these papers in stock and updated at any one time.

In many respects the CRS is a library within a library. Each of the seven research divisions will have its own working collection of from three to five thousand volumes of current books and looseleaf services that cover the activities in its assigned subject areas.

The Bill Digest

The Congressional Research Service has created its own tools to help it answer inquiries. Several of these have become popular with Congress itself and are used by congressional offices to do their own work—such as the *Digest of Public General Bills*, the *Monthly Status Report of Major Legislation*, the *Directory of Sources of U.S. Government Publications*, and the *Directory of Federal Commissions and Presidential Appointments*. The first of these, the *Bill Digest*, is published by the Government Printing Office, and, although it was designed for the use of the CRS and Congress, it is sold to the general public and scholarly institutions on a subscription basis. It comes out approximately every two weeks and during each session grows from a single issue the size of the *Playboy Annual* to two huge volumes as large as the Manhattan telephone directory. The *Digest* contains all the bills introduced in either house each day of the session. For the public bills (those dealing with matters other than the relief of a single citizen), it tells which member introduced them, when, and to what committee they were referred. Each piece of legislation is "digested" into a condensed statement of what the bill contains and is then indexed by the member who introduced it, the subject it is about, and the catchword or title by which it is known. A final "Action Section" keeps track of the progress of each bill as it marches through the legislative process from introduction to hearing to debate to amendment and finally to passage or defeat.

INFORMATION TECHNOLOGY

As we have noted, the Congressional Research Service uses the computer to control its reports and publications. The *Bill Digest* and the *Status Report* are also computer generated. But CRS uses a number of other devices to retrieve and transmit information quickly. It maintains reference rooms in various House and Senate office buildings. Each of these is staffed by trained librarians, backed by some 350 basic reference books, the thousand-odd CRS briefing studies, and basic newspapers on microfilm, all supported in turn by a facsimile transmittal machine, a Xerox machine, a microfilm reader-printer, and a computer terminal. The computer ties the reference centers to the home office in the Library of Congress. Back in the Main Building, the CRS maintains a hot line service from 8:30 in the morning to 9:30 at night, seven days a week, so that any immediate factual data of a while-you-wait nature that a member needs while writing a speech, drafting a letter, or responding to a debate can be supplied by a librarian working in the Congressional Reading Room. The librarian is backed, in this case, by some five thousand reference books and a battery of telephones. He can convert microcard and microfilm data in the central collections to hard copy and get it into congressional offices with minimum turn-around.

Thanks to the computer network, the congressman or the staff member need not ask himself where he should call to get a fact; rather he dials a single CRS number, and a team of thirteen inquiry recorders flashes the call through the computer so that it gets from the congressman to the most appropriate researcher literally within seconds.

The above system has been put together pragmatically over a fifty-year period. As Congress's needs have become apparent, the CRS has responded with Congress's man on . . . whatever subject. Through this process several rather unlikely forms of information transfer have been developed. The CRS has five full-time translators, who convert roughly six thousand letters and documents a year into English and, once the member has drafted a reply, convert the reply into any one of twenty-two different languages for sending back to inquirers. It has art design and drafting facilities and will provide charts and graphs for committee hearings and television presentations. It has voting analysts who can prepare a congressman's voting record at any given time, so he can see where he has stood on a particular issue as it has gone through previous forms on the floor, or can prepare a report for his constituents of his complete votes for one or both sessions of a Congress.

In Sum

The techniques described above work remarkably well. Congressional demands increase as much as 15 to 20 per cent each year, and, by dint of constant innovations, CRS productivity goes up faster than the increase in staff, while the response time goes down. (In the last twenty-five years the inquiries handled have risen from 23,000 annually to 189,000, while the staff has gone from 131 to 438.)

We could go into many details of CRS–Congress relations (the 1970 Reorganization Act could sustain a chapter itself!). But for the moment let it be said that the Congressional Research Service may well be one of the last vestiges of Victorian optimism left on the governmental scene. With an almost childlike faith and enthusiasm, it copes with tens of thousands of congressional inquiries each month in the belief that if the Truth is known it shall set you Free. Great quantities of unpaid overtime are sustained by the hope that a little more information, a few more alternatives, a little better understanding of an issue will raise the level of a debate, broaden the choices for action, and make the final solution of a problem a little more realistic.

The Congressional Research Service makes no recommendations. It draws no conclusions. It deliberately halts before the final step of "Therefore, the best action would be . . ." Instead, it simply says, "These are the facts, these are the choices—you, sirs, make the decision." Its present staff of nearly 450 is therefore acting in a direct line from Mr. Beckley. One hundred and seventy years later, they are still "librarians for the Congress."

VIII

The Law Library

The Law Library of the Library of Congress is the smallest of its six departments, but it is by far the oldest, antedating any of the others by a good half-century. It has the largest collection of legal materials of any institution in the world and not only covers the full story of American jurisprudence (captured as it all happened), but its strength in foreign law is so great that its American reputation is built on its non-American holdings and staff.

In any logical explanation of how the Library of Congress is put together, the Law Library acts as a bridge between the Reference Department and the Congressional Research Service. The CRS cares for the Congress, the Reference Department serves the public, but the Law Library works for both. It handles all the questions Congress asks concerning foreign law. (In a recent year it did 516 major congressional studies—3,000 typewritten pages—exploring how foreign governments used the law to solve their particular social problems.) On the public's side, its collections are heavily used by the federal executive agencies and the courts, and hundreds of students from Washington's five law schools seem to consider it part of their school campuses. In 1971, 60,500 public readers used the Anglo-American Reading Room alone.

You will recall that the Law Library was the first unit of the Library to be split off and set up as a separate department. In 1831, the Senate told its Judiciary Committee to look into the feasibility of putting all law books from the general library collection into a separate legal service. The committee found the idea good, and in 1832 a law was passed moving the appropriate books into "an apartment near to, and connected by an easy communication with that in which the Library is now kept." According to the act, the Justices of the Supreme Court were to make such rules and regulations for the new library as they saw fit, so long as they did not restrict its use by the President, the Vice-President, and the members of Congress. In those days the Supreme Court was itself housed in the Capitol, one floor below the Library of Congress. The Justices were given $5,000 to expand the collection, plus $1,000 a year thereafter to buy whatever books they wished for their law library. No doubt the separation was helpful to the Court, but by accident it was a greater boon to the nation, since most of the original Library burned to ashes in the fire of 1851, whereas the satellite law library was spared. The present collection of 1,202,000 volumes is thus the oldest continuously developed collection in the Library. "In the Library" is appropriate, because when the whole Library of Congress moved out of the Capitol, the Law Library came with it and was reabsorbed under Library of Congress control. No books have been selected for it by the Justices since the close of the century.

The legal collection has always been heavily used. Understandably, the Supreme Court has used it as it worked through its annual sessions, but the Congress has used it just as hard—not for interpreting the laws but for making them. From the beginning, the amelioration of many of the nation's ills began with the question "How are the British doing it?" Nowadays the question is more likely to be "What are the Swedes doing about it?" or "I hear the Japanese have changed their minds—how?" But the tradition persists.

To serve its many audiences, the Law Library has always built across the full spectrum of legal bibliography. It covers the works of all ages and all systems of law. Its shelves support rows of volumes in the traditional fields of jurisprudence, legal history, and legal philosophy—but they are filling even faster with the law of common markets, nuclear defense agreements, and multinational programs for developing countries. Similarly, its classification schemes embrace thousands of volumes of Roman, medieval, feudal, and canon law, as well as materials on the common, civil, Napoleonic, and Soviet systems.

ORGANIZATION

For the better part of this century, the successive Law Librarians have found it convenient to organize their staff and their collections around language/area legal systems. (This arrangement is not as obvious as it sounds. International law is so different from divorce law, and canon law from corporate law, that a strong case can be made for organization by content.) But staying with the language and area arrangement has produced five divisions: The American-British Law Division of twenty-four staff members copes with U.S., British Commonwealth, and Irish Republic material. The Hispanic Law Division with a staff of nine covers Latin America, Puerto Rico, the Philippines, Spain, and Portugal. The nineteen-man European Law Division handles the remainder of Europe, including Russia. Eight on the Far Eastern Division staff and seven in the Near Eastern and African Law Division complete the picture.

The extraordinary complexity of evolving law is bad enough, but when you add this to the fact that foreign law in particular lacks the detailed indexing and control system with which we are familiar in American-British law, it makes the selection of individual staff specialists particularly important in this department. The Library tries to get professionals who have actually been trained as lawyers within at least one of the countries they are paid to oversee. Each specialist must have passed a public law examination in his home country, and, to the extent that this is possible, each specialist is expected to have had a recognized career as a lawyer, judge, or administrator abroad. Thanks to the distressing turbulence in twentieth-century world politics, the Library has been able to secure some of the world's leading jurists from an astonishingly large number of foreign nations. At the present time, its attorneys work in more than forty different languages.

What Do You Use a Law Library For?

Obviously, it depends on who you are. The foreign specialist from a federal agency is most likely to be interested in commercial law relating to foreign taxes and trade incentives, the labor laws of the country the agency is dealing with, the regulation of private business within that country, the different treatment afforded foreigners (like Americans)—and the laws on motion picture censorship of exported American films.

The visitor from the Supreme Court or the Justice Department is likely to be seeking some looseleaf service relating to state and local statutes. The endless insertion into binders of literally tens of thousands of advance sheets, pocket parts, slip laws, decisions, and looseleaf pages occupies the full time of three Law Library assistants.

Attorneys need the journal articles and textbooks. Legal historians struggle with the great vellum codexes. And the day-to-day queries placed with the public reference desk add up to the full spectrum of legal research. In a recent year-end summary, the law librarians noted questions relating to:

the antiquity laws of Israel, Chad, and the United Arab Republic; the international movement of art treasures in Europe; marriage and divorce laws of the major religions of India; laws and regulations on the practice of optometry in the South Pacific Islands; the legal status of certain Latvian railroads after Latvia achieved its independence; and medieval laws in North Germany that give the church special rights to tax or even exert ownership over land that lay within the sound of the church bell.

THE K CLASSIFICATION

The Law Library is presently the scene of an unusual exercise, the like of which has not been seen in librarianship since the nineteenth century. The Gay Nineties and the ensuing turn of the century were the days of the great efforts in "organizing knowledge" into vastly detailed classification schemes, of which the Dewey Decimal System is the most famous and most pervasive. Dewey's system was only one of many at the time, but when, after several decades of experimentation, the smoke finally cleared, only it and the 5,000-page Library of Congress Classification Schedules had survived. Dewey was embraced by most school and public libraries and was fully developed from 001 through 999, covering all the ramifications of the human mind. The Library of Congress system was used most heavily by the nation's research and special libraries and was complete from AC 1 to Z 7999— except for the letter K! This had been reserved from the outset for the development of numbers to organize the subject of *law*, but for fifty years no one got around to doing anything about it.

The "K" exercise sounds trivial, but in the world of books and libraries it represents a fairly high order of irony. Most of the earliest American libraries *began* as collections of law books, yet from the early eighteenth century to 1967 no major law or research library in the country had developed a fully expanded subject classification for legal materials.

How did they handle the volumes they had? The traditional private law office library was always organized by the *kinds* of books on the lawyer's shelves. The Library of Congress followed this procedure at the start, then as the legal volumes grew from hundreds to thousands and then tens of thousands, it placed "temporary labels" on the spines and simply elaborated its basic form-sorts. Through the period from 1800 to World War II, the books were divided first into countries, and then within these countries into ten *kinds* of books (constitutions, session laws, compilations and codes, judicial decisions, simple legal treatises, and rules-regulations-decisions-and-orders). Within each *kind* of book the volumes were arranged either chronologically, numerically, or alphabetically, depending on which seemed appropriate. Considering that the collection had grown to over a million volumes (many floors of stacks of books) before anything was done about it, this arrangement would appear to have been confusing and clumsy. It was. Someone looking for books on divorce, for example, was forced to pick them out of thousands of legal treatises arranged simply by author from A to Z.

The legal profession was slow to complain about the situation, which was duplicated throughout most of the nation's law libraries, but when it finally faced up to the problem it concentrated its resources and expertise on the solution. Although the American Association of Law Libraries and the Library of Congress worked in concert, combining skills through committees, volunteer teams, and full-time personnel from the Library, it nevertheless took over twenty years to develop the detailed classification tables to the satisfaction of the many organized users. The schedules for U.S. law (KF) are now finished, and those for British law (KD), are likewise nearly done. The twenty years, recall, was required simply to decide what categories of subject matter should be isolated, how these subjects should be related to each other, and what numbers they were to carry. Not until 1967 did the Library begin to assign numbers to actual books.

This assignment is slow work. The Library is now trying to classify all newly received law material under the new K numbers, and to start reclassifying the million-odd volumes presently shelved with the temporary-form labels. In addition, there are between 250,000 and 300,000 books in the general collections that used to be classified as H's and J's (for Economics and Political science) that will now be withdrawn and recataloged under K (for Law). (Most books on Congress, for example, will be removed from the government numbers and moved to the legal ones.) The classifiers had transferred some 90,000 such volumes through 1972. At the present rate, this task should be completed around the year 2050.

A FUNDAMENTAL CHANGE

The philosophy represented by the K tables will have a profound effect on the use of books in the Library of Congress as well as on those libraries using LC printed cards and classification numbers. Traditionally, books have been classified by the subject they concern; books describing the *history* of education, the *financing* of education, *legislation* concerning education, and *techniques* of education have all been grouped together under the broad subject of Education. The same is true with other subjects. With the inception of the K classification, anything that bears on the *law*, the *legislation*, the *governmental processes* concerning a subject at the federal, state, or local level will be reclassified and placed with the legal materials. This will have a major impact on such topics as taxation and labor relations, which traditionally have been classified as aspects of economics. Since activities in these fields are almost entirely based on federal or state law, great numbers of volumes will be transferred to K. All congressional hearings and reports, regardless of subject (the aged, space, pollution, cotton subsidies) as well as all appropriation material (foreign aid, Indian reservations, the Library of Congress) will also be moved out of their present subject classifications and distributed among the law "numbers" KF 25 through KF 32.5. Social science scholars in particular will have to learn to search both the shelves of their H and J numbers *and* the legal shelves of the K's. Such moves, however, will finally rationalize the legal collections of both the Library of Congress and the participating national libraries— a century and a half after such moves might have been expected.

Let us now conclude our look at the kinds of things the Library does with a glance at what is probably the most unlikely set of activities of all the unlikely things the Library does do: Culture, with a capital C.

IX

The Library of Congress and Culture

The final area that we view has glamour. Here, not only do the materials sparkle with the riches of the fine and the lively arts, but many of their users seem to have come out of the Sunday supplements as well. The man at the Steenbeck viewer there is Gregory Peck, the gentleman in the next listening booth is Leonard Bernstein, the lady in the headphones across the table is Joan Baez, and that was Stephen Spender talking to Louis Untermeyer in the elevator.

The Library of Congress preserves culture in ink, wax, and silver salts. It has music, etchings, poetry, lithographs, motion pictures, photographs, and phonograph records, So do many libraries, but what is different about the Library of Congress is that it not only collects and preserves these products of the creative spirit, but it also generates, sponsors, and even underwrites the treasures it collects. Furthermore, while the material is fragile, incredibly valuable, and often unique, no portion of the Library is so involved in hard day-to-day use of its materials as the divisions to be described here. For want of a better way to proceed, let's take them one bureaucratic unit at a time and, within each unit, work from the prosaic to the sublime.

MUSIC

In 1971, the music collection reached four million items. In that year, the Library's five Stradivari instruments and its one Guarnerius were played in forty-five free concerts, which were rebroadcast over dozens of "good music" stations in North America and Europe. The same year the Music Division added to its vaults original manuscripts from the hands of George Gershwin, Franz Schubert, Fritz Kreisler, Sir Edward Elgar, Sergei Rachmaninoff, and Robert Schumann; it also put 30,678 new books and pieces of music on its shelves. We'll start with the latter.

How Do You Organize Musical Material
So You Can Find It?

If you, as a user, walk into the Music Division, you will find yourself facing four separate catalogs. The first is a typical dictionary catalog of *books* about music; the second has nothing in it but material on music theory and teaching; the third indexes the Library's huge collection of opera librettos; but it is the fourth that is the most unusual, for while the first three involve words, the last—and largest catalog—is limited to *music* (as in notes)—sheet music, collections, and full scores. The music catalog is in turn divided into three quite different parts. One part is filed by composer, the second by title, and the third (which in a typical book catalog would be by subject) in this music library is filed by call number. It is what is called a *classed* catalog.

A great deal of use in a library of music is for music of *kinds*: the reader wants carols; harpsichord solos; harpsichord, flute, and cello trios; Indian temple music; sea chanteys;

singing television commercials; Moog transcriptions. To accommodate this kind of access, the cards for thousands upon thousands of individual pieces of music are sorted into their classification numbers to permit browsing by "class," just as you would browse books on shelves by subject. A sample at random: M298 Drum and bagpipe music; M1958.D87 Songs and music of Duke University; M1682–3 Mexican music; M1507.9 Piano-vocal excerpts from motion picture musical comedies; M1527.25 Music for silent films in general; M14.6 Organ accompaniments to silent motion pictures in specific.

Working with this display of musical knowledge, you can make your own selections, and you will find that the actual shape your choices come in may turn out to be as varied as penciled manuscript sheets, printed scores, player piano rolls, phonograph records, or reel or cassette tapes. To get the pieces delivered to you in the division's reading room, you fill out a request slip just as if you were in a public library and the deck attendant disappears into the stacks to collect the goods. He will have a lively challenge before him because the materials themselves are housed in remarkable ways. Most sheet music is unbound, so it is kept flat in cardboard boxes, which are stacked tall on metal shelves. A few of the most frequently used pieces will be in thin cardboard covers, and the thickest scores are likely to be bound in buckram like oversized books. Where the piece is actually located will be determined by its format or where it came from. If it came from the copyright deposit, the attendant will have to paw through cartons of loose sheets arranged only by their copyright number. If it is on a phonograph record, it will be filed by manufacturer and then by serial number. (The Library owns almost 300,000 records, all of which are stored vertically and which produce literally hundreds of yards of discs, disappearing down aisles like cut stone courses in endless walls.) If your requested item happens to have been a part of one of a hundred special collections, it could be in one of a hundred different places arranged by the original *owner* (such as the cluster of 12,500 opera librettos collected by a single railroad man).

Ultimately, having assembled the pieces you want, the attendant will bring them to you and you can go into a sound-proofed room and either play them on the piano provided or listen to them via the appropriate audio apparatus. Qualified violinists can use the Library's Amati violin, which is available for this purpose.

What Do You Use a Music Library For?

On a typical recent day, the following situations arose and were resolved.

1. A Midwestern symphony director was preparing a program tribute to John F. Kennedy. *Query*: What were President Kennedy's favorite orchestral works?

2. An author writing a biography of John Philip Sousa was continuing his study of everything Sousa wrote (the Library has all Sousa's manuscripts as well as his published works) and was searching for duplication. *The problem*: Sousa would write a march for some special occasion and then throw the copies in a drawer after they had been played; years later when he needed something new, he would take a trio from one, an introduction or a coda from another, and write in a new body. Similarly, if some major piece he had written went particularly well in some parts but nobody whistled the rest, he would simply take the good parts, paste them to the good parts of another piece, and come up with a better whole. The author was trying to trace all the permutations.

3. Another author wanted a list of all the operas written by black composers.

4. A television documentary on Henry the Eighth was in production, and the music director (having abandoned "Greensleeves") wished to score the hour with contemporary

Tudor music that could legitimately be played on modern instruments. He wanted not only for the music to have been themes that Henry would have heard, but he wanted them to sound the way they sounded to Henry as well. What pieces would be appropriate?

The majority of the Music Division's reference questions come from people living outside Washington. The librarians will answer any legitimate musical query, and they rely heavily on photoduplication to provide copies of the original music, score, or libretto to the correspondent. (The copies are charged for at the Library's regular photoduplication rates.)

The Rarities

The Music Division's treasure vaults are filled with such an astonishing array of incredibly valuable material that the professional musicologist tends to be as awed as the "reader in the street." In the past seventy-five years, a series of aggressive, imaginative heads of the division have amassed original manuscripts from essentially all of the great composers of Western music—from Bach to composers of acid rock.

Some of the manuscript collections are simply "representative," with examples of particular kinds of works (as in the case of Bizet, Tchaikovsky, and Sibelius), while others are "comprehensive." The latter contain extensive holdings of most of a composer's musical production. (Recall, we are referring here to the scribbled worksheets and half-done rejected efforts, as well as the finished on-the-way-to-the-printer manuscripts, all in the composer's hand—*not* to the printed versions which resulted.)

The works of American composers fall into the "comprehensive" holdings, and thus here you can see thousands of manuscript pages from Samuel Barber, Leonard Bernstein, Howard Hanson, Victor Herbert, Frederick Loewe, Edward MacDowell, Walter Piston, Sigmund Romberg, and William

Schuman. All of the scores of the great Richard Rodgers' musicals sit side-by-side on a shelf, each bound in rich, red leather. Inside their slipcases (on common dime store music composition paper) the notes are in pencil, neatly marching along single staffs with the Hammerstein words jotted below. *Oklahoma!*, *South Pacific*, and *The Sound of Music* are written in simple, two-note chords that even a beginning pianist could play. The manuscripts of Gershwin's *Porgy and Bess* and his "An American in Paris," on the other hand, are in ink, also neatly drawn but fully orchestrated so a single chord can appear in 20 stacked staffs, each tagged to the proper instrument to which Gershwin assigned it.

The international "modern" scene appears in quantity: The Library owns the manuscripts of Bartok's Fifth String Quartet, Benjamin Britten's opera *Peter Grimes*, Honegger's Fifth Symphony, Villa-Lobos's *Madona*, Ginastera's "Bomarzo Cantata," and hundreds more.

The great masters of classical music are richly represented; their manuscripts have come from three sources. Some were given to "the Library and the Nation" by the composer or his family, some came as gifts from organizations such as the Beethoven Association of New York, and some were purchased from foundation funds (of which more later). The first major bloc arrived as far back as 1921, when the family of Leo Delibes presented the full scores of *Lakmé*, *La Source*, and *Sylvia*. Others followed. Herbert Witherspoon gave the full manuscript score of Leoncavallo's *Pagliacci*; Fritz Kreisler presented the manuscript of Brahms's Violin Concerto in D Major (this is in ink and is a fearful mish-mash of scribbled notes, fully orchestrated, almost unreadable to an amateur). On the other hand, the manuscripts of Robert Schumann's First Symphony (the *Spring*) and Mendelssohn's String Octet, Op. 20, are neat, precise, and easily read by any pianist. The original manuscript of Beethoven's Piano Sonata in E Major, Op. 109, is hurried and cluttered, but the ink chords and notations are thin and spidery, like snippets of black thread thrown on the page. Brahms's pages look like what one imagines Beethoven's should be—thick notes, spattered bars, generally black all over.

This exercise in name-dropping could go on for pages without adding to the point, but the yards of precious stuff so impresses *me* that I can't resist just a few more lines: The Library owns great masses of Stravinsky given by the composer himself; it has the 52nd Haydn Piano Sonata; the Coolidge collection has stacks of manuscripts, including Copland's *Appalachian Spring*, Prokofiev's String Quartet, Op. 50, Ravel's "Chansons Madecasses," and Respighi's *Trittico Botticelliano*. The Whittall collection contains Brahms's Third Symphony, Haydn's Symphony No. 90 in C Major, and the andante movement of his 94th, the *Surprise Symphony*. Sergei Rachmaninoff's wife donated an enormous collection of rare musical material (letters, phonograph records—many unreleased—and general memorabilia of the great), among which are the manuscripts of the composer's *Rhapsody on a Theme by Paganini*, the score of his Third Symphony, and the two-piano transcription of his Prelude in C Sharp Minor. Other great collections provided similar riches: the Heifetz collection, the Geraldine Farrar collection, the Liszt-Rosenthal, and the continuing gifts of Mrs. Gisella Selden-Goth, which include manuscripts of Liszt, Mendelssohn, Brahms, Schubert, and Paganini.

What Use Are They to Anybody?

The cynic might well ask why the Library should bother with all these manuscripts when music of any worth is available in printed form and much easier to use than the scribbled originals. Aside from the simple archival, historical, sense-of-presence justification, the treasure materials are heavily used in basic musical research for the following reasons.

1. Much of it was never published, and the unfinished and rejected manuscripts frequently tell more about the development of a composer than the final, polished product.

2. Even as many of the pages are nearly illegible to us, thanks to the work habits of the composers, they were almost as illegible to their contemporary publishers, and in many instances research has shown that accepted versions of the classics simply are not what the composer intended them to be; the engravers, working under pressure, misread many of the notations, and, once the pieces appeared in print, the printed version became the authorized one. (The discrepancy need not apply only to details. Examination of the Library's manuscript of Mozart's famous *Serenade for Thirteen Wind Instruments* reveals that Mozart had scored it for twelve wind instruments and a stringed, bass viol.)

3. Both musical editors and conductors have felt free to embellish or modify passages to improve them. Oddly enough, many of these changes or additions were gratefully accepted by the composers, but in other cases the manuscripts provide only means of returning to the purity of the original.

Folk Music

Not all of the Music Division's collections are as drenched with dignity and concert hall hush as the above would imply. In 1928 four private citizens gave the Library a thousand dollars apiece to start the Archive of American Folk Song. With this as a base, three Library of Congress employees, Robert W. Gordon and John and Alan Lomax, began threading their way from jail to jail, up narrow Appalachian valleys, and across Indian reservations, trying to capture authentic American folk music while it was still close to its antecedents. The music was picked up via wax cuttings, then wire, and ultimately recording tape and brought back to the Library's Recording Laboratory (established in

1940 with Carnegie Foundation money), where it was converted to formal pressings for public sale at cost.

The Archive now boasts over 125,000 specimens of songs, instrumental tunes, spoken tales, and other lore from all over the world. The Library offers some sixty-odd long-playing records of this music, much of which has become the primary source material for basic research in the field. (Such celebrated American performers as Harry Belafonte and Joan Baez spend hours listening to unreleased recordings to find authentic material for their own programs.)

The accumulation of the original sounds has not slackened in recent years, but it is now done differently. Whereas in the Archive's early days very few individuals had the tools to do what LC managed to do with its mobile truck equipment, nowadays, thanks to the ubiquitous tape recorder, anyone with the inclination can capture sound anywhere. This has resulted in less field work for the Library but more reproduction and distribution, and more drawing on the skills of trained folklorists around the country.

In 1970, for example, Professor Robert A. Black of California State College lent the Library for duplication seventy-nine tapes of Pueblo Indian music—principally Hopi, but some material from Acoma, Laguna, and the Zuñi. Carl B. Johnson of Arizona loaned the Library fourteen cylinders of Navajo music he had discovered, originally made by Geoffrey O'Hara in 1914. Charles Faurot permitted the division to copy twenty-two tapes of Texas fiddle and guitar music. Similar loan/reproduction arrangements were made for tapes of mountain church services, conversations with Negro healers and root doctors, and banjo tunes from the South.

Once the American antecedents were reasonably well developed, the Archive began to broaden its scope until by now the musical traditions of Latin America and the Caribbean have been covered in detail. Coverage of the African scene is being perfected, building on the already developed holdings from the west coast south of the Sahara, the Congo basin, and Morocco. The collection of the music of the Far and Near East is similarly growing, with present strength in the Korean, Japanese, Iranian, and Iraqi areas.

The Library as Patron and Impresario

The Library of Congress and the nation's audience for fine music are deeply in debt to two strong-willed women whose impact on the Library went far beyond their own areas of cultural interest. The first was Mrs. Elizabeth Sprague Coolidge (the "Sprague" was that of the Sprague-Warner Corporation; her father was the noted Chicago businessman). Mrs. Coolidge had been trained as a concert pianist; she had given critically acclaimed performances at the time of World War I and thereafter became immersed in a long career of musical philanthropy. In 1918 she founded the Berkshire Music Festival for chamber music and awarded her first Berkshire Prize for an original composition. In 1924 she approached the Library of Congress with an offer to build an auditorium in one of the courtyards of the Old Building and then give the Library an endowment with which to promote "the study and appreciation of music in America."

The Library, being a government agency, had no right to accept money and keep it in the bottom drawer, so Herbert Putnam turned to the Congress for help. The Joint Committee on the Library thereupon sponsored legislation that would permit the establishment of a Library of Congress Trust Fund, and after its passage on March 3, 1925, the Library could "accept, hold, and invest moneys" via a Trust Fund Board. The U.S. Treasury was directed to pay 4 per cent on all gifts so deposited—in perpetuity. The Elizabeth Sprague Coolidge Foundation then became the first of such private moneys to be accepted by the Library, but, thanks to the device her philanthropy created, *private* support of the

Library's cultural activities became possible throughout all its divisions. By 1971 there were no less than ninety-seven of these gift and trust funds, bringing in income "available for obligation" (cash to be spent) of some $6.6 million a year. There is scarcely a department in the Library that does not now receive some service or acquisition support from these nonappropriated funds.

But to return to Mrs. Coolidge—she did finance a 500-seat auditorium which proved to have almost flawless acoustics. She began a lavish tradition of free chamber music concerts played by the leading artists of our time, and she commissioned a seemingly endless series of new musical compositions by the "unknown but promising" as well as by established composers. She stated her purpose as:

> to make possible, through the Library of Congress, the composition and performance of music in ways which might otherwise be considered too unique or too expensive to be ordinarily undertaken. Not this alone, of course, nor with a view to extravagance for its own sake; but as an occasional possibility of giving precedence to considerations of quality over those of quantity; to artistic rather than to economic values; and to opportunity rather than to expediency.

Mrs. Coolidge lived to be eighty-nine, active to the end, and the proceeds from her original investments continue to flow in.

Mrs. Gertrude Clarke Whittall of Worcester, Massachusetts, came to the Library in 1935 and quickly joined Mrs. Coolidge in the role of patroness. Mrs. Whittall began by giving the Library five splendid Stradivari instruments (the Betts violin made in 1704, the Castelbarco violin, 1699, the Ward violin, 1700, the Cassavetti viola, 1727, and the Castelbarco violincello made in 1697). She accompanied the original gift with a Tourte bow for each instrument. As important as the Strads themselves were her explicit instructions that the violins must not become museum pieces but were to be played regularly for the sake of maintaining their tone and general well-being. To this end, Mrs. Whittall established the Gertrude Clarke Whittall Foundation to pay for free chamber music concerts to be held throughout the year. The Strads cannot leave the building, so the public and the performers must come to the Library. Under such rules the Music Division has now staged a rich series of concerts running from October to May every year for four decades. The Budapest String Quartet acted as artists in residence for many seasons, and since 1962 the Juilliard String Quartet has carried on the role. As the tradition has developed, the Library has varied the concerts between chamber groups and individual performers. In recent years it has offered with pride such artists as Menuhin, Serkin, Francescatti, Rubinstein, Bernstein, Arrau, and Firkusny. Mrs. Whittall lived to be ninety-seven and never missed a concert season until her death in 1965. Both the Coolidge and Whittall foundations continue to prosper and expand.

In 1949, the famous conductor Serge Koussevitzky established a foundation in his name to commission new works for the Library, and in 1968 Mr. and Mrs. Walter Louchheim established a fund so that all the Library's musical performances could be made available for little or no cost (via audio and video tape) to educational and good music stations around the country.

Consequence

The end product of these private, nonappropriated funds has been the sponsoring—and creating—of music in great quantity. Through its foundations, the Library has commissioned, paid for, and produced such works as George Crumb's *Ancient Voices of Children*, Britten's *Spring Symphony*, Menotti's *The Unicorn, the Gorgon, and the Manticore,* Stravinsky's *Apollon-Musagète*, Hindemith's *Hérodiade*, Barber's "Hermit Songs," and Schoenberg's Third and Fourth String Quartets.

In 1971 it staged forty-five concerts in the Coolidge Auditorium, and it commissioned new compositions from Luigi Dallapiccola, Milton Babbitt, George Crumb, Jean-Claude Eloy, Cristobal Halffter, Juan Orrego-Salas, Mel Powell, Charles Dodge, John Eaton, Milko Keleman, and R. Murray Schafer. How many of the resultant works will prove to be of enduring quality and how many will fade into obscurity in unopened boxes in the back stacks is, of course, the nature of the game—but it is what makes the game so fascinating. For simple quantity, 1971 was a typical year, about par for the course.

The Music Division is run with thirty-one people: five in the administrative unit, fifteen in the public reference section, three in the Archive of Folk Song, and eight in the Recorded Sound Section.

THE POETRY CONSULTANT

There is a splendid suite of rooms that sits across the brow of the Library of Congress, overlooking the Capitol Plaza. The rooms are carpeted, comfortable, furnished with antiques, overstuffed sofas, and casual chairs. If you pass through the French doors, you will find yourself on a high balcony looking down on the Capitol steps to the west (pictures of Presidential inaugurations have been taken from here for seventy-five years). The Supreme Court, Senate Office Buildings, and Union Station march in dazzling marble to the north. The view is one of the finest in Washington, and the rooms might be expected to belong to the Librarian himself—but they don't. The Librarian occupies a glowing baroque chapel buried in one of the Library's courtyards without a view of any kind. The peaceful rooms with the splendid view belong to the Library's Poetry Consultant. Since 1929, the Library has accumulated no less than sixteen consultantships and honorary chairs (Aeronautics, American History, Slavic Studies, Historical Cartography ...) but like Abou ben

Adhem, the one that leads all the rest in visibility and prestige is that of the Consultant in Poetry in English.

This unlikely office (the local press always refers to the incumbent as the American Poet Laureate) was created in 1937 by Herbert Putnam. By then Putnam had already established a half-dozen of his "chairs," and in 1937 an anonymous donor, who later proved to be Archer M. Huntington, gave enough money to support yet another one, and thus Joseph Auslander, the poetry editor of the *North American Review*, became the first Consultant in Poetry. He served for four years, during which time he compiled a catalog of all the American and English poetry in the Library, begged a substantial number of original poetry manuscripts, and gave innumerable lectures before poetry societies and university audiences.

In 1943, Auslander was followed by the eminent poet and critic Allen Tate, and from that time on the Chair of Poetry (according to Archibald MacLeish) would "be filled for annual periods by distinguished American poets whose interest in bibliographical and critical problems may be of service to the Library in the development of its collections." Auslander, Tate, and their successors, some of whom served for more than one year, add up to a truly breathtaking roster of the finest names in American belles-lettres:

THE CONSULTANTS IN POETRY IN ENGLISH

Joseph Auslander	1937–41	Robert Frost	1958–59
Allen Tate	1943–44	Richard Eberhart	1959–61
Robert Penn Warren	1944–45	Louis Untermeyer	1961–63
Louise Bogan	1945–46	Howard Nemerov	1963–64
Karl Shapiro	1946–47	Reed Whittemore	1964–65
Robert Lowell	1947–48	Stephen Spender	1965–66
Leonie Adams	1948–49	James Dickey	1966–68
Elizabeth Bishop	1949–50	William Jay Smith	1968–70
Conrad Aiken	1950–52	William E. Stafford	1970–71
Randall Jarrell	1956–58	Josephine Jacobsen	1971–73

Howard Nemerov, whose stint fell in the mid-1960's, was wont to say with a sad smile, "The Consultant in Poetry is a very busy man, chiefly because he spends so much time talking with people who want to know what the Consultant in Poetry does."

What Does *a Poetry Consultant Do?*

De jure, pretty much what he wants to. Like the typical college, which has just snared the latest Nobel Prize Winner to be its Something-in-Residence, the Library tends to be so awed by and grateful for the poets' presence that the poets can play their role in almost any way they see fit. *De facto,* however, each seems to struggle to do everything his predecessor tried to do, as well as adding a few innovations of his own, and the result is that the consultant's one- or two-year sabbatical becomes a frenzied attempt to keep up.

For example, Robert Penn Warren started an ambitious recording program, using the Music Division's Recording Laboratory, and during his tenure drew thirteen poets and three novelists into the Library to read their own works so that posterity might know how *they* heard and interpreted their writings themselves. The resultant long-playing records are available for sale by the Library. Louise Bogan compiled a checklist of a thousand belles-lettres published in England during and after World War II, which the Library published for the use of scholars. Miss Bogan expanded Warren's recording program, secured money from the Bollingen Foundation to broaden the selections, and prepared five albums of contemporary American poetry read by the poets themselves. She produced additional recordings by W. H. Auden and got T. S. Eliot to read enough of his works to fill an album of his own.

The succeeding consultants became involved in staging regular seasons of poetry readings in the Coolidge Auditorium. Free programs, underwritten by Agnes and Eugene Meyer of the *Washington Post*, were given by Carl Sandburg, Robert Frost, Robinson Jeffers, and Stephen Vincent Benet and became a major part of the Washington cultural scene. Mrs. Whittall (of the musical foundation) gave money to outfit the Poetry Consultant's rooms noted above, to expand the readings from poetry to literary criticism, and to support free, staged, drama productions.

Robert Frost embraced the growing obligations of the consultants by recruiting readers for the recorded series, planning programs for the Coolidge performances, and inaugurating an innovation of his own by teaching a year-long seminar for graduate students and professors from the five local universities. At the end of his stay, he declared,

> I have had a fine time, a whale of a good time, as Poetry Consultant; there hasn't been a boring minute. Of the talks in the Hall [the Coolidge Auditorium] at the Library, I have liked them all. The high school children were fine and I liked the Library group very much. These times when I had a chance to talk to people about poetry are the ones I recall first.

Richard Eberhart added the voices of some ninety poets to the Library's growing Archive of Recorded Poetry and Literature and continued the seminars for local students. He also worked closely with the Voice of America, conducting interviews for overseas broadcasts and preparing a short history of American poetry for the U.S. Information Agency. Louis Untermeyer staged a National Poetry Festival at the Library, bringing together some thirty-five of the nation's leading poets for three days of discussions on technique and purpose. (The Festival was underwritten by the Bollingen Foundation and resulted in a 367-page *Proceedings*, published by the Library.)

The National Festival proved so successful that Reed Whittemore staged an even larger event in April of 1965—the Symposium on American Literature. A hundred editors of literary magazines and many writers from abroad took part in this two-day conference (financed by the Carnegie Corporation), and by this time the accumulated "voluntary" activities had reached such density that when Whittemore turned in his final report he noted having given "about three dozen" poetry readings, thirteen radio programs for the Voice of America, a television show on poetry for children, and "innumerable lectures." He had held informal meetings with government officials on "The Useful Arts," had written a pamphlet for distribution at the Jefferson Memorial at the request of the National Park Service, and had participated in a University of Texas conference on "What To Do with the New Government Foundation for the Arts and Humanities." His Library of Congress lecture, "Ways of Misunderstanding Poetry," is still one of the Library's best-sellers.

Consultant Stephen Spender worried over the problem of translating poetry from one language to another, and his concern stimulated a 1970 conference of translators and the translated, under the leadership of Consultant William Jay Smith. James Dickey of *Deliverance* fame increased the consultants' television activities and introduced two of his own variations to the expected role: combined poetry readings and guitar concerts for children and the inauguration of three-man reading programs in the Coolidge—two guest poets reading their works, moderated (or baited) by a third.

In short, the tradition continues and accretes, enabling the Library of Congress to fan the flames of contemporary poetry with both hands. The weekly "Monday nights in the Coolidge" are not only bringing a lively stream of the spoken word to Washington audiences, but, via the tapes distributed through the National Public Radio network, the Library's poetry, literary criticism, drama readings, and festival discussions are becoming increasingly familiar throughout the country.

The Poetry Office operates with three people: the incumbent

Poetry Consultant; the Special Assistant in Poetry, who runs the office and manages the public programs; and the Poetry Assistant, who is research assistant and secretary to the enterprise.

PRINTS AND PHOTOGRAPHS

We come now to the last Library of Congress unit that we shall describe, and, since this final piece of the picture comes at the very end, more by accident than design, it manages to project an irresistible irony. The historians tell us that man's first written communications were by the pictures drawn on the cave wall and that the printed word came long after. Thanks to the educational film, the ubiquitous television tube, and the whole pictorial trend in publishing, there is now more than a hint that the preserved word is fading, and reliance on the picture is coming around again. If that is so, this final division of the Library may yet end up the central core—with all the books simply an adjunct in some peripheral annex down some as yet unknown street.

From the very beginning, one of the Library's major obligations was to preserve the experience of the nation. It was to store the story of our peoples, our national successes and failures, and the sense of our daily lives. During the early years this was primarily done via the printed word; then our social history began to be captured by the daguerreotypes, the Brady wet plates, the strips of jerky motion picture news films, then the wirephotos and the picture magazines, and now television tapes. There seems little doubt that our mental images of the past come from written descriptions for the first hundred years but from frozen pictorial descriptions for the second. The Prints and Photographs Division reflects this trend.

When the division was established, it was properly a part of "culture," as evinced in the fine arts, and we shall see it starting with Rembrandt and Dürer. It then passed into "culture" as in the lively arts (with theatrical history and the motion picture era), and now is overwhelmingly immersed in "culture" as in social culture, the record of the here and now. When this book was begun, the Library and the division had just inherited one and a quarter million news photographs from the New York *World-Telegram*; within weeks of the time this sentence is being written, the Library will receive the first of 20 million photographs—the entire picture file of *Look* magazine, covering the past forty years in incredible detail.

The Prints

The Library got into the picture business because of the feather-edge between art and printing. The art museums on the Mall seemed appropriate for the painting and sculpture, but the reproduced drawings of the printing press seemed to belong to the "national library." The copyright deposit thus brought in the first art prints in the nineteenth century, and at the beginning of the twentieth Mrs. Gardiner Green Hubbard donated her husband's splendid collection of Dürers, Mantegnas, and Rembrandts and pressed the Library to *buy* prints to reinforce the Hubbard holdings. While printmaking had long been a strong sideline for American artists (Benjamin West, the Peales,, Whistler, and Winslow Homer are well represented by their engravings and etchings), twentieth-century limners Frank Duveneck and Joseph Pennell built international reputations on their printed lines. When Pennell reached artistic stardom, he discovered to his surprise how very strong the gifts and the copyright deposit had made the Library of Congress in his field, and he resolved to use this as a base on which to build a collection by *contemporary* print-makers. Thus in the 1930's, the Library got Pennell's own collection of nineteenth- and twentieth-century masters, together with a substantial endowment "for the continuing purchase of prints of the highest quality, executed in the last hundred years by artists of all nationalities."

According to Pennell's will, the Library was to create a committee composed of a leading etcher, a recognized lithographer, and the chief of the Prints and Photographs Division. These three were to recommend prints for the Library's permanent collection. They have been doing so for nearly forty years. The Library wanted to be certain that its collections did not merely reflect the names of those who had "arrived" in artistic popularity, but that it would find and recognize the young and the unknown, those with potential and promise. To achieve this end, it instituted a "National Exhibition of Prints," which would be well advertised and open to any artist from anywhere. Starting in 1941, this LC Biennial quickly became the most important single event in American printmaking, and, although it is no longer unique, the competition still draws great quantities of entries. In 1969 and 1971, 1,168 and 1,700 works were submitted, from which 65 and 92, respectively, were selected for Library of Congress purchase and exhibition. After several months in the Library's exhibit halls the prints are sent out as touring exhibits for a year or two, working their way through other museums.

Incidentally, the Library prepares many exhibitions of all kinds for its public areas in Washington and then sends these materials and display panels on to local museums and universities for further viewing; in 1971 the "Papermaking: Art and Craft" display was exhibited in six cities, "Preservation Through Documentation" in six cities, the Twenty-First National Exhibition of Prints in seven cities; the Smithsonian borrowed and circulated two Library of Congress exhibits to seven cities; and 400 rare items from the LC collections were loaned to libraries, museums, and other public institutions for display.

But the point of the National Exhibition of Prints is that, like its musical counterparts, it puts the Library in the posture of supporting, underwriting, and then preserving such culture as appears in etchings, woodblocks, lithographs, serigraphs, and all the other forms of ink and paper the printmakers nowadays employ.

Posters

Posters, a dramatic art form, constitute a bridge between art-for-art's-sake and art that captures time and events. The Library has one of the largest, most diverse collections of public posters in the world. They range from nearly 3,000 nineteenth-century theatrical billboards (Jenny Lind, P. T. Barnum, *H.M.S. Pinafore, The Great Train Robbery*) through Art Nouveau to shattering sheets of al Fatah recruiting posters and the self-styled "revolutionary challenge" of the Parisian student uprising. In 1971, such unlikely additions as stacks of black light psychedelic hangings and the complete poster series for the Munich Olympics were slipped into the division's long, flat drawers.

Photography and the Social Scene

The early librarians of the division immediately recognized the camera's potential for preserving social history, and a catechism of their contributions serves as a sampling of the kinds of materials we now take for granted when we approach the division's files. Jeffrey Parsons headed the unit from 1899 to 1911 and loaded its drawers with rows of pictures from the Klondike gold rush, cartoons of the Russo-Japanese War, and rare views of Liberia and West Africa taken by the American Colonization Society in the nineteenth century. The rage for stereoscopic views sent photographers around the world, and Parsons carefully preserved their double-view cards, which he received in vast quantity through the copyright device. Parsons made prints of 2,000 portraits, built a collection on the development of equestrian statues, and scooped up political cartoons from any place he could find them.

He was followed by Richard A. Rice, who was sixty-six when he took the job and stayed with it until he was eighty! Rice acquired the Civil War drawings of Forbes and Ward, the Mathew Brady daguerreotypes, and such uncommon hoards as a huge collection of British railway posters.

Division Chief L. B. Holland, who managed the unit from 1929 to 1943, was a trained architect. In 1931 he instituted the Pictorial Archives of Early American Architecture. This started as a collection of photographic negatives and prints but quickly grew into a library of drawings and data sheets and now includes the photographs of the Historic American Buildings Survey. The Survey became real through the joint efforts of the Library of Congress, the National Park Service, and the American Institute of Architects and now contains 27,000 measured drawings and 30,000 photographs of over 7,500 buildings.

Holland also began what he called the Cabinet of American Illustration, a collection of thousands of original drawings used to illustrate books and magazines in the 1880's and 1890's. (Their modern counterparts are the thousands of original *New Yorker* cartoons that have been given to the Library during the past half century.) Holland was one of the first to collect and publish Currier and Ives prints, and as far back as 1931 he was having special exhibitions of the original copyright copies to draw attention to the remarkable social history they contain.

During the 1930's and the Depression, photographic social history became a near-art form in itself. The Library has all of the famous Farm Security Administration photographs of the Dust Bowl and other depressed areas made in that time of economic despair. The nation's memory of these desperate years is increasingly built on images caught by the cameras of Walker Evans and Dorothea Lange.

Indeed much of the national memory is preserved in the division's Master American Photographers collection. The pictures that have become an essential part of American publishing are drawn (and duplicated) from the division's files. The beginnings of photography itself—the calotypes of Henry Fox Talbot, the Brady Lincoln portraits, the Civil War pictures of George N. Barnard—are all here, as well as Roger Fenton's photographs of the Crimean War. The early pictures of the West—the Grand Canyon, Yellowstone, Yosemite—as seen through the lenses of William Henry Jackson and Timothy O'Sullivan are well represented and available for copying by anyone who needs them. The Library takes particular pride in its collections of the Photo-Secession Group represented by Alfred Steiglitz, Edward Steichen, Clarence H. White, and others. These records of the work of individual photographer-artists are still eagerly sought and acquired. Within the past few years, the Library has rejoiced in its receipt of the photographic files of Ansel Adams, Brett Weston, and Toni Frissell. Miss Frissell's magnificent collection of portraits of the great (de Gaulle, Churchill, Adenauer, Pius XII) and of the American society scene (Astors, Vanderbilts, Whitneys, and Mellons) runs to 40,000 color transparencies and over 270,000 black-and-white negatives.

Who Cares and Why?

Short of the comfort of knowing you have several million pictures stored in the attic, what good is all this vast collection to anyone, and who uses it anyway?

The audience is intriguingly varied. The television world is plowing the hoard daily—compilers of documentaries, costumers for period dramas, set designers. Museum curators use the fine and historical prints and secure duplicates of photographs for their own collections. Novelists spend hours browsing, looking for local color detail, and historians and book designers select pictures to elaborate and adorn their texts.

Oddly enough, the Historic American Buildings Survey material is the most heavily used single collection in the division, and the stream of visitors who use this collection range from trained architects restoring major national shrines to "ordinary householders" making repairs in their private but historical homes.

All told, the reference assistants in Prints and Photographs answer in person five to six thousand questions each year and another five or six thousand a year by mail.

How?

How does a publisher or a media man find the pictures he needs? There are various ways, of course, the major approaches being:

1. Certain rare items are cataloged individually, just like books, and these appear in the division's card catalog. Examples: the original plate of Paul Revere's Boston Massacre scene, Bellows's *Dempsey and Firpo*, and single posters like Jacques Villon's "Guinguette Fleurie."

2. There are book catalogs of the various individual collections. The Johns Hopkins Press published a splendid, illustrated, 568-page *American Prints in the Library of Congress*, and the Government Printing Office put out a more summary *Guide to the Special Collections of Prints and Photographs in the Library of Congress*. The latter describes some 800 individual groupings, such as the 18,500 photographs in 47 albums belonging to Field Marshal Hermann Goering—his private, chronologically arranged snapshot albums!—or the Detroit Publishing Company's 20,000 prints and 30,000 glass negatives of stores, town squares, courthouses, factories, and what-have-you that the company rented for picture postcards and advertisements. (Speaking of advertisements, thanks to the copyright deposit, the Library's nineteenth-century collection of soap wrappers, cigar box covers, beer

signs, cigarette packs, and playing card designs is without peer.)

3. The third approach is via browsing files—the Farm Security Administration and Office of War Information glossy prints are in this form—wherein all the pictures are pasted on cardboard, sorted by subject, and filed in upright file drawers so the user can simply flip and look.

4. Many thousands of pictures have already been published from the division's collections, so there is a continual demand for "the original of . . . " or "a big, copiable print of so-and-so picture of yours I saw in . . . "

The Product

Unless an item is still so recent it is covered by copyright or some special instruction from its living photographer, anything in the collection can be duplicated, and the Division will have the copies made in whatever form is most useful to the requester: slides, color prints, glossy prints, matte prints, blueprints, photostats, or what have you.

The operation runs with a staff of forty people, who divide their time among acquisitions (trying to determine what is *needed*), researching and cataloging (so the user can be certain about what he actually has as well as identifying it so he can conveniently find it), and preservation (a major task when you're dealing with everything from cigar bands to Win-With-Willkie campaign billboards . . . not to mention restoring the mildewed, water-soaked, stuck-together cavalryman's pictures of Kiowa chiefs at Medicine Lodge—or of Lincoln at City Point).

And with this we end our hurried, obviously superficial glance at a few of the many libraries that make up the Library of Congress. Not only could whole books be written about a single room—or drawer or item of the Library—but whole books *have* been so written!

For our present purposes, the best we could hope to do was provide a general idea of the *kinds* of things the Library keeps, and the *kinds* of things the Library does with them. We now turn to a more difficult matter. So far, everything we've seen has been bathed in the pleasant glow of stained glass and an operational Elysium. Experience tells us that even the best of man's creations have hairline cracks, and candor (and the publisher) require that we step a little closer to this institution and check out the glaze. We therefore proceed to the stresses and strains of administration—to competing customers . . . conflicting missions . . . difficult choices . . .

X

The Library of Congress
and Congress

Thus far we have tried to examine three things: how the Library of Congress came to be, how it is organized to do its work, and what its work is. We now turn to the question: How well is it doing its job? The Library is essentially a service agency. It secures and preserves great collections of written, audible, and visual records, which to a degree is a mission in itself, but the key to its activities is that the material is secured and preserved for use by someone else. It serves three external groups: Congress, the library profession, and the scholarly research world. Our question here will be: How well are these customers satisfied with what they're getting?

To find the answer, we will try to note what they would like the Library to do for them and what the Library is in fact doing for them already, and then see if there is any way to determine which of their additional requests are appropriate and which are not likely to be fulfilled. Incidentally, this makes for a noteworthy paradox. On the one hand, if each customer had his own way, he would have the Library abandon all its activities relating to other clearly less useful applications and would have it concentrate on his needs alone. But the resultant irony is that such an extreme position is probably quite legitimate and valid.

Congress, the parent elite, says firmly that the Library is *Congress's* library. Congress built it, funded it, and simply has no other place to turn to for printed legislative data. Indeed, why should it even look for an alternative? It properly feels that the Library of Congress should concentrate on serving Congress fully and adequately, and not until it has completely satisfied this purpose dare it consider the luxury of helping other customers. Yet Congress is not now getting as complete informational support as the Library knows how to provide, and it would take a major redirection of mission and resources to give it such.

When Library priorities are discussed, the case for Congress has an underlying element that has probably never been better expressed than by Representative Wayne Hays, speaking on the 1972 Library budget before the House Appropriations Committee. As the newly appointed Chairman of the Joint Committee on the Library Congressman Hays said:

> I have had conversations with Mr. Mumford before because I have been on the House Administration Committee and had been ranking member. He told me quite candidly this is not really a Library of Congress; it is a national library. I quite candidly said, "Why don't you get your money someplace else?"
>
> That sort of ended the conversation.

Similarly, both the federal librarians and the librarians of the nation's public, college, and research libraries can make a strong case for the Library's attention. They say with perfect validity: We are in the business of providing information to the various parts of the public with the public's money. We are buying and storing and retrieving information from essentially the same sources. We owe it to the public to buy materials at the lowest cost and organize them for use with the greatest efficiency. Since we are all using essentially the same materials, "someone" should act as the central point for purchasing, cataloging, record keeping, reducing duplication, and providing leadership, and, since the Library of Congress is the biggest and richest library and is run with the public's own money, it is clearly the library that should do these things.

The scientific community is a typical example of the multi-disciplined research world. It too is concerned with duplication, but with scientists the pivotal problem is the re-invention of the wheel. Their distress concerns the vast amount of public and private money being spent for research which could be done so much faster and so much more efficiently if "someone" would do a faster, better job of analyzing and retrieving technical literature and disseminating reports of solved problems throughout the interested research community. The "someone" would be both a storage unit and a switching, crossover point for the receipt and dissemination of scientific data. Thanks to its hundred-year-old Smithsonian Deposit and its ties to governmental research reporting, the Library of Congress is already the largest scientific library in the world and accumulates more technical data every day than any other institution anywhere. Ergo, it is the obvious candidate for "someone."

Thus the contending positions. Now, where does validity lie? Let's start with the customer with the prior claim: Congress.

WHAT DOES CONGRESS WANT OF THE LIBRARY OF CONGRESS?

Information

First, Congress simply wants information. Who, what, when, where, how much, how many. Information has been the traditional product of the Library's collections—its data base (in modern systems language), which happens to be stored in hard-copy books, magazines, and documents. Providing information to Congress is a service that the Library does very well and seems constantly to be doing better.

Most of the identification and transfer of this information is provided by the Congressional Research Service (CRS). In 1969 the Library conducted a detailed survey of congressional, senatorial, and committee staffs to test their satisfaction with twenty CRS products. The simple provision of information was rated the highest in use by members of Congress and their staffs (89.8 per cent) and highest in satisfaction with the material received.

The CRS provides information at many levels from many locations. It operates a professionally manned, while-you-wait, hot line telephone service, librarian-staffed reference rooms in the House and Senate Office Buildings, and a Congressional Reading Room in the Library itself. It has a librarian-staffed Congressional Reference Division tied to all the other outposts, so the flow of queries coming in via phone, letter, and personal visit is keyed to responses going out via computer net, phone, and messenger. The whole information complex involves fifty professionals handling 120,000 inquiries a year—1,000 a day at the height of the session. All together, these congressional requests for pure information, neither analyzed nor elaborated upon, involve 21 per cent of the CRS work time and 14 per cent of its professional staff.

The responses are quick and accurate, and the recipients appear to be satisfied with the way they are provided and the appropriateness of their being done by the CRS and the Library.

Briefing Assistance and Pro and Con Studies

The second product Congress seems to expect from the Library is its pro and con briefing reports on national issues.

Eighty-six per cent of the surveyed offices in the 1969 study said they used these and found the product to be satisfactory or better. These reports are prepared by subject analysts in the CRS research divisions. They are done by the transportation economists, the African specialists, the physicists, the Social Security experts, and specialists in the hundred-odd other disciplines distributed among the 300-man research staff. The briefing report endeavors to do four things: give a short historical background of an issue; enumerate the current federal and local laws concerning it; provide a statement of the present problem; and describe the identifiable alternative ways of solving it. The Service does several thousand such analyses each year, and ten times that many copies of the resulting reports are used to answer further congressional requests. In 1971, briefing and background studies were involved in 14,725 inquiries, which took up 49 per cent of total research time.

These reports are the proudest product of the Congressional Research Service. It believes the briefing papers have the greatest impact on legislation of any single service it provides. They are a unique tool unlike anything available to congressional decision-makers from any other source. There is strong congressional support for this service and for the appropriateness of CRS providing it.

Speech Drafts

Congress wants speeches written. Here we enter the area of controversial services. Until the mid-1940's, the Library and CRS were expressly limited to the provision of detached, balanced reports. ("Balancing a report" then and now merely means describing all the known positions possible on an issue. If there are twenty sound arguments in favor and two against, that is the way it is written. There is no attempt to make it 11 pro and 11 con!) But in the late 1940's Congress began requesting, first, outlines of speeches, then pro and con drafts, and finally completed texts representing either one side or another, admittedly one-sided and "unbalanced."

The CRS preference was to limit itself to factual presentations of all sides of an issue, urging a member of Congress to select the position he favored and then recast it in his own words within his own frame of reference. The members replied that this was time-consuming and dangerous. Why make a busy member of Congress or a staff member spend his time rewriting a CRS report when the specialist who wrote it originally had all the facts at hand? The researcher could do the job faster and better, releasing the staff member or congressman for legislative tasks, which *only* he could do. Furthermore, considering the complexity of modern issues, the original author is in the best position to identify subtleties of controversy and probably has access to more current data than the inquiring office.

The outcome of this twenty-year controversy is that at the present time the CRS does do speech drafts on one side or another of an issue, always according to the instructions of a member of Congress, but with the clear understanding that while the text is one-sided, the one side taken is wholly accurate. The draft will be the best possible, most honestly stated case that can be made for that particular position. The drafts must be limited to *issues* only, and they will involve neither praise nor blame for another member or for either political party.

There are two sides to this still current argument over the propriety of the Library's writing (or ghosting?) speeches for Congress. Some hold that speech-drafting is an inappropriate task for an unbiased, public-supported institution to engage in at all. Others maintain that a legislator has three duties to his constituents: to make needed laws, to act as their man-in-Washington (ombudsman), and to provide a two-way communication link between home district and the national capital. In that last role the congressman has two functions: telling Congress and the executive branch what his constituents want and need, and familiarizing the people at home with the national issues. The issues are to be presented, not as raw black-and-white, point-with-pride, or view-with-alarm orations, but as sophisticated, factual elaborations of true public problems. The CRS is expected to provide the latter.

In terms of consumer satisfaction, it should be noted that well over half of the membership of Congress calls on the CRS for at least one speech a year, and many request several dozen. In 1971 these added up to 1,677 drafts, requiring 7 per cent of the total research time. There is an irony here: While the same offices return time after time to request new drafts, there is a lower level of satisfaction with this product than with anything else the Congressional Research Service provides. The frustration seems to stem from the fact that the CRS makes little attempt to couch a speech in the style of the requester. It simply drafts a clear, speakable statement explaining an issue. It expects the congressman's staff to rewrite the material to make it conform to the occasion and the style of the speaker. The latter step appears inadequately understood.

Data for Constituents

A major battle rages among congressional users over whether CRS staff time and resources should be spent on "constituent inquiries." Constituent requests tend to be of two types. The first are those cases where a home town citizen writes his congressman about troubles he is having with "the Government"—federal government, in this case— problems of pensions, housing, the military; consumer complaints; tax inequities. Congress uses the CRS not to answer the complaint but to ask, "Where is the best place in Washington to get help for the writer?" or "What is the law on the matter referred to in the attached letter from my constituent?" In these instances the CRS helps the member of Congress to carry out his ombudsman role—and to help the citizen.

The second form of constituent request is for information about a particular national issue. These can come from a schoolchild, a League of Women Voters' president, or a Baptist Men's Club discussion leader. Usually they will want a general background briefing or a pro and con statement. Contrary to the myth, the CRS not only will not write term papers but it cannot do research for constituents at all. With legislative queries constantly on the rise and 1,500 inquiries coming in each day, the Congressional Research Service has had to set the following limitations to constituent work:

1. If documents, pamphlets, or CRS reports already stockpiled for congressional inquiries will answer the constituent's question, the CRS will be delighted to make them available to the member's staff (no constituents are answered directly);

2. If photocopies from clippings or reference books will provide the answer needed and the total effort can be done in minutes not hours, it will be done; but

3. If neither of the above is possible, the CRS will try to tell the member the best source of the information for the constituent, either in the writer's home town, in Washington, or in the nation, in that order.

The above type of constituent request comes under the congressman's role of communicator—helping the citizen at home to understand better the complicated national issues under legislative consideration. The Congressional Research Service answers constituent questions with junior personnel on a quick turn-around basis, but there are many of them. In 1971 congressional offices sent the CRS 75,000 constituent inquiries, which absorbed 16 per cent of its research time.

Policy Analysis

This brings us to the newest product of the Congressional Research Service and one that is changing its way of life.

Literally dozens of political scientists, consumer groups, environmentalists, and congressional reform committees have pointed to the need for formal, professional analysis of legislation *before* it is passed. They point to examples of major programs that went awry, which, they believe, had the enabling legislation been subjected to modern analytical techniques, could either have been avoided or ameliorated. They cite the ill-fated aircraft programs for the SST, the TFX, the C-5A. They point to Medicaid, many of the early "poverty programs," duplication in education programs, the "instant ghettos" of public housing, self-defeating tax exemptions—a protracted list of federal plans and programs that failed to work out as expected. These groups believe that if the Congress had its own think tank to provide it with the same impartial policy analysis and environmental impact studies that the executive branch buys at such expense, the tension between the two opposing points of view would result in better legislation. According to this belief, the executive branch tends to promote expansionary products for a self-perpetuating bureaucracy. The legislative branch, on the other hand, more perfectly represents the individual citizen and is more knowledgeable and responsive to what the electors back home really need and want. Thus legislative analysis provided by the CRS would introduce a greater sense of reality in the hammering-out process.

Such analytical support had been implicit in the Congressional Reorganization Act of 1946, but the reformers felt that the CRS had failed to embrace the broader mission and had clung too firmly to informational, reference activities through the ensuing twenty years. The Legislative Reorganization Act of 1970 therefore laid it hard on the line: The CRS was assigned responsibility for providing policy analysis support to all congressional committees. To accomplish this purpose, the Act's accompanying report of intent instructed the Congressional Research Service to increase its own staff of specialists threefold and then to hire, on short-term contracts, whatever additional expertise was needed to analyze specific projects beyond the skills of the permanent staff.

The CRS is taking these new responsibilities seriously. Computer-based programs for "issue tracking" have been installed. Liaison officers have been selected to maintain continuing contact with each congressional committee to be certain that the committee staffs are using CRS staff and capabilities to their full potential. Lists of expiring federal programs and new problem areas of potential legislative interest are being brought to the attention of the appropriate committees. The majority of all new employees hired are invested in the policy analysis effort. In short, the concept is broadening throughout all levels of the Congressional Research Service's work in response to the new legislation.

Program Analysis

The most controversial CRS function of all is program analysis. Many of the reformers who pointed out the need for policy analysis believed that it should be merely the first step in strengthening Congress's ability to legislate. *Program* analysis should follow: The CRS should not only help with getting better laws written but help to see that they are being properly carried out. What happened after the law was passed and the money was appropriated? How did the program actually develop? Is it achieving its original purpose? Are modifications in the legislation called for?

The CRS does next to none of this evaluating now. Indeed, since program analysis requires judgments and flat-out recommendations ("expand it," "kill it," "put it in another agency"), it runs at right angles to the most basic of CRS tenets: Get the facts to the member. Let *him* assess the values and draw the conclusions.

A corollary to program analysis has been operating for years in the General Accounting Office (GAO). Congress established this legislative agency in 1921, and it has now grown to 4,782 employees and a budget of more than $96 million. While the GAO has done only a limited amount of investigation about purpose, method, and effectiveness, it has always pursued the investigation of cost. GAO's question has been: Is the money Congress allocated to carry out a program being properly—indeed, even legally—spent? Certain reformers have urged a pairing of GAO and CRS skills. They recommend that the two work together, with the Library testing the effectiveness and operation of the programs, while the Accounting Office examines their efficiency and cost.

The apparently simple suggestion that the CRS move into program analysis has stirred controversy in many directions. One group holds that such an extension of the traditional CRS mission would require not only more staff but a radical change in its way of doing business. Heretofore its work has been heavily based on the printed word. Program analysis implies field investigations, interviews, and on-the-scene observation. Those who favor it say it would energize the CRS and give it a base of greater reality, and that it would be the logical application of the study and staff expertise already invested in the pre-passage legislative analyses. They believe that the same knowledge of a problem area that makes an analyst useful in perfecting the legislation in prior development would be valuable in appraising its implementation. They underline the need for legislative (versus executive) monitoring and suggest that the CRS would be in an unusually good position to evaluate the way the program is actually working and then be able to suggest appropriate repairs.

But the opponents are convinced of the contrary. They believe that to add this mission to the CRS charter would turn it into an investigative agency, looked upon with suspicion and dedicated to finding fault. They fear it would close off present access to executive agency staff, with whom there is now easy cooperation (the image of the CRS has traditionally been that of an agency eager to improve, perfect, and solve problems). They fear that program evaluation would destroy its traditional objectivity. They fear that once it began to approve or disapprove of specific programs, that once the

CRS researchers had made their reports, all further research by the participants would (even if unconsciously) tend to ratify and reinforce their earlier conclusions. The day of "no axe to grind" would have disappeared.

And probably most important of all, the representatives of the no-program-analysis position underline a stark fact: Capitol Hill is the real world. They note that it would take only an occasional instance in which CRS evaluations were used to destroy a favorite project of the congressional leadership—or of the committee chairmen—before the waiting political world would find the entire CRS missing from the Washington scene.

The Legislative Consul

There is a final role that has been urged on the CRS (though never tried) that probably falls into the category of program analysis: the legislative consul. For several years, a senator active in foreign policy affairs has recommended that the CRS be staffed and funded so as to place a CRS foreign policy analyst in each of the major U.S. embassies and consulates abroad. The senator pictures this legislative consul not as a legislative watchdog and inspector general but as a reporting officer who sends back to Congress independent summaries and analyses of foreign affairs in general and of affected American interests in particular. Additionally, he would act as Congress's man on the scene "liaisoning" with the legislative branch of the host country. There are increasing contacts between parliaments through such groups as the Inter-Parliamentary Union and its numerous subcommittees. The senator believes legislative consuls would help to nurture these contacts.

CONFLICT IN EDEN

These, then, are the kinds of services that Congress has requested of the Library, especially of the CRS. The majority appear to be obvious and desirable and presumably represent the consensus of Congress's will. But it is not really so. If anything, they are but knots on two sides of a tug-of-war rope. Except for basic reference work, no two congressional groups seem to agree on any service or any product.

Example I: The Congressional Reorganization Act of 1970 stresses the CRS's primary responsibility to congressional *committees*. Of the sixty-four lines in the Act defining the services CRS must render, the first forty-two relate solely to committee support. The justification for this primacy was simply that it is in the committees that the actual laws are written, choices made, and programs challenged or developed. The CRS is above all oriented to *legislative issues*, and the committee work is the payoff. Logical, obvious, essentially a truism.

But the truth is precisely the opposite, say a large and increasingly vocal number of individual senators and congressmen. They note that each committee has its own substantial, well-paid staff of experts. What Congress needs most from the CRS is support for *individual* congressmen, who have small staffs without great subject expertise but who are asked to debate and vote on complicated issues and to initiate legislation for the good of their state or district without objective subject specialists to assist them. They claim that the heavily funded committees do not need experts to call on; the individual congressmen do—yet the CRS is supposed to give priority to committees.

Example II: The CRS is repeatedly told to emphasize legislative matters, to staff with high-level experts, and to provide the Congress with outstanding professionals in all the major fields of public issues—yet 41.8 per cent of the requests actually sent to the CRS are for *constituents*.

Example III (which is more fundamental): The Congress repeatedly praises the Congressional Research Service for its objectivity and detachment. When addressing foreign parliamentarians, one of the most frequent points made with the greatest pride is that Congress can trust the CRS to transfer facts and information, while avoiding opinion, conclusions, and recommendations. The researcher's personal point of view is never allowed to intrude. But what is the most frequent criticism made of the CRS by the members of Congress? Across the board, it is: "You can never get the kind of answer you really *need* out of the CRS! They hire all those expensive experts, but when you ask them how you should vote or what would be the best solution, they always give you on-the-one-hand and then on-the-other-hand . . ."

Final Example: The rhetoric of policy analysis points with pride to the efficacy of *research* to give the widest span of choices and the greatest depth of analysis re cost, impact, social results, and resource tradeoffs. But a substantial number of thinking members of Congress believe this is unreal. They believe the most the CRS can do is identify and transmit facts. They believe that all that people can do who are located in a library and dependent on what someone else has happened to get printed on paper is locate and send data. What is supposed to be provided by "research" can really be found only in the field ("out there where the people are"). In short, they challenge the whole idea of policy analysis as being an outgrowth of campus activity ("doing a paper on . . ."), which is essentially meaningless in the harsh world of politics. They believe the CRS and the Library of Congress should perfect its information-handling techniques and avoid the costly distraction of professional "report writers." (The latter is to them a pejorative noun.)

CONGRESS-LIBRARY RELATIONS

Enough. These are simply samples of the kinds of contradictions with which the Library must work as it attempts to satisfy Congress's research and reference needs.

Two things occur to the observer: First, there must be *someone* who has the authority to decide on priorities and purpose. Who is it? And second, the CRS comprises only 450 out of 4,000 Library of Congress employees. How does the rest of the institution relate to the Congress?

The fact is that there are many areas of Library activity that require Congress's approval and funding if they are to continue, and in these areas Congress is not asking the Library for assistance; it is the Library that is the supplicant. Thus Library-Congress relations differ from the usual executive agency–congressional dialogue. Each is requesting support from the other. Who does what for whom ... under whose instructions ... by whose approval ... with what funds ... brings us to the Library's congressional oversight committees. These determine how all three of the audience elites shall be served—Congress itself, the library world, and the nation's scholars. What the Library of Congress is to be and what it is to do lies in their hands. *Videlicet*:

The Appropriations Committees

There are two appropriations committees—one in the House and one in the Senate—and it is they who really run the Library. They rarely say, "We want you to do this, we don't want you to do that," but they either provide money to staff an activity or they do not. These signals from the appropriation committees—plus tradition, protocol, and common sense—provide the Librarian with his instructions.

There are some unusual elements in the funding process. To begin with, unlike the typical obstacle course that an executive program agency must run, there is no annual "authorization committee" to convince. When HUD wants to float a new housing program, it must first sell it to the House Banking and Currency Committee and then to the Senate Banking, Housing, and Urban Affairs Committee. Once these approve and agree on the purpose, magnitude, and necessary funding, the idea must be presented and defended all over again before the two appropriation committees.

Not so the Library of Congress. The Librarian starts directly with the House Appropriations Committee's Legislative Subcommittee, and, after enumerating his ongoing services and requesting continuation of enough money to sustain them at a viable level, he presents whatever new services or expanded programs he desires and requests the committee's approval by appropriate funding. He repeats the procedure before the equivalent committee in the Senate (the two bodies operate as if they had scarcely heard of each other), and the representatives from the two committees meet in executive (secret) session, where they decide how much of his program they want to buy. Their decision is announced some two or three months after the hearings. The two houses vote the money with little demur, and that ends the process for the year.

By and large, the Library fares very well. This has been particularly true under L. Quincy Mumford's leadership; he has been exceptionally effective in keeping Congress's confidence. During his tenure, the Library's annual appropriations have increased from $9,561,000 to $68,093,000, with a staff increase from 1,564 positions to 3,667—not including the acceptance and funding of a new, third building for $90 million. Ironically, until recently the appropriations committees have been reluctant to spend money for those parts of the Library that serve Congress itself but have been reasonably generous in supporting the acquisition and processing programs, which aid the nation's research libraries. At the present moment this situation is reversed, but Congress continues to underwrite new programs and new services—within reason.

The fact that the Library is a legislative agency asking the Legislature for funds is only a partial help. Programs have to be defended sharply and always with varying degrees of success. In the last twenty-five years the Library has suffered actual cuts in staff on three occasions (the 1954 reduction eliminated fifty-two jobs), and it has always had its requests pared back at hearing time. For fiscal years 1969–73, funds requested by the Librarian have been cut by $4,260,000, $1,867,000, $1,054,000, $1,679,000, and $1,624,000 respectively.

The House subcommittee is composed of nine members, and the Senate's Legislative Appropriations Subcommittee of five. There is no telling from year to year which will turn out to be sympathetic and which critical. Over the long pull the House side has tended to be more probing and somewhat more distant, treating the Library more in the relationship of a "stranger" executive agency, which is slightly suspect and not to be trusted too far. The Senate usually approaches the hearings with an "Are you giving us our money's worth?" attitude, but with the assumption that the Library's function is at least that of an accepted congressional support body.

The annual appearance before the two groups is always the occasion for a mixture of hope, delight, and despair, and it has produced an endless series of anecdota. Among my own favorites is one occasioned by a committee chairman being called to the telephone in the midst of the Librarian's presentation. When he returned, he apologized profusely for the interruption and said, "Now let's see, you were explaining why you wanted the additional eight hundred million." Mumford corrected him, "Eight hundred *thousand*, sir," and went on with his presentation. The chairman also serves on several committees dealing with the executive branch.

The Joint Committee on the Library

The Joint Committee on the Library has long been LC's friend at court. With only an occasional exception, its chairman has taken great pride in the Library's activities and collections and has been a frequent visitor to its public events.

In this relationship the Joint Committee and the appropriations committees are analogous to the governing bodies traditionally concerned with a public or university library. The Joint Committee is much like a library board or library committee that assists a librarian with his problems and confers with him about how and where he invests his library's resources. The appropriations committees are the counterpart of the mayor or the college president. Eager as they may be to support and expand, they must divide their resources among many competing customers and they play the part of the no-sayers. (Not so much. Not now. Not ever.) The Joint Committee on the Library tends to be the mediator.

The Joint Committee was established in 1800 at the same time and by the same legislation as the Library of Congress itself. Through the years it has conveyed to successive Librarians Congress's needs, and it has urged adequate and enlarged support from fellow members of Congress. During periods of the expansion of the collections—the purchase of the great treasure holdings of the 1930's and the initiation of the broad international programs of the 1960's, such as "Public Law 480" and the National Program for Acquisitions and Cataloging—the Joint Committee has lent active support in providing both Congress and the nation with the library we know today.

The Joint Committee is composed of ten members, all of whom are drawn from the two legislative supervisory committees: the Committee on House Administration and the Senate Committee on Rules and Administration. The chairmen of the two administration committees act as the rotating chairmen of the Joint Committee on the Library. The House chairman serves during the first year of a congressional session and the Senate chairman sits during the second. The remaining eight members are selected from the two administrative committees, four from each and equally divided between the two parties. The fact that you have here three separate and independent committees but with one made from parts of the other two has an interesting result. While the Joint Committee on the Library is the parent oversight committee, if there is disagreement between the representatives of the two houses within the joint committee, its members can "go home" and with full authority instruct the Library in the role of the *Administration* Committee membership. Any one of the three groups has the authority to send the Library directives or even hold critical hearings or investigations as an independent administrative body.

There are a number of anomalies built into the Joint Committee's relationship to the Library, with the "ill-definition" usually found in British parliamentary practices: The Joint Committee has no authority to consider or report legislation that affects the Library; it has no relationship to the money that is appropriated for it; the Librarian is appointed by the President, and his confirmation is recommended by the Senate Committee on Rules and Administration. On the other hand, by "custom and tradition," the Joint Committee is deeply involved in the ways the Library spends its money, in the kinds of programs it supports, and in the Library's public image. (And the Joint Committee on the Library does have full legal responsibility for the Botanic Gardens and the monuments in the Capitol's Statuary Hall!)

The Administrative Committees

Most legislation relating to the Library (other than appropriations) is sent, not to the Joint Committee on the Library or to the appropriation committees, but to the Committee on House Administration and the Senate Committee on Rules and Administration. Thus these bodies are in the strongest position to modify the long-term objectives of the Library by changing the Library's statutory charter. If the plan so often suggested by the nation's librarians—moving the Library of Congress into the Office of Education—were to materialize, it presumably would be considered by these two committees.

In addition, on the House side, the all-powerful Rules Committee has had a particular interest in congressional reform and thus was the committee that handled the detailed development of the Legislative Reorganization Act, which impacted so heavily on the Congressional Research Service.

The Joint Committee on Congressional Operations

The newest oversight body, the Joint Committee on Congressional Operations, was created as a part of the Legislative Reorganization Act of 1970, specifically to watch over the implementation of the Act and to make continuing recommendations for improving congressional procedures. Its interest in the Library is focused almost exclusively on the Congressional Research Service, and it has already taken issue with the appropriations committees for failing to provide funds for staffing the policy analysis and legislative transactions directives as quickly as it would have liked. In this contest, the CRS is a shuttlecock being flailed between contending parties (with frequent advice and criticism offered by the chairman of the Joint Committee on the Library and the membership of the House Rules Committee).

And Many Others

In addition to the above, there are many congressional committees that are concerned with specific activities of the Library. Thus in a typical year the Librarian may testify before such committees as the two Judiciary committees (copyright matters), Foreign Relations (UNESCO, ratification of treaties re the exchange of books and documents), Ways and Means (tax deductions for charitable contributions to libraries), Agriculture (foreign book funds obtained under the Public Law 480 program of agricultural exchange), Public Works (expansion of the Library plant), Post Office and Civil Service (postage rates for materials to the blind and physically handicapped, and LC staff "supergrades"), Science and Astronautics (Library support for technology assessment), and more.

Who decides what the Library shall do? Who resolves differences between conflicting aims? All of these committees, individually and in concert. The resulting problem is self-evident.

A LIBRARY FOR CONGRESS

Congress started a library to serve itself and ended up with the greatest library in the Western world both for itself and for the nation. With this library, the Library of Congress staff provides vast assistance to the Congress (over 1,500 questions of reference, research, and analysis answered each day), but there are ways it could provide greater informational service with only a little imagination and a great deal of money. These improvements are all quite plain to the Library's administration and the oversight committees, but they have been either delayed or denied for the simple reason that no one is sure they are worth what they would cost.

Improvements in the Collections Themselves

In spite of millions of volumes preserved and cataloged, they are not particularly the ones Congress needs the most. The collections are heavily oriented to long-term preservation of book material—increasingly in foreign languages. The Congress needs current, documentary material in English. The Library's collections of federal materials are far from comprehensive, and its holdings of state and local publications are less adequate than many state and university libraries. This startling condition stems from the fact that most documentary materials are unbound, often near-print, sequential, and voluminous. Struggling to keep up with the world's publishing, the Library has had to stop somewhere, and unbound serials, which must be hand-collated and hand-bound, are vastly time-consuming and expensive and thus were one of the first categories to be cut back. The Library receives over 700 U.S. newspapers, for example, but can keep only 300—although it both receives and retains over 1,000 foreign papers.

When it comes to official documents, what with the overwhelming flood of daily, weekly, and monthly reporting of every town, city, county, state, and interstate unit, what with the bales of expenditure summaries, employment figures, area surveys, and grants-in-aid reports, the task of simply collecting such quantities of materials would require an acquisition effort as costly as the one now required to cover the book publishing of the entire world. (The CRS itself tries to keep up with some 3,000 serials, but, being unbound, the majority must be pulped after four or five years of use. But regrettably, it is just such day-to-day reporting of governmental affairs that Congress needs most. For example, while LC retains the legislative gazettes of 115 countries (their "*Congressional Records*"), it contains none for the 50 U.S. states.

What About the Computer?

Is the computer the answer to legislative informational support? Is the Library too committed to print? Should it be moving more deeply into automatic data processing for public issue data?

If the Library is to be Congress's primary supplier of information, a strong case can be made for placing a Library of Congress computer terminal in each of the 535 congressional and 65 committee offices, so that an awesome display of data could be made immediately available to the membership.

The Congressional Research Service already has abstracts of all current legislation in the Library's computer. It updates the status of each piece each day (30,000 bills in each two-year Congress), and these can be retrieved by number, sponsor, or subject at will. The CRS already places 20,000 citations to major government reports, periodical articles, and CRS studies into the Library's computer annually, and these can be retrieved by author or subject. But think of the following possibilities: access to the records of all federal program spending now kept in the Treasury Department's computer; access to census data kept on Commerce Department tapes; access to the U.S. Code kept in computer form by the Air Force; access to computerized crime statistics kept by the Justice Department. The Library could act as the switching point for all these data collections, securing and manipulating them in response to queries from Congress—and displaying the answers on the inquiring congressman's own cathode ray tube screen.

The only caveats to this golden future are: Does Congress really need these raw data? Is it not better to let the Library collect and digest the data first, as it does now? Is it worth the money it would cost? (The skilled research staff that could be bought with the sums required to create and maintain a computer program of such magnitude might well be more productive and flexible than the computer equipment.) And would it really work? While the computer clearly can handle numbers with ease, the application of the human mind to the intricacies of social research has consistently proved more effective than the computer. The data processing literature is filling with reports of intelligence programs, social science programs, bibliographic programs, and legal retrieval programs that have been abandoned in favor of the filing cabinet and the three-by-five card. Where does truth lie here? Diogenes has yet to blow out his lantern and go home.

So what is to be learned? Probably something of the following. Congress relies heavily on its Library for information and has been willing to support it with substantial funds. Some of its membership believes that the Library is the appropriate agency for giving it informational parity with the executive branch, while other members question this or feel that there is no real need for such a service. Inasmuch as the oversight power is distributed among a number of units, each of which views the Library's role in a different manner, the institution's relationship with Congress can be expected to follow a wavering course but will probably develop into a strengthened and broadened interdependence, for there is no portion of the Congress opposed to Congress's library as an institution.

Whose Library?

Is it Congress's library or the nation's library? It must not be assumed that this aspect of Congress–Library relations is so trivial that it need not be discussed. On the contrary, it is paramount to every question that can be raised about the Library and its future. But let us first get some feel for the position of the other two contenders in this three-way tug-of-war before we try to face the most difficult dilemma of all: Whose library is it?

XI

The Library of Congress and the Library World: Cards and Catalogers

We have looked at the Library and its first customer, the Congress, and asked, "What does Congress want of the Library?" And we have come up with a fairly confused answer. Congress hasn't decided just what it wants from the Library, much less how it wants it done. But there is no such confusion with the Library's second client, the library world. What do the nation's librarians want from the Library of Congress? The same thing Samuel Gompers said Labor wants: "More."

The "more" relates to four areas of great importance to librarians: their catalogs (cards and uniform cataloging), their grip on the world's publishing (bibliographic control), efficiency and totality in acquiring the world's publishing (centralized acquisition), and innovative technological leadership (automation, preservation, uniform technical standards). In generality these sound dull; in detail they relate to some remarkable activities involving tens of thousands of professional librarians and tens of millions of dollars each year.

THE PRINTED CATALOG CARD

The whole thing began with the simple, printed Library of Congress (LC) card. It was the first benefit the profession wanted from its "national library," and it has proved to be not only the most popular service the Library ever rendered the profession, but the foundation on which a dozen other services have been built.

For twenty-five years before Herbert Putnam took over the Library in 1899, the nation's librarians had been pleading for a single source of cataloging, so every library need not process the identical same books in a thousand different institutions, each performing precisely the same exercise as its neighbor and nine times out of ten coming up with the identical answer. Solution: Let the largest library do the work. Let everybody buy copies of the largest library's cards and spend the money they saved (by employing fewer catalogers) on more books. Putnam was one of the most ardent of the recommenders, so it was appropriate that when he became Librarian of Congress he should start the card service at once, an act that he justified in four ways.

First premise: It would cut down on duplication of effort. In this he was right. The concept has been embraced by the library world beyond his wildest dreams. In 1902 there were 212 subscribers with cash sales of $3,785. By 1968 there were 25,000 subscribers, who bought in that one year alone 79 million cards for $7 million. For the benefit of the statistically minded, 79 million cards would produce a single deck of cards 15 miles high. *One* year's sales! Of these subscribers, 2,500 were foreign libraries, many of whom not only bought LC cards for their American books but used them for books that had been printed in their own countries.

Second premise: Since LC was going to have to make the cards for itself anyway, running some extras for sale would be next to automatic and have little impact on the Library. Mr.

Putnam was wrong on this one. From the very beginning, the Card Service has been operated primarily for "outside" subscribers and through the years has actually told LC what to put on its cards and even what books to keep in order to get cards made. (Until quite recently, the choice of which congressional documents were to be retained and bound was based on which titles were most likely to generate the most card orders!) Modern librarians will identify with Mr. Putnam's November 30, 1901, circular to his brand new subscribers. In it he explained why the cards they had ordered were so late in coming, but he assured them that a number of useful new things would soon be added to the cards for their benefit.

LC has been adding elements to the cards ever since, elements which are of little use to the Library of Congress itself. At the present time an LC card carries: the Dewey Decimal number for the benefit of libraries not using the LC classification system; children's subject headings for special juvenile collections; audio-visual information to serve public libraries with collections of film strips, educational motion pictures, and phonograph recordings; the Superintendent of Documents classification number for depository and other libraries filing by these numbers; the price of the volume for libraries who wish to order from "proof sheets" of LC cards; and the International Standard Book Number for institutions using this bibliographic device.

While these elements are of limited use to readers using LC's catalogs or collections, many other improvements incorporated at the library profession's request have been of vast benefit to LC readers as well. The cards began with only the author, title, publisher, and date on them. The following year the Library added some "collation"—description of pages, plates, maps, and multiple parts. In the 1920's uniform subject headings were included, each one prepared in accordance with American Library Association cataloging rules. In the 1940's more detailed biographical information was added, plus more descriptive notes. In the 1960's the contents of the cards were put on computer tapes and the tapes made available to subscribing libraries (of which more later).

Third premise: LC would get all of the books that smaller libraries would want cards for, so it would automatically have a card for every book any library would want. Mr. Putnam was wrong on this one too. By the mid-1960's, the presses of America had become so fertile that LC was cataloging barely half of the books kept by all those "smaller libraries." Further, the huge research libraries had taken to buying so much abroad that they could find LC cards for barely half of the foreign books that they were purchasing—but that LC was not. (In 1965, for example, LC created some 100,000 cards for books on the way to its own shelves, but in the same period the card subscribers were acquiring over 200,000 *more* titles that LC did not have, had no intention of getting, and for which LC had therefore prepared no cards to sell. The outside libraries had to catalog these themselves.)

Fourth premise: Mr. Putnam's final justification was, in his own words, "to place in each center of research as complete as possible a statement of the contents of the national collections in Washington." His hopes here have been dramatically fulfilled. In his lifetime, it was done by passing out depository sets of every card printed. In the 1950's, enormous book catalogs were produced of every LC card arranged by author and by subject, and thus over 2,500 libraries now have these complete indexes to the LC collections on their own reference room shelves. The computer and the telephone wire appear to be the next step, but we anticipate ourselves. For the moment, the card service—

How Does It Work?

The printing, storage, and sale of 70 million cards a year is astonishingly straightforward. It is done just about as anyone would expect it to be done.

1. The catalogers send the Card Division a typed copy of the card to be printed.

2. The copy is cast into slugs on one of the twelve, half-ton Harris-Intertype machines sitting right in the Card Division. The machines and staff belong to the Government Printing Office, which runs a branch plant on Library property. The Harris-Intertypes set cards in five type fonts beside the Roman: Cyrillic, Armenian, Greek, Hebrew, and Arabic. Cards in oriental languages are set by photocomposition.

3. The experts in the division estimate how many copies of each card they will receive orders for. The guess is based on the usual popularity of the book's *subject*, the usual size of the *publisher's* market, and how many sales this particular *author* had on cards for his last book (if the author has been published before). The number of copies runs from as few as 200 to as many as 10,000 on the first printing. (They know a book-of-the-month selection will need more cards than this, but there is simply no place to put them until they're needed. They are thus reprinting cards constantly—60,000 titles a month.)

4. The cards are printed on huge sheets of high-grade rag paper; they are cut, and the rod hole is drilled at the bottom of each card. They are then stored in long steel trays to await the arrival of the orders.

5. Thousands of these orders will come in before the book is actually published, before it is received by the Library, or while it is still being cataloged! The reason for this is that libraries are eager to have the cards already on hand and waiting, so the moment the volume arrives in the mail it can be processed and placed on the shelf for use. The libraries can order by author and title (which is slower and costs more) but most use the LC card number assigned to each cataloged publication. (The one for this book is 72–189909 and can be found on the back of the title page.) To avoid having to wait till a librarian gets the volume in his hands before he can find out what its LC card number is, LC pre-assigns numbers at the request of some 7,000 cooperating publishers. The

publishing world has been remarkably generous with its time and product in support of the card service. Not only do publishers accept the task of requesting numbers in advance, but some 9,400 of them are sending the Library free pre-publication copies of their books so it can get the books cataloged and the cards printed before the books actually go on sale. Further, at their own expense, publishers collect and announce forthcoming books with their pre-assigned card numbers in such trade publications as *Publishers Weekly* and the *Cumulative Book Index*. With all these advance data available, any library can order the cards from LC at the same time they order the book from their jobber or bookstore.

6. The orders arrive at LC on little red and white slips of paper, which are provided free to all subscribers. The slips, some 40,000 a day, are dumped into a strange Rube Goldberg machine, which is a glorified combination of a computer and a sorting rack. With blinding speed, the machine examines each slip, turns it face up, "reads" the order number from left to right by electronic eye (it can cope with over two dozen typewriter typefaces), sorts the slips into numerical sequence, checks each for its inventory status, and re-sorts the slips into the appropriate status pile.

7. Until now the slips have been "untouched by human hands." At this point the flow slows abruptly to a walk. For each order, eight copies of a card are withdrawn—by thumb and forefinger—from one of tens of thousands of drawers.

8. The eight-card sets, plus the order slips, are then re-sorted by requesting library, wrapped, addressed, and debited against the library's pre-deposited accounts at the rate of 35 cents a title. The price is set on the basis of a 1902 statute passed specifically for Putnam's benefit that required him to charge "a price which will cover their cost and ten per centum added," proceeds to go directly to the Treasury. The eight-card pack gives the buyer enough cards to provide one each for a Shelf List card, an author card, a title card, one each for

all the subjects and "added entries," and a few for branch library or bookmobile records as well.

Troubles

The result of all this effort is that tens of thousands of libraries in the Western World—from the Vatican to the smallest storefront library in Appalachia—have as fine a bibliographic apparatus as the library profession can produce. For 35 cents any library can get many dollars' worth of skilled cataloging, plus eight crisp, attractive cards for its catalog trays.

But things are going awry. The halcyon days of the card service appear to be over. There is no particular reason for distress—most of its "troubles" are for heartening reasons— but Putnam's idea of a national library selling its *cards* has probably crested.

Merchandising. The Card Division keeps 5.5 million titles in master stock at any given time. Of these, 10 per cent of the titles account for 90 per cent of the sales. Thus the Library is spending a great deal of time and effort cataloging and storing cards which will be used by a very limited number of libraries. Since it has promised to make *any* of its cataloging products available to the library profession and since the most difficult cataloging usually goes into the 90 per cent (because of esoteric language or recondite subjects), LC cannot throw the 90 per cent away, but producing and reprinting the 90 per cent runs up the cost of all LC cards and slows down LC's response to the ordering libraries.

This has resulted in many outside firms buying one set of the most popular cards, reprinting selected ones by offset, and storing the cards for a very limited number of titles (the 10 per cent or less). They will thus be able to sell the "easy ones" more cheaply and within a shorter time period than LC. This is private enterprise in the best sense of the word. The "easy ones" are, of course, the cards most needed by public libraries, and the public libraries are going to these jobbers for cheaper, faster service. At the present time it is estimated that 75 per cent of the cards purchased in this country now come from private sellers using LC cataloging copy! Since, by law, LC must charge enough to pay for the cost of the service, as more of the cheap, easy ones are sold elsewhere, the hard, slow ones will have to go up in price. As in the case of bus fares, this would appear to be pricing LC out of the market. In fact, by automating so many of its handling procedures, the Library has managed to hold the line thus far, but it is unlikely that the service will ever get appreciably faster or cheaper.

Time. There are now an increasing number of faster ways to get cataloging information into a catalog tray and the book on the shelf than by sending for a packet of cards from LC—or anywhere else, for that matter:

1. For $420 a year, you can buy the LC proof sheets of one each of all its cards, and keep the sheets in the back room until the books come in. When the books arrive, you can put the appropriate parts of the proof sheets on a Xerox machine loaded with card paper, push the button, and instantly produce the exact number of cards you need at the exact time you need them.

2. By dint of an astonishingly complex but effective piece of cooperation between publishers and LC, more and more publishers are sending galley proofs of their yet unpublished books to the Library; LC is rush cataloging from the proofs, and the publisher is printing the information he gets in return on the back of the title page of the book itself. (For example, see the "verso" of the title page of this volume.) As of this writing over 200 publishers are cooperating in this "Cataloging-in-Publication" (CIP) Program, and the number is increasing each month. As the CIP Program spreads, it will become increasingly simple for a clerical assistant in a local library merely to type up a single card from the data on

the verso. He can copy out the entry, the subject headings, and the call number, and put the card on the Xerox machine, for instant, at-home card production. The book goes from incoming mail to the public shelf that same afternoon.

Format. But labor costs are rising for cards handled outside LC as well as in. Public, university, and industrial libraries are all finding it increasingly difficult to hire staff to stand around filing individual cards into catalog drawers. The computer, infinitely faster and mechanically more flexible, is increasingly being used to print *book* catalogs—fat bales of computer paper, repellent to handle but so easy to update and so cheap to distribute. A few years ago, in many communities the downtown public library, the local high school library, the college at the edge of town, and the factory library out on the highway all began reporting to the local bank's computer what magazines they took and what issues they had. The computer ran off this "union list" and sent copies to the contributing libraries. Suddenly patrons in any library could know what was available anywhere else in town. The device strengthened every collection so dramatically (and cut down duplication so quickly) that more and more library communities are doing the same thing for all the *books* in town or county. Result: Computer-generated book catalogs seem to be nudging the old-fashioned library card into an ever shrinking environment.

In Fine

The idea of libraries without cards is a fascinating topic but scarcely appropriate here. What seems to be appearing from the convergence of changes in mechandising, time, and format is this: The content of the old traditional catalog card—the professional description of the book and author and the skilled control of subject and indexing—is just as important as it ever was, but the techniques for storing and transmitting the information are changing radically. If costs of filing cards are going up, costs of analyzing and cataloging the publications are going up even faster. The need to eliminate duplication is even greater than it was in Putnam's day. Only the little piece of cardboard is under attack. So what does the library profession want? The cataloging data. How it gets the data into its hands is the least of its worries so long as the means are fast, cheap, accurate, and comprehensive. It is up to LC to continue innovating and to make sure it is responding appropriately.

In the meantime, the Card Division still sold 74 million cards in 1971 in response to other libraries' requests, and it still employs four hundred staff members, struggling to keep time and turn-around to a minimum. It is far from moribund (as Churchill said: "Some chicken") and continues to make a major contribution to the nation's libraries.

GREATNESS THRUST UPON IT: THE NATIONAL PROGRAM FOR ACQUISITION AND CATALOGING

But, the librarians say, we expect LC to provide us with centralized cataloging to eliminate duplication throughout the American library system. How can this be done if LC is cataloging less than half of what the library system needs?

The question was raised repeatedly in the 1960's when the gap between what ought to be and what was appeared to be widening day by day. A lot of people talked about it; the leaders of the national Association of Research Libraries did something about it. Their thinking ran as follows: The reason LC was not providing them with the cataloging data they needed was that the Library of Congress was not getting the material itself (inadequate funds for acquisition and overly narrow selection policies); also, the Library had insufficient catalogers to handle broader acquisitions even if it had gotten them (inadequate funds for processing). Where could more money be found and who had the authority to broaden the policies? Answer: the Congress. Could Congress be sold on the need? Rather easily, for a change. Frightened by Sputnik and claims of Russian technical superiority, Congress had just passed a series of programs pouring millions of dollars into strengthening the American educational scene through such broad-ranging legislation as the National Defense Education Act of 1958 and the Elementary and Secondary Education and the Higher Education Acts of 1965. What would be more logical than to request money to identify, acquire, and catalog the materials on which all of these educational and research efforts were going to rely? The Association of Research Libraries asked LC, "If we can get you the money, will you assume the responsibility and do the work?" The Library replied with a barely audible affirmative, and spokesmen from the Association of Research Libraries and the American Library Association began approaching the appropriate members of Congress and committees all over Capitol Hill.

When the smoke cleared, the Higher Education Act had been amended so that its Title II C instructed the Library of Congress to acquire "all library materials currently published throughout the world which are of value to scholarship." LC was to provide "catalog information for these materials promptly after receipt" and to distribute this "bibliographic information by printing catalog cards and by other means." As William S. Dix, Librarian of Princeton and a prime mover in the plan, said with remarkable understatement, "The role of the Library of Congress as the *de facto* national library, stimulated by frequent new initiatives proposed by organized librarianship, was substantially enlarged and strengthened."

Here was a real challenge. The money became available in 1966, and the Library was expected to find, ship, and catalog "all library materials currently published throughout the world which are of value to scholarship." How could this be done? The answer took the form of a bureaucratic *tour de force*. With astonishing vigor, in six years the Library's Processing Department geared up an operation blanketing forty-two countries and doubled the rate of books cataloged into the

LC collections. In 1965 LC had processed 109,787 titles; in 1971 it cataloged 233,517 titles and was still accelerating its procedures. How?

NPAC*

In carrying out its role in the National Program for Acquisition and Cataloging (NPAC), the Library decided to go down two paths simultaneously. In the twenty-four "developed" countries of the "West," it decided to rely on the foreign book trade to act as its acquisition officers (expanding on the old practice of blanket orders—"buy one copy of everything published in your country that meets the following criteria"), and it decided to use the cataloging and bibliographic know-how of the countries themselves to do the processing rather than attempt to hire platoons of foreign-language experts to describe the material in Washington. Thus, by working with the libraries and booksellers in the parent countries—the people responsible for or knowledgeable about their own national bibliographies— a highly refined program of shared cataloging was established. The initial descriptive work was thus tied to such national bibliographies as the Norsk Bokfortegnelse in Norway, the Nōhon Shūho in Japan, and the Bibliografija Jugoslavije in Yugoslavia, and then, when each book arrived at LC with a "foreign" catalog card in it, all LC had to do was make minor adjustments to fit it into its own catalogs, assign subject headings and classification numbers, and the card copy was on the way to the Card Division.

Renting space in medieval basements, new glass-sided office blocks, and a pair of cells in a one-time monastery, the Library's dealers created ten LC Shared Cataloging Centers in London, Vienna, Wiesbaden, Paris, Oslo, the Hague, Belgrade, Florence, Tokyo, and Barcelona. Each was tied to a major bookseller and employed a substantial team of foreign nationals. The ten centers were responsible for getting and

* Pronounced EN-PAK.

processing the materials of the country in which they were located. In addition, they divided up the neighboring states so together they achieved saturation coverage of the book publishing of sixteen "developed" countries. Like the countries of Western Europe and the British Commonwealth, Bulgaria, Czechoslovakia, East Germany, Romania, Yugoslavia, and the Soviet Union all cooperated in the plan and moved materials toward Washington by the tens of thousands of pieces.

A second approach was used in the "developing" countries. While the ten cataloging centers were being staffed and opened in the sophisticated and organized West, three regional *acquisition* centers were established in areas where there was no organized book trade or comprehensive national bibliography. These acquisition centers are now operating in Nairobi (which covers the publishing of Ethiopia, French Territory of the Afars and the Issas, Kenya, La Réunion, Malagasy Republic, Malawi, Mauritius, Seychelles, Somali Republic, Sudan, Tanzania, Uganda, and Zambia); Rio de Janeiro (for Brazilian materials); and Djakarta (which covers Indonesia, Malaysia, Singapore, and Brunei). The three centers invest their energies, not in processing and forwarding, as do the shared cataloging units, but primarily in trying to locate and acquire virtually all current publications in their assigned areas. They use any device that will work—purchase, exchange, or plain begging. Materials secured in the acquisition centers are sent to Washington for cataloging, but what has been gathered in and forwarded is described in printed "Accession Lists" distributed monthly for Southeast Asia and bimonthly for Eastern Africa.

Distributed to whom? To the research libraries which started the idea in the first place. The purpose of the program, it will be recalled, was to round up the products of world publishing and get them described and prepared as cataloging copy for America's research libraries. To achieve this, both comprehensiveness and speed are paramount. Materials from all forty-two countries are flown by weekly air freight to LC, where the cataloging data is processed, printed as cards, and then distributed as complete depository sets or proof sheets to some seventy American libraries. Is the system working? Apparently yes. The same major universities that formerly reported 30 to 40 per cent success in finding LC cataloging for the books they bought are now reporting 70 to 80 per cent. The purpose of the program was to support American research, and all professional feedback is positive; NPAC appears to be doing a better job, faster, at less expense than even its originators had hoped. The money, roughly $7 million a year, is spent as follows: 16 per cent for buying the books themselves, 69 per cent for cataloging them, 9 per cent for printing and distributing the cards, and 6 per cent for administering the program.

The Eternal Exception

In spite of all this effort, there is still a major bloc of American librarianship that is frustrated by the lack of centralized cataloging to avoid wasteful duplication: public libraries and the so-called special libraries. At the very time the large research libraries are reporting 70 to 80 per cent support, the small and medium-sized public and high school libraries, and the governmental, religious, business, and industrial libraries are reporting the same old 30 to 50 per cent success with LC cards to avoid costly in-house cataloging.

How can this be? It seems to stem from several causes: (1) The main thrust of NPAC is foreign acquisition, which has little impact on public and special libraries, which rely on English-language materials. (2) Public libraries must process their volumes quickly to satisfy their clients' demands. Thus, if LC has not cataloged an item within two months or so of its release, the public library must go ahead and do it itself. A research library can afford to wait the longer time it takes for LC to get the information through the processing pipeline.

(3) LC's acquisition policies still emphasize books and other monographs, especially hardbounds at that. A great proportion of public and special library collections are based on paperbacks, state and local government documents, reports of nearby colleges and industries, local history, and other items that LC does not catalog. Even the most optimistic survey estimates that the Library of Congress catalogs only half of the product of American publishing.

Is there hope of help here? Undoubtedly the situation will improve. The Cataloging in Publication program (itself created in response to impassioned pleas from the public library sector) is forcing LC to do a faster job in handling American trade publications and thus will make these available sooner—indeed, by definition, upon receipt of the publication. As more publishers join the CIP program, public libraries can be assured of faster, less expensive processing. The document situation may be relieved as more private firms offer federal, state, and local publications in microform and supply indexes to the material as a part of their services. From the point of view of the local institution, the material can then either be preserved on film, or the accompanying indexing can be used to process the library's hard copy. Whether the profession will feel that LC should be the center for this kind of cataloging as it is for foreign material has not yet been expressed. Finally, the gearing up to NPAC tended to draw LC's energies and attention toward servicing the foreign material first. As procedures become routinized, a return to normalcy will probably re-emphasize English-language material again. But the question of how close to totality the Library can be expected to come has not yet been fully faced by either LC or the library world.

TOTALITY AND THE AMERICAN NATIONAL BIBLIOGRAPHY

One other aspect of the bibliographic control of the world's publishing should be noted before we move on. You recall that Mr. Putnam's final justification for a card service was "to place in each center of research as complete as possible a statement of the contents of the national collections in Washington." Putnam intended to do it by sending complete sets of every LC card to the major research libraries around the country. This was actually done for forty years, until the libraries became so buried in proof slips they found they were devoting more staff time and floor space to preserving the record than their clients' use could ever justify. So, in 1941, the Association of Research Libraries (again) attacked the problem and convinced the private publishing firm of Edwards Brothers in Ann Arbor, Michigan, to make pages of LC cards laid top to bottom, shrink their size so that thirty could fit on a page approximately the size of a page of the *Encyclopaedia Britannica*, and sell the resultant set as a profit-making venture. LC organized and provided the cards free, and the first two printings were enormously successful. They contained only author entries and covered the years from August, 1898, through December, 1947. Tiny as the miniature entries were, it required 229 huge volumes to print the original series.

But the success of this approach—space-saving *book* catalogs—was so convincing to the scholarly and bibliographic world that a whole series of these catalogs is now published regularly. Without taking time to describe how each index came to be (or what particular scholarly group pressed for its creation!), we note in passing that a research library can now buy the following: The Library of Congress catalog of *Subjects* only; the LC catalog of *Motion Pictures and Filmstrips*; the LC catalog of *Music and Phonorecords*; the *National Union Catalog of Manuscript Collections*; *New Serial Titles* (which does for periodicals what the other catalogs do for books, films, and music); and the towering *National Union Catalog* itself.

The National Union Catalog

The National Union Catalog is essentially the great, total index to the world's publishing that Putnam and the Association of Research Libraries dreamed about, and many people believe it to be the most valuable service the Library renders the scholarly and library world. It is an enormous author index to practically every book printed anywhere! It contains column after column of LC cards, each reduced to half size. Each year's catalog lists the quarter of a million titles that LC adds to its collection annually—but this is literally only the half of it. Eighteen of the nation's major libraries, two from each geographic/bibliographic area (Cornell, UCLA, University of Texas, University of Chicago, and so on), report to LC essentially everything they add to their own shelves. In addition, 1,100 more U.S. and Canadian libraries report their unusual volumes, most of their foreign-language works, and essentially all of their local publishing. When these hundreds of thousands of cards come in, the outside "locations" are added to the LC cards. If LC does not have the volume, a special card is made up and filed into the proper alphabetic place with the symbol of the reporting library on it. The result is that there are another 250,000-plus titles included beyond those for which LC creates cards. This bibliographic *tour de force* comes very close to organizing the monographic publishing of the world. It sells for $750 a year, runs to some 15 volumes annually, and is bought by 2,440 libraries in the U.S. and abroad. Its impact on scholarship and librarianship can scarcely be overstated.

World scholarship, in fact, has come to rely so heavily on LC's book catalogs that a great deal of outside pressure built up during the 1960's for LC to produce a single, huge catalog of the world's books from 1440 to 1956—a union catalog of all known works held in North American libraries from the birth of printing to the start of the National Union Catalog (NUC). LC finally agreed to do so and is now involved in the largest bibliographic exercise ever undertaken by the Library. This "Pre-'56 NUC" is being printed in London by Mansell Information/Publishing Ltd. under the aegis of the American Library Association. It is expected to run to over 600 volumes of 700 pages each, will take ten years to complete, and is costing the A.L.A.'s publisher $4 million. Two hundred volumes have appeared to date (through Goldsmith, Oliver), and the 1,250 libraries currently subscribing are paying $26 a volume for 60 volumes a year. Barring too great a fluctuation in world currency, the completed set will have cost each of them $15,000 apiece. Nothing Putnam ever started worked out as successfully as the national bibliography. It requires 120 staff members to prepare the ongoing, current NUC, and 60 to create the "Pre-'56." The actual printing and distribution of all the various index sets is done by private firms; neither the government nor the Government Printing Office has a role in publishing the works. LC contributes half of the cataloging and all of the assembly work, but it is the conscientious, dedicated contributions from the 1,100 contributing libraries that make the National Union Catalog the astonishing research tool that it is.

UNIFORM CATALOGING

It is self-evident that the "outside" library world and LC are locked to each other's activities like two close-fitting gears, and it is extremely difficult to determine who is driving whom. With 25,000 U.S. libraries relying so heavily on LC's products—and with LC using so much data from these libraries' catalogs in its own—the necessity of everybody operating under the same rules has been recognized for years. Librarianship has literally hundreds of rules. Rules for selecting authors from complicated creative sources, for transliterating non-Roman-alphabet languages into Roman letters, for tracing subject headings through thickets of synonyms, for elaborating classification numbers by way of place, time, form, profession, edition, and translation.

LC, not being a *de jure* national library, has never had or wished to have the role of legislating these rules, or of telling "all American libraries" what to do. But LC has had such an intrusive role in all these libraries' catalogs that the outside libraries are practically strong-armed into following LC's practices. The result has been a need for close cooperation between LC and the nation's libraries (usually represented by the American Library Association) to be certain that LC's procedures are efficient, constructive, and compatible with the needs, procedures, and audiences of the dozens of different kinds of library institutions in the United States. Since Putnam's time, LC has worked closely with the nation's cataloging specialists.

The history of these cooperative activities could fill a book, but a simple enumeration of some of the landmark products may illustrate the point: In 1908, the American Library Association (A.L.A.) produced its *Cataloging Rules* for author and title entries. This actually was the first *Anglo*-American code and was developed with the working cooperation of the Library Association of Great Britain. The editor and the chairman of the American committee was James C. M. Hanson, chief of LC's Catalogue Division.

In 1941, after many months of public professional hearings and internal committee meetings, the American Library Association brought out its new *A.L.A. Catalog Rules.* The executive assistant to the committee and its general editor was Nella J. Martin of LC's Catalog Division. In 1949, a committee of the A.L.A. produced the *A.L.A. Cataloging Rules for Author and Title Entries*—whose editor was Clara Beetle, principal cataloger of LC's Descriptive Cataloging Division. The same year LC published its *Rules for Descriptive Cataloging in the Library of Congress*, edited by LC's Lucile M. Morsch, and these rules were subsequently adopted by the A.L.A.

For many years in the mid-1950's and 1960's, committees and representatives of the American Library Association, the (British) Library Association, the Canadian Library Association, and the Library of Congress met and in 1967 promulgated a grand revision of the *Anglo-American Cataloging Rules*, which was essentially based on the work of Seymour Lubetzky, long of LC's staff. The general editor of the *Rules* was C. Sumner Spalding, on leave to the project from his job as chief of LC's Descriptive Cataloging Division.

The ever shrinking world (plus the impact of overseas reliance on the National Union Catalog and NPAC's use of foreign bibliographies) has forced closer cooperation with the international library community. There was a major conference on cataloging principles in Paris in 1961, which made significant strides toward international bibliographic uniformity. This work was reactivated in Copenhagen in 1969 and is continuing to produce international cataloging standards. LC has been in the forefront of all these activities, marching under a banner with the legend: "LC will not go a separate way; we will find grounds for agreement with all other bodies and other organizations."

All of the above activities fall into what librarians call rules for entry, heading, and description. A similar list could be drawn for work in subject cataloging and the development of both the LC classification system and the traditional Dewey Decimal System. Changes in and additions to Dewey have been the responsibility of the Library of Congress since 1953, working under contract with the system's governing foundation.

The point need not be labored. For seventy years the Library of Congress has shared its role with the library community at large, developing new systems of library processing and the techniques by which the bibliographic apparatus is refined and perfected. The greatest work in this area is not in the past. The advent of the computer has made uniformity, "compatibility," and precision more important than ever before. If the parts of the American library system are ever to be electronically linked, the *real* problems of uniform cataloging are just beginning. The Library of Congress is expected—and willing—to assume its share of the task.

XII

The Library of Congress and the Library World: Acquisition and Computers

We are trying to note in this and the preceding chapter the kinds of things the Library of Congress does for the national library community outside its own walls and also to identify those other things the community wishes LC would do. The first of these activities was related to providing cards, book catalogs, and general bibliographic data—especially those services that cut down on duplication of effort by the cataloging profession. LC has been doing these things for a long time; it does them well, and, while they are a long way from perfection, this is a fully developed area of service.

Much the same could be said for the second area: providing leadership in establishing national and international standards of library techniques. We note now a third kind of service, which has been needed and discussed just as long as the first two but has only recently been applied and developed.

CENTRALIZED ACQUISITION

If the Library is up to its waist in cataloging data and rules, it is barely over its instep in *centralized acquisition*. Centralized acquisition is the other side of the coin from centralized cataloging and logically should have come first.

Example: The justification for the National Program for Acquisitions and Cataloging (NPAC) was that hundreds of large university libraries were buying foreign books, and, without LC to catalog them, each library had to do them itself. Had the acquisition librarians been complaining (instead of the catalogers), they would have pointed out that each of those hundreds of libraries had to write off to the foreign publisher to order each of the titles, each had his account charged separately, and then each had to pay for the books by separate transfer of funds. Wasn't there some way books could be bought in lots of several hundred, paid for en bloc, and distributed back in the U.S.?

Second example: This concerns the same sort of single-point purchasing but for all kinds of special libraries tied to single areas of interest—medical schools, the fifty state legislative reference services, or the national consortium of Asian area studies. The chain of 2,800 federal libraries appears to be a classic example. Can't at least the government buy and process en bloc and cut down on duplicative ordering, billing, and accessioning?

For nearly a hundred years, library association conventions have been urging that the Library of Congress be the central point for such central acquisition, buying in quantity (with resultant cheaper prices), and then distributing the pieces among the participating library customers. LC is actually doing this in one small area that deserves our notice because it could well be the pilot experience for the way of the future.

Public Law 480

The story here starts back at the end of World War II when the large research libraries of the country were fretting over what to do with the five-year hole in all their collections. Not only had they received no publications from Germany, Italy, and Japan during the war, but they had received next to none from Sweden, Switzerland, France, or indeed from any occupied country of Europe or Asia. Rather than each library independently trying to put together all the thousands of fragments they were missing, the librarians of the largest institutions met at Farmington, Connecticut, to make a concerted, rational attack on the problem.

The members of the Farmington Plan, as it became known, decided to proceed down two paths simultaneously. Some things (like records of parliaments and general statistical documents) were wanted by everybody, so the group sought enough copies of these to go around to all—but everything else was to be distributed in single copies, by subject, to specific individual libraries. Institutions that were already strong in certain fields would agree to accept *everything* from all the countries in the assigned areas and then make these materials available to the other members via interlibrary loan when needed. The distribution of subjects covered the entire span of knowledge, and some of it was most intriguing. Brandeis University agreed to take all publications issued in the Arab World; Brooklyn Public Library accepted responsibility for all works on clothing and costume, "including applied art, design, fashion, history & manners & customs relating to dress"; Dartmouth—exploration and history of the polar regions; Duke—history of Bolivia, Ecuador, and Peru; Georgia Tech—the technology of textile industries; University of Missouri—"outdoor life, including camping (but not tourist camps), hunting and trapping . . . & wildlife (i.e. bird & game) preservation, but not mountaineering." The University of Rochester was to be responsible for all foreign works on light; the University of Southern California would take and keep publications on "moving pictures, including acting, actors, and actresses; animated cartoons; costume; direction; management." The Library of Congress, which was simply a partner in the project and neither leader nor servant, had its assigned areas along with everyone else.

The activity began by sending a team of librarians into freed Europe, and by September, 1948, they had collected 820,000 books and serials (over 2 million pieces altogether), had gotten them to the U.S., and distributed them among 113 participating libraries. Once they had filled in the gaps in their collections created by the war, the libraries agreed to continue buying at their own expense everything available abroad in their assigned area. The Catch 22 was that, once a library became responsible for a subject area, it was obligated to acquire whatever appeared relating to that area, no matter how trivial. With this, the first step was taken from "get the best works on . . ." toward "take anything you can find that seems to be about . . . " There was an added obligation: All the participants agreed to catalog the material as quickly as possible and send a copy of the catalog card to LC's National Union Catalog for the purpose of making the material available on interlibrary loan. The National Union Catalog thus became the central directory of a system of bibliographic location and control for North America.

The Farmington Plan started with Western European countries, then added Eastern Europe, the major Latin American nations, and finally Asia and the Middle East. By the 1970's, sixty-two major libraries were grimly hanging on, still buying everything in their subject fields from some ninety-nine of the most developed nations of the world.

The significance of the Farmington Plan is that it got everybody's feet wet and gave the participants a good deal of experience in what it would take to operate a really global program of acquisition. The Farmington Plan was based on purchases through booksellers under blanket orders. It lacked even respectable coverage (much less comprehensiveness) in the developing countries, where there was no sophisticated bookselling industry to support it.

This led to Public Law (P.L.) 480. In the late 1950's, it struck library leaders that the solution to the bibliographic problem of the "missing countries" lay in all the money that was piling up around the world in currencies for which the U.S. had no use. Since 1954 the U.S. had been selling surplus agricultural commodities to some forty nations who paid for them in their local money. The money built up in U.S. government accounts in each country and was drawn on to run the local embassy and pay for whatever American military presence there was, but there were usually vast sums left over.

The American Council of Learned Societies and the Association of Research Libraries pressed for access to these monies for scholarship, and in 1958 Representative John Dingell of Michigan got an amendment passed to the Agricultural Trade Development and Assistance Act that permitted these surplus funds to be spent on library materials printed and sold within the countries involved. The Library of Congress was to acquire the material, index it, and distribute it to the other libraries. It took several years for Congress to fund the plan, but in 1962 it was launched with LC setting up outposts in India, Pakistan, and the United Arab Republic. Indonesia and Israel were soon added to the list, and LC was shortly collecting books in these countries, cataloging them on the spot with local personnel, and shipping the material back to the participating libraries in the U.S. (This differed from the later NPAC approach, which acquired *one* copy of a book and sent it to LC.) The P.L. 480 Program collected complete sets of materials and sent them directly to the requesting institutions. Some wanted the publishing of only one country, others of several. For example, sets of publications from India and Pakistan were crated and sent simultaneously to ten university libraries (U.C.L.A., Berkeley, Columbia, Harvard, Illinois, Michigan, Princeton, Utah, Virginia, Indiana), the New York Public Library, and LC itself. Hartford Seminary and Portland State shared a set.

The original list of "P.L. 480 countries" has changed slightly through the years (Yugoslavia, Ceylon, Nepal, and

Poland have been added, and the surplus funds were exhausted in Indonesia), but since 1962 LC has secured and distributed over 14 million items from nine countries. Forty-one major libraries are currently receiving the shipments, whose total in the past ten years has added up to: India, 6.5 million pieces; Israel, 1.5 million; Egypt, 2 million; Ceylon, 100,000; Indonesia, 100,000; Nepal, 200,000; Pakistan, 1.5 million; and Yugoslavia, 1 million.

The idea, at least in this limited application, works. Many librarians feel LC should do more of this kind of thing. Others believe that centralized acquisition is a mixed blessing—it cuts down duplication at the expense of flexibility. The cooperating library loses control over what it gets and sacrifices both control over priorities and responsiveness to its audience in order to buy comprehensiveness and economy. As philosopher Mort Sahl says, "The future lies ahead." We won't know till we get there and by then it'll probably be too late.

TECHNOLOGY

The library world looks to LC for a final area of innovation and service: the applied technology of librarianship. This might seem the last possible activity of the bookman, but in fact librarians in general have a fair track record for professional exploitation of current inventions. They have embraced new methods of photoduplication, "keyed" charging systems, audio-visual innovations, and imaginative storage and architectural solutions, as quickly as they have appeared. They have repeatedly urged LC to be more experimental in its search for answers to library problems and have rejoiced at LC's laboratory work on preservation. LC has built a nationally known staff of preservation specialists, who are currently involved in such Strangelove-sounding investigations as the effectiveness of vapor phase methods of deacidification, the restrengthening of old paper by graft polymerization, the stabilization of photographic print emulsions, freeze-drying methods for the restoration of water-damaged books, and the establishment of international standards of long-lived paper. Incidentally, in the world of technological standardization, the late Verner Clapp used to say that the library *card* was one of the all-time triumphs: Cards are identical in size (precisely 75 by 125 mm.) in every library in every literate location, anywhere in the world. The hundreds of thousands of standardized card drawers in standardized library furniture are an inevitable by-product.

But, for librarians, computer applications and automatic data processing tower above all other technological interests, and LC has indeed had a major role in the profession's development of computerized bibliographic support.

The Library of Congress and the Computer

LC's experience with the computer so closely parallels that of most American libraries, it might well serve as the stock plot for the drama. Its computerized synopsis could well read: LC avoided computerization as long as possible, was intimidated into exploration, suddenly realized the potential, became fascinated and wildly hopeful, received the icy shock of reality, and is now grimly trying to make it work among those day-to-day procedures where it seems to be genuinely appropriate. The brave new world still seems to throb in shimmering Technicolor, but it is so far down the path that no one can be quite sure what it is he thinks he is seeing.

In a nutshell the story runs thus: In 1961, using money from the Council on Library Resources, the Library hired an outside computer group to do a feasibility study to see if LC's operations were appropriate for automation. In 1963, to no one's surprise, the report said they were. The report concluded that the process would be reasonably simple in terms of procedures, but something of a problem because of size. However, since each item (the equivalent of a catalog card) was a tiny, finite block, each could be loaded into the computer and then controlled, added to, and recalled without trouble. The study pictured a system where one of these tiny binary "documents" would be created when a book was ordered, expanded as it was cataloged, annotated as the book was charged in and out or sent for rebinding, and in general manipulated so as to reflect everything that happens to a book through its lifetime in a library.

The survey (done by a team under Gilbert W. King and therefore referred to as the King Report) pictured LC's great reading room cleared of bulky card catalog cases, whose space was taken by dozens of desk-sized computer terminals before which readers would sit and ask questions. What is the call number for such and such a book? Answer appears on the terminal's 12-inch television tube: Z 733. W 38. How many books do you have on thus-and-such a subject? Answer: 150. Let me see those written in English, printed after 1950, that contain a bibliography. The tube shows a catalog card for each, one at a time, at the reader's command, and if he wants to retain the citation, he presses a button and a copy of the card slides out the side of the machine for him to take with him. The King Report recommended a timetable that would bring all these magical visions to reality by 1972.

The system would clearly permit great flexibility and economy for the Library of Congress, but it would have an even greater impact on American librarianship in general. The computer would hold in its "memory" not only the equivalent of the LC catalog but the entire National Union Catalog as well. With this the computer would indeed have a record of almost every item held in every library anywhere in North America. Thus all a library in Phoenix or Bangor would have to do was tell LC to add its symbol to the LC "card" for every book it got, and Phoenix and Bangor could throw away their catalogs, too. An Arizonian would ask the Phoenix computer terminal, What books do you have on thus-and-such, written in English, printed after 1950, with the symbol for the *Phoenix Public Library* on it?, and the machine would work as well in Phoenix as in Washington. The cost of a rented telephone line was appreciably less than all the catalogers' salaries that could be eliminated. Assured by the computer specialists that the system was feasible, LC went to work.

Work began with the building of the tiny block that represented a catalog card in the computer's memory. Recognizing that if the King Report was right, this block or document would some day be the basis for a nationwide bibliographic network, the Library designed it in close cooperation with all the major library groups. Months of meetings involving representatives of the American Library Association, the Special Libraries Association, the Association of Research Libraries, the Committee on Scientific and Technical Information, the British National Bibliography, the International Atomic Energy Agency, the National Library of Medicine, and the National Agricultural Library produced a "format" known as MARC (pronounced "mark" and standing for MAchine-Readable Cataloging).

With the MARC established, LC began producing computer tapes containing all English-language books cataloged by LC and made these tapes available to sixteen carefully chosen libraries representing several different types. With the tapes went computer programs that would print out such basic products as individual cards or book catalogs. Once the pilot program was shaken down, a refined MARC II was produced, and it is now the basic format at LC. Tapes were made available to any library, and in 1969 there were sixty-eight individual subscribers, each buying a weekly 300-foot reel containing some thousand new records.

So far so good. But from this point on almost nothing worked out as the computer industry had predicted. Through the 1960's, literally dozens of computer "hardware" and "software" manufacturers visited the Library to get pieces of the action in the hope that being in on the automating of the national library would open all other libraries to their product—only to withdraw, shaken with the immensity of what they found. (A team from the second largest software house in the country told me with only half-humorous hyperbole, "We just checked out the Central Charge File operation; just the electricity it would take to drive the discs for that thing would cost more than the six girls you've got doing it by hand!")

The original estimates had concentrated too heavily on how a reader would get information *out* of the computer, and too little on what it was going to take to get it in. They had failed to anticipate the multiplicity of printed characters that would be necessary, not to mention the fact that rather than being a finite size like a bank check, the "document" could run to many hundreds of characters, and thus there could be no uniform lengths or localities established in the finding programs for retrieval. The complex relationships between order files, charge files, accession files, Shelf List files, subject files, language files, and scores of others proved far more complex than originally expected.

The result was that by the end of the 1960's the Library had all but dispensed with the services of the contract firms, who time and again failed to understand how the data was actually created or manipulated, and in their place built an in-house Information Systems Office of approximately sixty people. The staff is a mixture of librarians and lawyers, who have been trained as computer specialists, and computer technicians, whom the Library has trained as librarians.

The new system is working very well. The idea of a great computerized system of bibliographic cradle-to-grave information has been pushed back on the shelf, and LC is now automating specific chunks, one procedure or product at a time. Each is designed to operate alone, but each is being built in such a way that, when all the parts have been completed, they will form a total integrated system.

By 1971 the Card Division was using the computer to control its inventory and do its billing. The Order Division controls its orders, claims, and payment releases through its own terminals. The Reference Department is creating automated demand bibliographies and book catalogs of specialized reference collections. The National Referral Center accumulates its directories of participating institutions on tape. Subject Cataloging is updating its subject heading catalogs via the machine and sending the tapes to the Government Printing Office, where they are printed out by high-speed computer-driven Linofilm.

The Congressional Research Service has thirty-eight computer terminals distributed through its nine divisions. It uses the computer to print its *Digest of Public General Bills* and displays the resulting knowledge via cathode-ray-tube consoles. It maintains its SDI (Selective Dissemination of Information) bibliographic system, produces calendars for congressional committees, and produces the CRS *Legislative Status Report* on its automated equipment. Such management statistics as numbers of inquiries, time spent, grade level, method of answering, and task force interdivisional commitment are computer produced, and the thirty-eight terminals are used for instantaneous transmittal of query data among its divisions, its outposts in the congressional office buildings, and to other parts of the Library (such as Order Division for purchase orders, Loan Division for congressional book requests, and so forth). LC's Administrative Department has computerized its personnel files, and all of its fiscal and payroll operations are on tape and disk.

And the Library World?

But what significance has this for the Library world? The MARC format has become the basic international bibliographic module, and it clearly was an LC contribution of major proportions. However, all of LC's other applications are useful only as experiments and case studies. LC wrestles with the problem and solves it—but then the outside libraries must buy and build separate systems for their own use. This irritating duplication is a frustrating and expensive result of the automated guild system. An innocent taxpayer might think that once a library—any library—has worked out a computer program to print its book catalogs or support an SDI system, this program could print *any* book catalog or accept *any* bibliographic entry. This is almost never so. The automators force expensive "installations" and "modifications" for each institution, so the library world finds each unit re-inventing its automatic data processing wheels. At this point then, LC's solutions are essentially feasibility demonstrations for its fellow libraries. Its solutions and shortcuts can rarely be adopted without expensive changes by its friends.

And the future? Almost everyone involved believes that the glittering world of the King Report will come to pass, but it will be seen by the next generation. Not this one.

Two Points

LC's relations with its library audiences need not be summarized; the cumulated activities speak for themselves. There are, however, two aspects which deserve some underlining.

Why Is LC So Conservative?

For the past hundred years, one of the standard dialogues at library conventions has started with the question: Why is it so hard to get LC to do something new? The profession has always been ahead of the Library. (Even so obvious a benefit as a legislative reference service in a congressional library caused great pain to Herbert Putnam, and the record shows he hoped to the very last it would go away; he finally bowed to the pressures when all hope of their disappearance was gone.) Again and again throughout the Library's history, the Librarians of Congress and the department heads have been selected because of their imagination and because of the aggressive, innovative ideas they have demonstrated in their home libraries—only to have these qualities apparently evaporate when they reach the great gray building on Capitol Hill.

I would suggest that we are seeing here a very complicated phenomenon. It operates in a veritable thicket of contradictions. To begin with, the Library has always had a tradition of professional excellence. The programs that are operating *today* must be executed at the highest level of professional standards. To take on a new program for *tomorrow* means that today's programs must be diluted or eroded because staffing rarely catches up with new responsibilities or, if help comes at all, it arrives much too late. At the same time, LC management feels its leadership role acutely. The Library has traditionally been involved with new professional developments, and each successive generation wants to embellish its share of the tradition. A division chief recently dramatized the dilemma when he sat down wearily after an impassioned and successful plea for a new program and said, "I hope to hell I know what I'm doing; we're doing such a lousy job of everything already, do we really dare take on this much more?" Of course he was not doing so poor a job, but the present performance failed to match his standards and expectations.

But this is scarcely news. Any administrator in any effective program suffers the same dilemma in launching new programs. The main pain is always to select the present programs that should be dropped to find personnel, space, and funds to support the new direction.

It is here LC's administrators suffer so much trauma, because, as LC works in the national scene, each continuing program builds its own out-of-house elite. Thus, when the Library responds to the needs or demands of Elite A to initiate New Program Z, Elite Groups B, C, and D (having just lost long-time Programs Y, X, and W) exert all their collective resistance to the shift of resources. Thus the interruption (for whatever reasons) of the *Monthly Index of Russian Accessions*, the *Index to Presidential Manuscripts*, the Cooperative Cataloging Program, the *World List of Future International Meetings*, or the aerospace technology services causes as much distress outside the Library as in. These agonizing trade-offs are particularly difficult in librarianship, where the long-time, continuing product cannot be independently assumed by the libraries relying upon it.

Another aspect of LC's delayed reaction to the library profession's demands (and there is no doubt that it is delayed: the Cataloging in Publication Program, the Union Catalog, and improvements in card service response were pressed for years before LC responded) relates to where the money comes from. In a university library (theoretically, at least!) the better the library serves the teaching departments, the easier it is to get funds. In a public library, much the same holds true in service to the community. But at LC, successful service to the national library community makes next to no difference at all to the two congressional appropriations committees. Not only does national professional success or failure matter little in the committees' scale of values, they rarely even hear of such things except in the Librarian's pleas for funds, which are promptly discounted as self-serving. Thus the Library, rather than making Brownie points with its money source when it adds a useful, innovative outside service, frequently must initiate the service almost covertly to get it off the ground.

...When It Adds an Outside Service

The other point that should be underscored is that the library profession's needs and demands are indeed, in the eyes of many members of Congress, quite "outside" the Library's true concerns. Most, if not all of LC's efforts in the very things we have enumerated in this chapter—the Card Service, Cataloging-in-Publication, NPAC, the National Union Catalog, the Dewey Decimal Classification Scheme, PL 480, and the MARC tapes—are primarily done for *other* libraries. They are of fractional use to LC itself. If LC could devote a fourth of the manpower spent on the above programs strictly to in-house, Washington-centered activities, the Library of Congress as a self-contained institution would improve immeasurably in service and (that word again) in excellence.

So why doesn't it? Because it truly believes itself to be the National Library, regardless of its name. And the fact that for seventy-five years a succession of critical appropriations committees has voted hundreds of millions of dollars to support these very out-of-house services would suggest that Congress supports this national role and recognizes LC's obligations to the library profession at large—albeit, on occasion, somewhat belatedly. "But you just got through saying ... How can you have it both ways?" That's the paradox. You can't, but somehow you do.

XIII

The Library of Congress and the Scholarly World

We have noted that the Library of Congress has three customer elites: the Congress, the library world, and the nation's scholars. Let us now examine the last of these three to see what the world of research wants of the Library and how well its wants are being satisfied.

We should first note precisely who these scholars/researchers/users really are. They can be grouped into eight classes, and the word "classes" is singularly appropriate because, although it is never officially admitted, there is in fact a pecking order in the way in which these classes are treated. Given conflicting pressures of resources, time, staff, space, or priority, the daily users of the Library line up in the following order:

1. Members of Congress and their staffs pursuing public or private research
2. Federal employees engaged in official studies for their agencies
3. The Press—representatives of newspapers, TV, radio, and the wire services

4. Established individual scholars writing books and scholarly papers
5. Ph.D. candidates doing doctoral dissertations
6. Adult citizens following personal interests
7. College students doing undergraduate and Master's work
8. Local high school students doing class assignments

Ignoring such subtle decisions as who gets the long-term study carrels, and which groups get the full-time research assistance, the simple integer of *chairs to sit on* has become a major problem for the Library.

There are 425 seats in the two general reading rooms and 300 more in the twelve special reading rooms. During the peak use weeks of the year, over a thousand readers will pour into the Library in a single day. On such occasions, the visiting scholar may find himself joining rows of readers hunched on stair steps, propped in window wells, or simply leaning against those wall spaces undefended by the fire marshal. This situation has forced the Library to re-examine its obligations. On the one hand, it meets pressures from the local schools, taxpayers, and news media to make the Library available to anyone who seeks the written word. Their position is that the collections belong to the American people and should be made available on the basis of first come, first served. On the other side are the users who emphasize that the Library of Congress is in fact a unique collection of the fugitive, the uncommon, and the rare, and its resources should be saved for "serious" research. This group holds that the local school libraries should support the educational activity and the area public libraries should care for the routine reference needs of the citizens.

Caught with an intolerable situation but recognizing the legitimacy of both positions, in 1958 the Library reluctantly closed its doors to local high school students and thus began to lift its threshold of accessibility. For a decade this eased the pressure on its facilities, but in recent years the same situation is building again—and is now threatening access to college students as well.

The Library dreads having to make a decision on this problem, but it is under increasing pressure from the organized professional societies who feel that space and attention are being denied their "senior, serious" scholars, who are forced to compete with the teaching-assignment clientele. There is little doubt that the dozen or so local colleges have failed to spend money on their libraries simply because the tax-supported public Library of Congress was available. Similarly, the amazing mobility of today's college students continues to shake the library world everywhere. (A survey in the central library at Newark revealed that, of five thousand readers questioned, 64 per cent were full-time students, 48 per cent were working on school assignments, 50.8 per cent neither lived nor went to school in Newark, and a substantial proportion actually came from outside the state. Director James E. Bryan noted, "Students treat all libraries as though we were a system and we [librarians] are not ready for that.") In short, although LC's Madison Memorial Library now building will make more chairs and more desk space available, the Washington area population is booming and the nation's students are getting increasingly mobile. Is LC the library of senior scholars, of any scholar, or of any citizen across the board?

What does the scholarly world expect from LC?

Five things: The materials of research. Appropriate, sophisticated indexes and guides to these materials. Well-organized, easily accessible collections. Professional personnel to help the user use the material efficiently. And modern photoduplication services to support the mechanics of scholarship.

Obviously we have been examining aspects of all these

things for the past hundred pages. There is thus no need to re-state the details, but a few generalizations and an occasional elaboration may be useful.

SCHOLARS EXPECT THE MATERIALS OF RESEARCH

What does this mean to LC? It means that a scholar can come through the doors of the Library of Congress and either go to the Main Catalog or to a specialized reading room and find there waiting for him the precise information that he seeks. In order for him to do this, it means the Library has had to identify that material, get it to the Library, and process it months, years, possibly a century ago, so it is neatly and quietly waiting for the user. Getting the material cannot have been left to chance in the hope that in the fullness of time the collections would accumulate to the point where they would be helpful to someone. They have had to be plowed endlessly by nearly ten generations of librarians to achieve the purpose required of them.

So how good are the collections? Have the nearly ten generations of librarians brought it off? There is no question but that they are, in *general*, the finest of any library in the Western world. Those of no other single institution even approach them in comprehensiveness, in quantity, in variety. Similarly, some parts of the collections are the finest in the world in *detail* as well. Scholars who have spent their lives researching on five continents underscore the excellence of the special collections. The manuscripts, music, law, and many of the foreign specializations exceed any individual collection anywhere.

At the same time, the Library has never claimed totality. Spofford abandoned primacy in medicine, and Putnam gave up agriculture once federal libraries were founded in these areas. Putnam refused governmental records saying that there must be a clear distinction between "archives" and "library materials." And with the Farmington Plan not only did LC deliberately withdraw in many subject areas, it assisted other institutions to "pass it" by declaring many new receipts surplus and making them available to the designated specialized institutions.

The collections are relatively better the farther back you go. For example, from 1640 to 1940 the materials relating to Americana are superb. If you are seeking European humanities in this period, they too are strong—but other foreign material is not. Those in the know refer to the foreign volumes as "adequate or less." However, the post-1940 foreign collections have become "excellent," exceeding the hopes of the most optimistic scholar, but the U.S. holdings become less comprehensive after 1940. This reversal involves two elements: currency and totality.

Of these the improvement of the collections because of age is the easier to explain, so let's look at it first—and start with a trivial element which really is a footnote but one that frustrates the daily user of the Library because it is unexpected.

Item. The user's batting average improves the longer he waits, simply because of binding practices. LC thinks in terms of the long pull. This is easiest to see when you compare LC's procedures with those of a local public library. When the latter gets a magazine, a document, or a pamphlet it hurriedly puts it out for *use* and keeps it unbound but available, for as long as it is in demand. Once the pressure is off, it goes to the bindery to ensure its preservation for the future.

In LC the preservation process begins immediately on receipt. The moment an item is cataloged or accessioned (in the case of documents, pamphlets, and paperbacks) and just as soon as a bound-volume's worth has accumulated (in the case of journals or magazines), the pieces go to the bindery before anything gets lost or worn. Because of this, the Congressional Research Service must operate a complete, independent, 3,000-title serial library so the congressmen have access to current material, but the public is left facing a frustrating hiatus of some two years' worth of material until the bound volumes get back on the shelves.

Does this make sense? Yes. LC is more interested in the future scholar a decade or a century from now, who must have complete sets to use, than in today's user, who can rely on the local public library for today's news. Can't LC satisfy both? No. It would raise the cost of all its acquisition and processing techniques so astronomically it would jeopardize the whole operation.

Item. More significantly, the collections become richer as they age because of the method used to acquire the material. Again, a comparison between LC's approach and a public library's points up the contrast. A public library builds its collection a piece at a time, selecting each item so it contributes to a planned, controlled, balanced collection—the brick-and-cinderblock approach. LC does it by accumulating great mounds of material and then picking out what it wants—the blast-the-face-off-the-mountain approach. The result is that the average library misses material because it failed to ask for it; LC misses material because it is simply impossible to take the face off of *every* hillside.

LC tries to get its masses of materials by establishing automatic flows of material—hence the automatic copyright deposit of Anglo-American books, the automatic receipt of government documents, and the automatic receipt of foreign materials through blanket order contracts.

This approach is cheaper but it leaves gaps, and to fill the gaps the Reference Department takes over and methodically, year after year, searches the collections for lacunae. Its subject specialists travel, visit auctions, comb bookdealers' catalogs, and identify scholars' demands that the collections were unable to satisfy. The Reference Department staff orders as many as a hundred thousand pieces a year just to plug gaps. Obviously the longer you refine a subject area, the better it gets; thus older is better.

Item. The collections are better the farther back the user goes, because the simple statistical odds of comprehensiveness improve for years when "everything" was less. Thus for the period from 1640 to World War II, the Library was at least heading toward the Sunday supplement writer's conviction that "the Library of Congress has one copy of everything ever printed." Its holdings in Americana through these years are splendid and only begin to fail with the detonation of the information explosion after 1945. And this brings us to the question of totality ... comprehensiveness. Can LC ever hope to have everything? Should it even try?

Totality

LC has never claimed it would keep every shred of print known. It did say it would keep the materials needed by the government, it would endeavor to record the history of the American people, and it would support American scholarship. It did all these things reasonably well in the days when this was possible. But after World War II several elements of the picture changed. The federal agencies began to build their own departmental libraries, and LC shared the governmental support with them. The state libraries and the state historical societies began to share the responsibility for Americana, and it soon became evident that local institutions could do a more efficient job collecting regional materials, town by town, county by county, than distant LC. Finally, the great universities began to build huge, well-supported library systems so that serious research could be supported through decentralized campus and regional research collections.

Thus as LC recognized the impossibility of acquiring "everything," pure pragmatism suggested it ease off on areas where others could do as well or better. Conversely, it should retain those areas of strength either where it was already preeminent or where it could support scholarship more efficiently than any other single institution.

The current emphasis on foreign acquisitions reflects this. It will be recalled that the present annual mix is one part American to three parts foreign. This is reinforced by the aforementioned division by subject, which appears in the medical/agricultural move to the national libraries, and the subject assignments of such agreements as the Farmington Plan.

In the early 1950's, the National Archives declared the logic and efficiency of its taking over LC's traditional role of Keeper of the Presidential Papers. The Congress agreed, and thus LC custody of the great manuscript series from Washington to Coolidge was terminated. Since Hoover, each successive Presidential collection has been housed in a hometown memorial library under the supervision of the executive branch. While the shock of this decision was hard on the LC staff (to add insult to injury, the engrossed copies of the Declaration of Independence and the Constitution were moved from LC to Archives at the time), the result of the decision has had an even greater impact on manuscript deposits ever since. Traditionally, when a President's papers were given to the Library of Congress, the papers of his Cabinet officers, generals, political advisers, and the leading national figures of the time followed along so the totality of the collections gave a detailed history of each individual period. With the Presidential nuclei gone and Archives actively soliciting peripheral political and social papers, the emphasis in LC's manuscript collection has shifted to American culture and the arts. This has caused a fundamental change in the character of the holdings and has altered LC's traditional role in the preservation of the nation's heritage.

But who can say where the proper division of labor falls in any corner of the collections? At the present time, if we are to believe National Union Catalog figures, the Library of Congress is funding, acquiring, processing, and adding to its collections one-half of the significant monographic production of the entire world! Should it try to specialize more and achieve absolute totality in a limited universe of specific areas? Or should it attempt all-encompassing control, embrace ultraphotoreduction techniques and the computer, set up a depository in the Antarctic where space is cheap and deterioration (like the temperature) is zero? Both such extremes have been seriously considered, and there are proponents for all the steps in between.

One LC manager maintains that the best LC can hope for in the way of pre-eminence is the following: LC has the best collection of Hebraica outside of Israel; the best collection of Chinese literature outside China; the best collection of Africana outside of Africa—it also has the best collection of Massachusettsiana outside of Massachusetts, the best collection of Oregoniana outside of Oregon ... and the best collection of maps, music, and motion pictures anywhere!

Scholars Expect Indexes and Guides to LC's Materials

The difference between a library and a warehouse of books is the way a library tells the user what is *in* the materials stored. Both are organized so a book can be found, but the library goes inside the book and explains what is on the paper pages. To oversimplify, this was one of the major differences between Librarian Spofford (who was essentially a collector) and Librarian Putnam (who was a user). Putnam invested an enormous amount of energy and resources in analyzing the collections and telling everyone who would listen what was in them. He worked closely with the American Historical Association, and they jointly produced the fifty-odd volumes of *Writings on American History* from 1902 to our own time. He made the heads of his special collections publish bibliographies, guides, check lists, calendars—anything that would make known to the sophisticated scholar what was in the materials on the shelves.

From this came literally dozens of such publications as the 293-page *Check List of the Literature and Other Material in the Library of Congress on the European War* (1918); the 219-page *List of References on the Treaty-Making Power* (1920); and the 401-page *Check List of American Eighteenth Century Newspapers in the Library of Congress* (1936).

Likewise, Putnam wanted the scholarly world to have a simple inventory of LC's holdings and to this end established the depository sets of LC printed cards throughout the library world. From these came the comprehensive National Union Catalog and with it the elimination of much of the pressure for LC bibliographic publishing. Individual check lists of "Books in the Library of Congress on Such-and-such a Topic" are no longer essential, now that the *Library of Congress Catalog—Books: Subject* is published every ninety days, but LC guides and indexes to special and retrospective areas of the collection are still needed and are still prepared, distributed, and sold. Two representative examples may tell the story better than a hasty generalization.

Guide to the Study of the United States of America: Representative Books Reflecting the Development of American Life and Thought

This splendid volume, bound in red, blue, and gray buckram, is about the size of an unabridged dictionary and is printed and sold by the Government Printing Office. It was completed in 1960 after eight years of preparation and has proved to be both a critical and commercial success. Well over 25,000 copies have been sold to date, and it is a basic handbook in its scholarly field.

It is divided into thirty-two chapters. Some chapter divisions are obvious: Literature; Art and Architecture;

Politics, Parties, Elections. Others are less so: Entertainment; Medicine and Public Health; Travel and Travelers; Population, Immigration, and Minorities.

The idea for the *Guide* got its impetus from European nations who were rebuilding their bombed-out book collections and needed to know what basic books they should have about the U.S. As American study courses began to multiply on U.S. campuses and more scholars began to dissect the American culture, it seemed appropriate to come up with a basic handbook of essential volumes in U.S. culture and history. It was hoped that such a bench-mark guide might prevent, as the editor explained, "wasteful duplication of work resulting from repeated attempts to give individual attention to questions that might be more satisfactorily answered within the compass of one carefully prepared reference book."

Special scholars in each subject area were called on from the various divisions of the Library, and ultimately some 10,000 volumes were selected for inclusion in the 1,200-page *Guide*. Each selection is annotated to explain why it contributes to an understanding of the United States. The bibliographers had a refreshing purpose in their annotations. They designed them less to say how good the selected volumes were than to act as "aids which readers may use to eliminate materials irrelevant to their purpose and [as] guideposts to lead them as quickly as possible to the heart of what concerns them."

The basic volume has been so popular that scholars have insisted on updated supplements. The first, covering the decade 1956–65, contains 2,943 new entries.

A List of Geographical Atlases in the Library of Congress

This equally impressive volume, bound in red, blue, and gold, weighs three and a half pounds and contains descriptions of 2,647 atlases of Europe, Asia, Africa, the oceans, and the polar regions received in the Library between 1920 and

1960. It is in fact Volume 6 of a series begun in 1909. Volume 5, published in 1958, described 2,326 atlases of the world. Volume 7 will include only atlases of the Western Hemisphere. The volumes appear—with all deliberate speed—every decade or so.

The atlases in this current Volume 6 are arranged neatly in descending order by continent, country, subject, date, state, city, and region. The noncartographer is surprised to see whole chapters about nothing but atlases full of maps of such specialized subjects as Ecclesiastical Geography, Climatology, Postal Service, Telecommunication, and Terrestrial Magnetism. Similarly there are chapters of atlases that contain nothing but maps of water bodies: Strait of Dover, Mur River, Salzach River, Bay of Biscay, and the Nile. *Geographic Atlases* describes each volume in terms of compilers, sizes, and descriptions; it frequently provides short essays about the antecedents or importance of the work and, for atlases printed before 1820, it provides complete tables of contents.

National Events

During periods of national celebration, the Library reminds involved scholars of its resources in the field. For the Centenary of the Civil War period, it published a variety of volumes, among them such items as *Civil War Photographs 1861–1865, A Catalog of Copy Negatives Made From Originals Selected from the Mathew B. Brady Collection in the Prints and Photographs Division of the Library of Congress* (74 pages), and *The Civil War in Motion Pictures; A Bibliography of Films Produced in the United States Since 1897* (109 pages).

As the nation looks to the Revolutionary Bicentennial, the Library has already issued *The American Revolution: A Selected Reading List* and *Periodical Literature on the American Revolution: Historical Research and Changing Interpretations, 1895–1970*, identifying over a thousand articles and essays. The Library is now assembling its major project for the Bicentennial, the forthcoming *Letters of Delegates to Congress, 1774–1789.*

At the time of this writing, a guide to LC's manuscripts dealing with the Revolutionary period is on its way to the printers, and a check list of prints, cartoons, and contemporary graphics in the special collections is in final draft. The Geography and Maps Division is preparing a cartographic check list of its Revolutionary holdings, and the first of LC's five planned symposia has been held, this one under the banner of "The Development of a Revolutionary Mentality." Over five hundred historians attended the initial two-day session and papers were given by leaders in the field from nearly a dozen universities. The keynote address was delivered by the distinguished historian Henry Steele Commager, professor emeritus from Amherst. (Funds to support the *Letters of Delegates* publication are coming from the Ford Foundation, and the symposia are underwritten by the Morris and Gwendolyn Cafritz Foundation.)

While Putnam's drive for published indexes, guides, and bibliographies has slackened, given the funds available, the Library continues to keep faith with the tradition he set seventy-five years ago.

The Public Catalog

Now here is a depressing situation. We said that the scholar has the right to expect the finest guides and indexes to the collections possible, and clearly the Main Card Catalog is the prime example of the latter. But as it ages and grows, it becomes an increasingly crippled tool and is steadily drawing the criticism of its users and the librarians who are struggling to maintain it.

As we noted before, the catalog now contains 16.5 million cards filed in hundreds of thousands of separate alphabets under author, title, and subject. It is well into its seventh decade, and it has problems. Inefficiency—or general clumsiness from elephantiasis—is one. Error is another: 5 per cent of its cards are misfiled! Thousands of the cards are incorrect or illegible or lack any sign of a call number, and the catalog is slowly accumulating obsolete, blind, or conflicting cross references.

How could this have come about? Rather easily, if you think about it. Take the problem of filing. Filers stand eight hours a day looking for the precise place each card should go. If the filers make only one error out of every thousand cards they file, they will have loaded in 16,000 filing mistakes. These mistakes frequently trip another series of alphabetizations, which create another 8,000 or 10,000 mistakes, and so on. Correcting them is costly and time-consuming. If a reviser were to spend only 10 seconds per card, it would take 22 years to get from one end of the trays to the other, during which time the catalog would have grown by another 39 million cards (assuming that the present annual increase of 1.8 million cards does not rise, which it will). But 39 million cards would take 54 years to scan, by which time ...

What to do? In the 1960's everyone believed that the catalog would either be abandoned completely or stopped by 1975, and the computer would take over. By the early 1970's this was seen to be impracticable. New approaches were considered: (1) Freeze the present catalog and start a new, fresh, and (at least for the time being) accurate one. As the old one got older it would steadily be needed less anyway, and the new model could assume the task. (2) Use the printed book catalogs and give up cards completely. (3) Get by with make-do arrangements, but press all possible speed on the auto-mators and try for a "machine-readable" system by 1985. (4) Break out the subject cards and have two catalogs: author/title in one and subject in the other. Since most people looking by subject want "the latest book on," the separate subject set could be restarted every ten years. This would at least cut down on the maintenance problem.

The above "solutions" have generated furious discussions in the Library. The reference librarians say that the card catalog is the most efficient, flexible retrieval system ever invented, that it is the only way four or five hundred readers can be served simultaneously, and every effort should be made to continue and improve it. The catalogers say it is hopeless to think the device will work forever, and, with the steadily increasing number of items added to the collections each year, the reference librarians are going to have to face up to the real world and make the best of it.

Any so-called solution of this issue will damage someone, yet unless something is done everyone agrees the catalog tool will become a travesty, actually retarding effective scholarship. The catalog is requiring ever more staff to service it, and the lag in updating grows longer by the year. With a device so intertwined with every aspect of the Library's life, the old navy adage of "Do *something* even if you do it wrong!" may not hold. An error in judgment here could be devastating, yet the present choices are all based on negatives. The riddle in this problem is to decide which choice is least bad.

SCHOLARS WANT WELL-ORGANIZED COLLECTIONS AND EASY ACCESS TO THESE COLLECTIONS

How is the Library meeting this obligation?

The organization of the Library's collections by intellectual content is above reproach. If there is anything the Library of Congress can do well, it is "subject catalog." The general collections are logically arranged for both philosophical consistency and hard day-to-day use. The special collections are equally well controlled. Intellectual organization—yes. Physical organization—no.

Thanks to the dreadful overcrowding in the Main Building and Annex (Mumford began pleading for a third building as far back as 1959), the collections are spread all over the capital area. Maps and atlases are in a rented warehouse in Alexandria, Virginia. Catalog publications are in a converted apartment house on Massachusetts Avenue. Motion pictures are in film vaults in Suitland, Maryland, and at Wright-Patterson Air Force Base, Dayton, Ohio. All copyrighted materials are received and processed in an office building in Arlington, Virginia. Bound newspapers and gazettes of foreign governments are in a surplus Air Force hangar at Middle River, Maryland. Materials tied to card preparation are in the former Naval Gun Factory beside the Anacostia River. With the hoped-for completion of the Madison Building, the Library will be physically together for the first time in over twenty years.

The problems of geographical spread are troublesome, but not nearly so troublesome as the problems of locating what is stored in the two great buildings themselves. Here the "easy access" requirement is all but nonexistent and the scholar meets his greatest difficulty in using the Library of Congress: simply getting the materials out of central storage into his own hands.

If the reader coming to the Library goes to the special collections of manuscripts, music, prints and photographs, or oriental languages, or visits the map collection in Virginia, he rarely fails to be awed by the speed with which what he wants is placed before him. But if he is one of the greater number of visitors who use the general book collections in the two great reading rooms or the Law Library, he finds himself playing a frustrating game of bibliographic roulette. For example: If he requests a book on fine arts, his odds of getting it are roughly seven out of ten. If he asks for a book on economics his chances drop to five out of ten, and if it is for an economics book published during the past fifteen years, his chances of success drop to two out of ten. So if he places ten call slips for recent economics volumes, he can expect to receive two books and eight call slips marked "Not on Shelf"—and canceled. The same holds true for volumes in political science, international affairs, urban problems, race, education, etc.

This is shocking, and the Library is the first to admit it, but it is a furiously difficult situation to untangle. The problem can be seen in the use of contemporary social science publications. The present over-all score for these materials is 50 per cent—out of every ten requests the reader will get five books delivered and five rejection slips. The rejection rate for material printed since 1960 will run higher, for books printed before 1940 lower, and, if the books sought were printed before 1895, the reader may receive as many as eight books out of ten (rejection rate barely 20 per cent). From the point of view of the frustrated reader, the 50–50 batting average is irritating enough, but it can take an hour or more to receive word that *none* of the books requested are available. These troubles stem from two causes:

First, the general collections are simply worked to exhaustion. Most English-language volumes are kept in two copies, shelved side by side in the stacks. But the potential number of readers zeroed in on these two volumes is astronomical. On a routine day, 7,000 volumes will be off the shelves simply in transit to or from the scholars in the public reading rooms. The Congressional Research Service, with nearly 500 staff members, will be drawing on the volumes to answer 1,500 congressional inquiries a day. Three thousand congressional staff members with borrowing privileges will be borrowing the books directly. The hundreds of federal bureaus and agencies in Washington will be borrowing materials on precisely the same topics the Congress is interested in. Such agencies as the CIA, the National Academy of Sciences, the National Agricultural Library, the National Gallery of Art, the National Security Agency, the Smithsonian Institution, the U.S. Information Agency, and the Army Topo-

graphical Command rely so heavily on LC's collections that
they maintain permanent desks and stations in the building,
continually manned by agency personnel.

In 1971, aside from in-house use, 240,000 volumes were
loaned out of the building—37 per cent to scholarly libraries
around the country. All of this circulation occurs before the
private scholar even reaches the reading room. Once there,
he must compete against his fellows who are looking for
many of the same books as he.

The first reaction of the frustrated visitor is always: How
can you have 16 million volumes and it be so hard to get one?
The problem, of course, is that the overwhelming majority of
the 16 million are in a foreign language and/or printed before
World War I. If he is seeking something on highways in Mali
or Afghanistan or on the construction of the Appian Way, he
will find himself in a bibliographic paradise. But if he wants
something on the U.S. interstate highway system, he finds himself in competition with a dozen users who got there first. Unfortunately, the majority of the readers in the general reading
rooms are concerned with contemporary national social
problems.

The second obstacle to service and one, for the time being,
equally difficult to remove, is the physical condition of the
storage stacks. They are almost certainly in the worst shape
of any time in this century.

Existing stack space was headed for exhaustion in the early
1950's, and since that time new books, flowing in at a rate of
half a million volumes a year, have had to be distributed
through the collections by shelving them on floors, in make-
shift wooden cases across ventilation shafts, in unfloored
crawl spaces, and down aisles and public corridors. Adding
to the difficulty of finding space for individual volumes
(which must be forced into already filled shelves, one at a time,
each according to its specific call number) is the fact that the
stacks are "open." While the general public is denied access to

the decks, many senior scholars, many researchers engaged in long-term study programs, all the 4,000 LC employees, and the federal agency people engaged in official business can browse the collection and take away any volumes they require. Such browsing, with books withdrawn and improperly replaced, is highly disruptive. Volumes shelved fore-edge down on floors, laid flat on folio shelves, and running in unpredictable sequences around staircases and elevators make a nightmare of shelf-reading, and attempts to keep order are so frustrating that maintenance staff morale is low at best.

There is little that can be done about these conditions until the new building is complete. Temporary expedients are time-consuming and expensive. A recent attempt to reshelve those volumes whose call number began with the letter H involved the handling of over 1.5 million books—more than exist in the total collections of most of the nation's university libraries. The Madison Building will not be available until 1975 or 1976 at the earliest.

Scholars Want Professional Personnel to Help Them Use the Materials Efficiently

We need not elaborate this requirement of the scholarly world overmuch, because it appeared in every aspect of our previous examination of the work of the various divisions in the Library. LC has been unusually fortunate through the years in the quality of professionals it has attracted. In almost every field of its specializations it has managed to get out-standing—frequently nationally and internationally known—practitioners. Even as Harvard draws "names" in the educa-tional world, the reputation of the Library has attracted the mobile able in librarianship and the special subject fields.

LC's managers have long faced the choice either of "getting good young people and bringing them up in the system" or of exploiting its reputation to attract established leaders in its needed skills and knowledge areas. It has opted roughly down the middle on this one, and, throughout the present century, the staff has been divided about 60–40 between in-house career staff and recruits at all levels from outside the Library.

Traditionally, the Library has had to offer its reputation and prestige in lieu of the higher salaries paid by other libraries. At the present time this is not the case, and LC finds itself in the pleasant position of being slightly ahead of both the campus and local government when it comes to competing for professional personnel. The recent contraction in educational and library employment permits it the luxury of hiring from among many well-qualified applicants.

In short, there is little criticism and much praise from the scholarly world about the caliber of assistance it receives when it turns for help to the specialists in manuscripts, foreign law, maps, music, or the foreign-language areas, or to the reference personnel in the general reading rooms.

SCHOLARLY USERS EXPECT MODERN PHOTODUPLICATION SERVICES TO SUPPORT THEIR RESEARCH

LC runs one of the largest nonprofit photographic laboratories in the world. In 1971 it made 6.7 million Xerox shots, 15.2 million individual microfilm exposures, 39,900 photographic prints, and thousands of other reproductions.

The Photoduplication Service operates in a strange organizational configuration. In 1938 the Rockefeller Foundation recognized that there must be some technique by which the Library's research riches could be made available to the outside world of publishing and scholarship, so it gave LC a $35,000 grant to buy some photostat machines and cameras and to hire the men to run them. Since that time, the staff has grown to 166, and in 1971 they brought $1,957,000 into the revolving fund.

This perpetual, appropriation-free account has some odd

side-effects. By contract, the Photoduplication Service must be kept rigorously separate from LC. It must be self-sustaining, and, while it cannot make a profit, it must charge enough to cover its operating costs at all times. This forces prices to be set in real terms and precludes the usual absorption of peripheral costs as is done in most research libraries as a part of providing research assistance to the users of their collections. LC itself must pay hard cash for each Xerox or microfilm it uses, and the distant scholar must pay in advance for his order, rather than being invoiced on receipt. (Prices now run, after substantial minimum handling charges, 25 cents for a Xerox, $1.25 for a Photostat, and 7 cents for a frame of microfilm.)

But the product is flawless. Since the Library can never know how its copies will be used, on every order it must assume the highest requirements for precision and durability. The copy may be for inclusion in an "art book"—the resultant picture may become *the* cut known around the world for the Gettysburg Address; it may be *that* picture of Teddy Roosevelt shouting over a rostrum—indeed, any picture you ever saw with the credit "Library of Congress" in tiny letters at the bottom. The microfilm may prove to be the world's only copy of a manuscript or codex or document, thanks to wartime destruction of the original. The Photostat may be incorporated in a legal file where its paper and dye must stand as long as the accompanying court record. For all these reasons, the camera work must be as fine as machines and skill can make it, the film as long-lived, the paper as acid proof.

From these conditions come good news and bad: The standards set for LC photoduplication have come to be accepted as the model for fine research photoduplication and preservation throughout the Western world—and the time and cost of LC work runs higher than the casual user expects, since all he usually wants is a "quick and dirty" product for one-time use!

What kinds of things does the Photoduplication Service do for all this money? First, it responds to tens of thousands of requests from outside scholars for copies of LC materials. It will seek them out in the collections, photocopy them, and send them to the requester without his having to come to Washington.

Second, it assists the Library and other scholarly organizations to record research material beyond the Library's walls. Example: In 1949–50, LC technicians set up shop in a tiny sixth-century Nestorian chapel in Jerusalem and, working with a gasoline generator for the camera lights, filmed 1,030 ancient manuscripts and made 1,187 4-by-5-inch negatives of as many miniatures and illuminations. This project, a joint effort of LC and the American Schools of Oriental Research, was followed by an expedition to Saint Catherine's Monastery on the 5,000-foot face of Mount Sinai. The second project was organized by LC, the American Foundation for the Study of Man, and several private scholars. LC specialists spent months living alongside the monks in the great medieval shrine, carrying in supplies across 275 miles of desert track— but bringing out 1,700 rolls of film and 1,284 4-by-5 negatives of early Christian writings.

Third, the Library hires the Photoduplication Service to convert many of its newspapers into microfilm (the originals are then discarded), and it buys more thousands of frames to capture deteriorating "brittle books" each year. Finally, it microfilms copies of LC's most useful research materials to preserve the originals and to make the contents available to distant libraries and scholars. All this microfilm can be purchased by anybody at cost, and thus LC is providing the smallest community colleges with the kinds of primary research materials once available only at the greatest university centers. A random selection from the current catalog demonstrates the variety of these riches:

Fifty thousand pages of the Japanese "War Crimes Trial." 36 reels, $430.

The complete works of Johann Sebastian Bach. 47 volumes, 12 reels. Likewise 73 volumes of Mozart in 11 reels and 44 volumes of Beethoven in 9 reels.

The Soviet newspaper *Izvestia* for 1917 through 1938. 63 reels, $535.

Copies of LC's papers of 22 Presidents—a total of 3,000 reels plus indexes. You can buy them separately, if you wish: 97 reels of Lincoln, $950; 485 reels of Theodore Roosevelt, $4,695; 124 reels of George Washington, $1,293.

Twenty-eight African newspapers from their founding to the present.

Fifty-four different LC manuscript collections, such as Henry Clay in 22 reels, Samuel Gompers' AFL letter-books in 340 reels, everything the Library owns of Alexander Hamilton in 46 reels.

Or the complete *U.S. Statutes at Large* from 1789 to 1962. 118 reels, $1,085.

The only thing about the vast microfilming effort that bothers the layman is: How do you know the microfilm is going to last any longer than the paper did? The scientists assure us that there is no need to worry. It has been artificially aged for hundreds of accelerated years and is holding up beautifully. Since 1953 the Library has been testing all the film it uses for quantity of residual hypo left after processing, for the safety base characteristics, and for the degree of definition tied to the emulsion—its resolution, contrast, focus, and brilliancy. Be assured, the specialists tell us, we need not give a second thought to the possibility of its turning brown or brittle, sticking together, shriveling up, separating, granulating, or collapsing into dust. (Unfortunately, if the experts are wrong, they won't be around to sue.)

In Conclusion

As you can see, service to scholars is a Herculean effort. The complexities, the simple mechanics of scholarly support, are extensive, but the rewards are splendid. It is a cliché to say that a library is only as valuable as it is used, but that is precisely the name of the game. All the elements we have just looked at—materials, indexes, organized collections, professional staff, and duplication support—have to be dragged along together in order to bring it all off.

So what happens next? Where do the reference services go from here? Obviously, everything we have talked about can be done better, and that is the first challenge. But there is a second, broader challenge that is revealed almost by indirection. It will appear when you set out to find which aspects of the reference process really work well. If you query a hundred LC users, you will find that a clear-cut pattern soon develops. The scholars, the skilled researchers, and the most knowledgeable clientele will always heap their praise upon the special divisions. The Manuscript, Music, Geography and Map, Prints and Photographs, Foreign Law, African, Slavic, and Latin American units come off with the kudos. And the secret of their success seems to be the element of "special." Every one of these administrative elements has been given the luxury of a special, finite collection, a special reading room, a staff of specialists in the particular kind of material or subject area encompassed in its particular, specialized fragment of the total collections. Within these little duchies, the users would have us believe, the research material is complete. It is well-organized and can be placed quickly, efficiently, and surely within the visitor's hands.

This condition would seem to suggest something for the

future. A case can be made that it demands (and the sooner the better) splitting up the great public reading rooms into smaller, more specialized units: a Social Science Reading Room, a Humanities Reading Room—possibly even a Federal Government Room, or a German Literature or a Western Europe Room. (Carried to its logical conclusion this suggests a re-examination of the present general Law Library Reading Room to see if it could not be more effectively split into special kinds of law with special lawyers and special legal collections pulled together; it suggests another look at the generalized Congressional Reference Division in the Congressional Research Service to see if it should not be fractured into at least seven parts and these pasted back on to the specialized CRS subject divisions like Environmental Policy, Economics, or Foreign Affairs.)

But if you press the point a little further, you find the success of specialization of books and service staff may not be the point at all. The operating element here may be the almost accidental specialization—the natural selection—of the user public. Relatively few general readers or undergraduate students ever get into the special reference divisions. Rather it is a numerically limited audience of user experts and senior researchers, the most highly trained and experienced seekers of information, who turn to these special areas—where they deal with the most highly trained and specialized LC staffs. The clientele in the special areas is small and limited to the skilled and knowledgeable. Rather than attempting to be all things to all men like the personnel in the general public reading rooms, the staff of the special reading room can focus its service and collections on the sophisticated few. Does this imply that LC and the taxpayer would get a bigger bang for their buck (the highest cost-benefit ratio, as we have been taught to call it) if the Library restricted its role and made its service rules hard, limited, and precise?

What would happen if LC held firmly to a code that stated:

"Don't even come here until you have exhausted your local and your general information sources, wherever they may be; but in return for this inconvenient division of labor, we will save for you the finest, rarest, best organized, best analyzed special materials you can find anywhere. We will see that your final research time will be spent efficiently. You will be served by the most able, experienced, highly trained specialists in your particular discipline that we can assemble for you." While this rings with quality, excellence, and all such good things on the one hand, it smacks of elitism on the other. Democracy turned upside down. The long-suffering, tax-paying citizen barred from the very resource he funded. Is efficiency in information storage and transfer of sufficient importance that it can be legitimately focused and refined at such cost? And is this really the only way to achieve it?

Rough choice. Enough said.

XIV

Congressional Library
Versus National Library

Books of this kind always end with a chapter: "Whither the Institution?" "Quo vadis?" This will be no exception.

As tempting as it might be to be original for a change, the fact is that such a question is singularly appropriate for the Library of Congress at the present juncture. LC stands on the threshold of a new experience and probably faces a new direction as well. The great Madison Memorial Library is rising across the street. It will be filled with the most complicated computer, television, facsimile transmission, automated delivery, and mechanical storage systems yet devised by the mind of bibliographic man. With it will come the reassembly of the Library for the first time in a generation, an obvious take-off point for a new pattern of services.

With it, too, will come the final resolution of many things for which the present Librarian has been struggling since his accession in 1954. There have been eleven Librarians to date, and it seems likely that L. Quincy Mumford will take his place among a select group of three who have had the greatest impact on the character and personality of the institution.

Strangely enough, each of the big three managed to come up with the same scenario. Spofford dedicated a career to accumulating the collection itself and then spent twenty-six years begging, designing, and building a building—which was occupied by his successor. Putnam spent a lifetime converting the materials into a great research library, and then spent twelve years begging, designing, and building a second building—which was, in turn, occupied by his successor. Mumford's impact has been twofold. He has developed a larger, more professional, legislatively involved congressional service department than any of his predecessors, and he has shaped a vigorous *national* library more deeply involved with the world of professional librarianship than any of those that went before. Like his illustrious predecessors, he has already spent thirteen years on *his* building. He started begging for it in 1959, got it authorized in 1965, and saw it scheduled for completion in 1975 or 1976. It has not been easy.

Where does this library now stand?

It is in good shape as far as details go. It has its problems, as we have seen, but most of them are the result of too successful service or size-out-of-control, and they are copable. They form the stuff of which interesting administration is made. But across the broad picture there are major stresses. Two fundamental questions hang over the institution that we have met at every turn in the past pages: Whose Library is it? And what should it do? Let's explore these for a few moments to see what choices we've got.

WHAT'S THE PROBLEM?

The problem is that the three audiences we have just been describing are each convinced that they are being shortchanged because of the presence of the other two. Since the purpose of each is rather dramatically different, the devices and procedures used by the Library to satisfy all three—never the very best for any one audience—are always slightly debased to do what any *one* of them wants.

The Scholarly Position

The scholarly world and "the public" have been the most vocal. They resent competing with the governmental world in general, and with Congress in particular, for the books, space, and resources that would give them a Bibliothèque Nationale, a British Museum, or an American National Library. They point to the fact that, while the great collections of the Library are without peer in the Western world, all the administrative fiddlings of different reading rooms and refined access rules will be meaningless so long as the "national library" is considered a by-product of Congress's working legislative collection. It is competition with *government* that is causing the trouble, the scholars hold. Competition in acquisitions, space, staff, and service is dragging the great research resource toward mediocrity and aborting its purpose. If LC is to recover its thrust toward scholarly excellence—especially in the broad areas of applied social science and in the role of Keeper of the American Heritage—there must be a change in ownership. Jurisdiction over real estate, staff, and mission must shift.

The scholars offer two solutions: One, split off the portions of the present Library required to serve applied government, leave these with Congress, and then declare the rest an independent national library in the executive branch. Or, two, call the present library the National Library, give it to the President, and build a more precise, focused congressional library from scratch. With the Congress-only library comes the assumption that the departmental libraries in the executive would assume responsibility for information support around the Mall, and the Supreme Court Library would be expanded to support the courts system. Congress's Library would be a strictly legislative operation.

Not long ago an Australian visitor became frustrated with

the competition in LC's reading rooms and filled five columns of type in the *Washington Post*, in which the public's solution was crisply stated:

> Is there no body of librarians and legislators who will advocate the radical but real solution: Establishing a National Library, independent of Congress and its demands, along the lines of the flourishing Smithsonian, operating under executive jurisdiction and advised by a council of scholars? ... Is this country not sufficiently wealthy and sufficiently concerned with the nation's heritage to afford two libraries, as other nations do, one for Congressmen, their aides and other privileged borrowers, and another which functions as repository for the nation's recorded culture, making its collection democratically available to all?

This Australian's proposal—an independent executive agency library—is the solution most often suggested by the public, but proposals occasionally appear in which the national library becomes a subunit of the Smithsonian itself, like the National Gallery of Art or the Kennedy Center, or a subunit of the National Archives and Records Service, like the Franklin D. Roosevelt Library at Hyde Park or the Lyndon B. Johnson Library in Austin. Regardless of which administrative structure is selected, the proponents of this solution insist that independent status would permit the Library to be more flexible and sensitive to the public's needs, would permit it to concentrate on collecting and processing those materials that the scholars require, and would leave the satisfaction of governmental needs and library world support to someone else.

The Congressional Position

Congressmen are equally irritable about lack of attention and diversion of purpose. It is their library; they thought it up and nursed it along through all these years, and, simply because they graciously permitted "outsiders" to use its facilities, it now develops the outsiders want to walk off with it. The whole thing has gotten completely out of hand.

When critics deplore the "dreadful cost" of the legislature, one of the most popular proofs is to divide the Library of Congress's annual appropriation by 535 senators and congressmen and thus charge each member with $127,000 worth of personal library services each year. An offended Congress asks if this is the thanks it gets for broadening the Library's collections for the nation.

While this arithmetic frequently puts Congress on the defensive and increases the Librarian's difficulties at budget time, Congress's real concern comes from two serious sources: a longtime fear that LC will become so distracted with other obligations that it will fail to fulfill its purpose as a legislative library and a more recent concern that the Library's divided purpose will compromise the independence and effectiveness of the Congressional Research Service.

The first of the fears can be demonstrated in a rather bizarre fashion. Librarian Mumford's predecessor was Dr. Luther Evans, a political scientist, scholar, internationalist, and ultimately a distinguished Director-General of UNESCO. Evans had resigned from LC to take the UNESCO post, and, when Mumford was nominated, his first "official" act was to appear before the Senate Rules and Administration Committee for confirmation hearings. Instead of exploring his professional background, as is somewhat more usual, the committee began by presenting Mumford with a series of rhetorical questions that added up to a catechism of what they expected him to do through the coming years. The questions, albeit of vintage 1954, have a timelessness about them:

1. "What about the public services? Do you think they have been expanded to the detriment of the services rendered the Congress itself? ... If you found that the Library of Congress was neglecting its primary duty—that for which

it was established—that of service to Congress, and was
going into other fields to the detriment of Congress, you
would be willing to correct that situation?"

2. "Since the primary purpose of the Library is for the use
of Congress, just how far should it go in the maintenance
of bibliographical materials for the executive branches
and agencies? Do not other agencies have their own
libraries?"

3. "[Are your] intentions to devote full time and attention
to the work of the Library?" [This stemmed from earlier
distress with MacLeish's public role in general, and
Evans's interest in international scholarship in particular.]

4. "Would he act as a censor?" [This was in the middle of
the so-called McCarthy era, and the committee chairman's elaboration on this query made it clear the Librarian was to have books on *all* sides of every issue. They
did not want sanitized selections.]

5. "We would like you to discuss the methods which might
be put into force which would increase the services to the
Congress even at the expense of services to the public. . . .
The committee would have your comment on the means
that you may have decided upon which would halt and
perhaps decrease the ever-growing load of public demands, both locally and nationally, upon the Library's
facilities."

The chairman noted tangentially that in "the present problem of arrearages in the processing of accessions . . . there
should be some survey made of what is necessarily obsolete,
for junking purposes." He could not understand why they kept
giving the Library ever more catalogers, who never seemed
to catch up, and he summarized by saying, "The Librarian
exercises enormous powers and assumes the right to put the
Library in the many activities for which there exists no clear
authority."

The fears that "the Library" might distort and limit LRS

(the Legislative Reference Service, as the Congressional Research Service was then called) surfaced during the many hearings on the Legislative Reorganization Acts of 1965–70. (The dialogue throughout the hearings used "the LRS" and "the Library" as if they were opposing entities, barely related to each other!) The concerns expressed by both committee staff and some committee members fell into the following areas:

1. Fears that the LRS tradition of unbiased, nonadvocative, and detached analysis of issues would be compromised by the Library's official position on specific legislation (The committee was concerned that LC might exert "pressure" on such volatile questions as the funding or elimination of the Public Law 480 Program, the revision of the copyright laws, or national-aid-to-library bills—all dear to LC's heart. The dialogue here frequently stressed that the incumbent Librarian had always demonstrated meticulous regard for the needed detachment and objectivity, but there was the fear that some day the Library might inherit a popular public figure from the extremes of the political spectrum who would exploit the Librarian of Congress's national position to press some pet public issues. The Librarian is chosen by the President, they noted, not Congress.)

2. Fears that, when new public issues arose and Congress wanted the LRS to hire specialists to help Congress deal with them, the Library would limit LRS resources in order to keep all the competing LC departments "happy" thus thinning the funds available for expert legislative support

3. Fears on the part of some of the more bureaucratically sensitive committee members that, as the Library moved toward a national library role, it would create personnel practices and internal administrative orders that would unthinkingly pull the Legislative Reference Service toward the other mission and away from its attention to Congress itself

With the above thoughts in mind, the Legislative Reorganization Act of 1970, Title III, was written into the statutes with the following introduction:

> It is the policy of Congress that—
> 1) the Librarian of Congress shall, in every possible way, encourage, assist, and promote the Congressional Research Service in—
>   A) rendering to Congress the most effective and efficient service,
>   B) responding most expeditiously, effectively, and efficiently to the special needs of Congress, and
>   C) discharging its responsibilities to Congress; and
> 2) the Librarian of Congress shall grant and accord to the Congressional Research Service complete research independence and the maximum practicable administrative independence consistent with these objectives.

Competition with the rest of the Library and "complete research independence." Oddly enough this rather threatening language was the work of the conservatives. The reformers had a more dramatic solution, which was expressed among "outside" advisers and some "inside" committee staff members.

The reformers, who were then members of the Joint Committee on the Organization of Congress, pressed a solution which would break the Congressional Research Service out of LC as an administrative unit and move it, geographically and administratively, into Congress itself. They analogized it with the administrative mode used for the Architect of the Capitol or with the services of the Joint Committee on Printing. They would have had it overseen by a Joint Committee, paid from the House or Senate Disbursing Office, housed in the Capitol or one of the congressional office buildings, and given the highest-priority access to LC's collections. High-priority access would have been a temporary arrangement until the CRS accumulated a current, governmentally centered research collection of materials tied directly to national issues. Once this was organized, it was believed that further reliance on LC holdings would drop to a fraction of the total CRS work load.

The outsider's (noncongressional) solutions to the problem embraced a corollary position. They too urged that the CRS be detached and given a smaller, more focused collection with more responsive acquisition and classification procedures, but they based their argument on different analogies. The Council of State Governments had surveyed the history and effectiveness of the state legislative reference services and found that an overwhelming majority had started as adjuncts of the state libraries but had been forced to become independent because of the incompatibility of the two missions. The state library was dedicated to long-term, archival, historical collections of the state's history and traditions, while the legislative reference service was organized for day-to-day pursuit of state and local issues requiring immediate response. Various specialists in comparative government pointed to the Canadian and Australian divorcement of their legislative reference services from their national libraries and underlined the tradition of independence and self-sufficiency in the House of Commons Library and the parliamentary libraries in Bonn, Tokyo, and Stockholm. (The solution proposed by the Australian scholar quoted above was the result of an unfortunate experience that the Australian parliamentary service had had while functioning as a part of the National Library but which had led to a successful separation of the two.)

Thus the outsider's answer to the congressional dilemma.

The Position of the Library Profession

The library world proposes an equally self-evident solution —but different, of course. For years, librarians have been urging that the Library of Congress be put into the Department of Health, Education, and Welfare (HEW) and be run either as a separate bureau or as a unit of the Office of Education in the same way that Howard University and Gallaudet College are overseen by that agency. In the days of the great HEW grants for higher education, library matching funds, and the original $6 million annual grants for the National Program for Acquisitions and Cataloging (it was originally funded by the Office of Education), the HEW affiliation was appealing. However, as the grant money has dropped away, many library groups have swung toward the idea of a separate executive unit similar to the Smithsonian. Here the Library's fortunes would not be so tied to generalized feelings for or against education, and it would eliminate the bureaucratic competition and infighting found among many subunits competing for a limited amount of departmental funds.

One library group was represented by the so-called Bryant Memorandum (this was a 1962 formal recommendation for a *de jure* national library; Douglas W. Bryant was Associate Director of the Harvard Library, and the study was sponsored by Senator Claiborne Pell of the Joint Committee on the Library). The Bryant group maintained that, although they preferred an independent library in the executive branch, they would tolerate a legislative location if the effective control could lie in a National Library Advisory Board. The board would include "leaders in research, scholar-administrators such as university presidents and deans, librarians of major research libraries, members of the Congress, and other distinguished citizens." The Bryant recommendation included formal criteria for future Librarians:

> The Librarian of Congress must be a man who can administer an extremely diversified and organically complex institution; in addition, he must make important decisions on technological innovations in bibliography profoundly affecting the access of scholars to information, supervise the building up of enormous research collections, exercise imaginative leadership nationally, and take advantage of the Library's unique opportunities for contributing to American cultural life.

(There was talk at the time that if future Librarians could be found to fit these specifications, after a respectable term in office they might be considered for the Presidency of the United States.)

As a rule, what the library world wants is less a great national storehouse than a central library that would act as the hub of a national library wheel or (different image) a powerhouse at the center of a voltage grid. Properly named the National Library, this central library could more effectively achieve uniformity of cataloging, more appropriately develop shared computer ties, and more efficiently eliminate acquisition duplication. It could concentrate on serving the national library community full time rather than trying to keep Congress and the visiting scholars happy at the front door, while surreptitiously serving the librarians at the back door. Again, international models are cited. Britain, Canada, and Sweden all have highly centralized library systems, which process materials more cheaply than we do, flash loans back and forth more efficiently, provide better service to the constituent units, and reduce duplication everywhere.

The three insurgent positions could be enlarged on and various authorities quoted, but the essential positions are clear. Indeed, they all sound quite logical and appealing: better division of labor, better focusing of energies and resources, more responsive service. What possible case could be made for the status quo?

The Other Side

The opposition, consisting of equally distinguished scholars and analysts, says the above solutions are meretricious. The Hoover Commissions on federal reorganization studied the problem and recommended leaving everything just as it was. A growing body of public and library administrators conclude

that, in spite of minor tensions, the present mix of govern-
mental/national library tied to Congress is the best of
this possible world. To embrace any of the radical moves
could throw the baby out with the bath water. They work
from the following premises.

Funding

The reformers have always believed that the Library of
Congress would have access to larger sums of money with less
stress if it were a part of the executive branch. They point to
the fact that, while it is difficult to get an agency established,
once in being, it will run indefinitely and Congress will
tend to fund it adequately to accomplish its purpose. They hold
that if the national library were established as a national
treasure, just as in the case of our great museums and cultural
monuments, Congress would see to it that it could serve its
audiences as required. Furthermore, they contend that when
the appropriation committees deal with the executive agencies,
they distribute moneys by the hundreds of millions, leaving
it up to the agencies to use them effectively. They believe that,
with LC immediately under Congress's eye, it tends to be
nickled and dimed into mediocrity.

The conservators maintain that all this is quite at variance
with the facts. They hold that year in and year out Congress
has done marvelously well by the Library. While some institutions like the Smithsonian and the National Parks are frequently in favor, in just as many instances they are ignored for
years at a time. Furthermore, being a part of the executive
branch would subject the Library to all the fluctuations of
Presidential freezes, grade reductions, and denials of budget
increases to which all Administrative agencies are subject.

The conservators maintain that over the long pull, the
Library has consistently been the darling of the Congress, that
the legislature has always had a paternal feeling for its library,
and that many of its leaders have taken great pride in the fact

that in this democracy the people's representatives have been the patrons of the cultural heritage.

(This argument brings out some of LC's most intriguing stories—for example, the one about the time that Putnam asked Congress for $1.5 million to buy ten cases of incunabula, which included the Gutenberg Bible. No one was more surprised than Putnam when the money was appropriated with scarcely a demur. On the way back to the Library, still shaking his head in amazement, he met an arch-conservative congressman from an agrarian district who had voted in favor of the money. Putnam thanked him and then timidly asked, "Why?" He was told: "Mr. Putnam, we are a young country. We have no monuments. If we know where they are and can be got we ought to get 'em.")

The conservators' point here has been that with rare exceptions Congress has supported its own Library. If Congress would be equally sympathetic to "just another federal agency" could well be a dangerous "if" to test.

Leadership and Efficiency

Those who have embraced the conservative side of the argument maintain that many of the words used by the library profession to describe its stand sound very well, but the ideas they express simply would not work. They believe that the repeated cry that LC should "lead" or be the "center of a great library system" ignores the very delicate balance presently existing between LC and the nation's libraries—a balance which, if replaced by statutory leadership, would quickly move toward "government interference." Now LC and the library world get along reasonably well because each needs the other, and each has to be civil to achieve its own purposes. If the arrangement became *de jure*, the natural corrosion of even the best bureaucracy would begin to erode the common aims. Strong leadership and an aggressive national board would soon lead to firmer demands for uniformity for efficiency's sake. Once the official manner of operation was established for the good of all, demands for "better communication" would follow. Better communication would lead to a growing stream of memoranda, bulletins, official programs, orders, and then firm dicta with sanctions against the constituent that failed to play the what's-best-for-everybody game. The conservators would have us believe that it is almost impossible to think of a more independent, heterogeneous group than the nation's libraries, which reflect different audiences, incredibly diverse sources of funds and resources, and various purposes, traditions, and means of responding to their immediate clienteles. They believe that strong leadership at the center of a great system would shatter this fragile system and soon bring on either open warfare or withdrawal—or, most likely, domination by the largest elements in the system.

The conservators challenge the idea of efficiency at many levels. They question it in macrocosm under the above charge. They question it within the Library itself or with Congress under a different rationale. The idea of separate elements—a *congressional* library, or a *scholar's* library, or a *governmental* library—being able to serve their special audiences better is equally unreal, they say. One librarian compares the present missions of LC to the Ballantine Ale trademark of interlocking rings. He claims that the three rings symbolize the congressional/scholarly/library-world programs and audiences but that the overlapping center is the processing aspect. He believes that LC has developed the fastest, cheapest, most comprehensive processing techniques of any unit in the library world. He claims that because of LC's multifaceted acquisition systems, it can serve any constituency better than that constituency could serve itself. While any library could handle the "easy ones," the marginal, ephemeral, fugitive materials can be found and processed more quickly by a large, centralized processing unit than by fragmented, specialized ones.

Thus, he says, any detachments or splits off the present whole would weaken the then independent parts.

The Library Keeps the CRS from Concentrating on Congress

The conservators attack this concept on many counts. They maintain first that the CRS already is substantially independent of LC. It receives a separate budget, which "the Library" cannot touch. It already runs a separate library within a library, getting thousands of books and serials for itself while being saved the distraction of their acquisition, purchase, and processing, now supplied by the Library's processing services. If it wishes more responsive acquisition in public areas, all it has to do is add specialized acquirers itself or tell the processors what it needs.

The idea of getting the CRS back in the congressional establishment and congressional halls, the conservators believe, is a two-edged sword that would cut into the very area that the reformers thought they were securing: more independent, unpressured analysis. They note that with CRS housed in its present gray temple—psychologically detached from the cut and thrust of politics while physically connected to the intellectual, Olympian Library of Congress—it can examine volatile issues with minimal fear of partisan reprisal. It involves itself in congressional committee activities and the legislative process by going *to* this audience daily or weekly and then symbolically withdrawing to do its analysis. If CRS were placed in the very halls of Congress, it would find itself caught between the pressures of patronage and direction by strong chairmen or by the leadership itself. Its involvement in and evaluation of day-to-day issues, all of which matter deeply to someone, would make it a sitting target for the defeated, who would blame CRS for their loss and retaliate. Moving into the partisan area in order to be more receptive of needs might well cost CRS its image of a detached, objective, uninvolved source of accurate, honest data.

And the Intangibles ...

The conservators underscore the dangers of tampering with a good thing. They claim there are an unknown number of delicate balances in the present arrangement, which were probably achieved by accident and which it would be shocking if our generation were the one to destroy.

The conservators point to the almost miraculous sequence of able, honest men who have been Librarians of Congress for the past hundred years. The conservators wonder how much of this is luck, and how much reflects the pressures of the multiple elites and the demands placed on the job, all of which act as a process of natural selection. Specifically—if the Library of Congress were solely a governmental or legislative library, would the Librarianship have been a routine plum with which to reward partisan supporters or an easy place to put the current *éminence grise*? If LC had been solely a national library, would the office have become a battleground for representatives of the great research libraries, or the public libraries, or the school libraries, or possibly even the publishing world?

How much of its pre-eminence in the intellectual world stems from the unusual crossing of Presidential selection, congressional funding and oversight, and scholarly, professional standards and demands for excellence? If the institution into which the nation seems to have muddled were broken up or relocated to increase efficiency and response, might we reduce it to being "just another government agency" and destroy the tensions which were in fact the very source of its energies and drives to excellence?

The conservators want to be certain that some drastic administrative changes do not derive from resentment against a temporary incumbent, from the personality of someone seeking professional attention, from the search for better things simply for the sake of the search, or from the reflection of a passing administrative fad that revisionists will loudly challenge when the next generation of graduate students comes along.

QUERY

So where do we come out in this quite fundamental argument? I have tried to reflect the mixture of emotion and substance in the conflict, and I hope I have reflected the head-splitting dilemma. There was a time when the argument could be passed off with the simple "Ah, it's academic anyway. Congress would never give up the Library no matter what anyone says." This may no longer be true. To the continued astonishment of long-time Capitol Hill watchers, Congress seems to be increasingly short-tempered with obligations that are presently mixed blessings on the way to becoming more trouble than they are worth.

Ten years ago no one would have believed that the legislature would have written off the entire postal service with its limitless opportunities for rewards of political support. But all the postmasters, all the rural routes, all the new post offices are now selected and set by nameless civil servants in a barely governmental operation. Five years ago it seemed incredible that Congress would give away its two-centuries-old control over government salaries. The dreadful impact this has on budget balances plus the splendid opportunities to court gratitude in election years would seem to have kept this high on Congress's priority list. It has now passed it over to the President and all but washed its hands of the whole subject.

So Congress's relations with the Library cannot be taken for granted. If separation is wise, it might be achieved. If only an improved form of the status quo is best, care should be taken that Congress continues to receive sufficient benefits and that accumulated aggravations do not find the Library unloaded in a fit of pique.

So which way is best? Like so many of the dilemmas we have found in this library, the answer is not obvious. There are probably enough data already in; more study is not required. Just more wisdom.

Appendix A

Careers in the Library of Congress

The Library of Congress employs over 4,000 staff members who deal with almost every area of human thought. It requires specialists in music, science, all foreign languages, and politics. Indeed its areas of work are so varied that it offers ideal opportunities for anyone seeking challenging careers at any level of professional, technical, administrative, or clerical work.

The Library is part of the legislative branch of the government; this means that it works directly for Congress in contrast to the executive branch, which works for the President. Because of this relationship, the Librarian of Congress can select employees "solely with reference to their fitness for their particular duties" without reference to Civil Service registers. Applicants for positions in the Library are not required to compete in the Civil Service Commission's examinations, since the Library has its own merit system. The Library's positions are organized under the same position classification system that applies throughout the federal government, and its salary schedules are the same as those in the executive branch. The government-wide leave and retirement systems apply, and staff members are eligible for federal life and health insurance programs.

Almost all positions at the Library require that the employee be at least eighteen years of age and a citizen of the United States. Tests are given by the Library to applicants for clerical positions, and applicants applying for positions requiring a knowledge of specific foreign languages may be requested to pass a qualifying examination in the appropriate language. However, written examinations are not normally required for administrative or professional positions. As a rule, a professional position requires a college degree in an appropriate subject field, and graduates are requested to submit transcripts of their academic training when they apply.

Applicants must fill out and submit a Personal Qualifications Statement (Standard Form 171 of the federal government, available from the Library or most U.S. post offices). This may be sent to:

> Placement Office
> Library of Congress
> Room G-108, Main Building
> Washington, D.C. 20540

Lists of vacancies are posted daily throughout the Library and circulated to library schools, libraries, educational institutions, and various government agencies. Interviews are conducted in the Placement Office Monday through Friday from 10:00 A.M. to 3:00 P.M., but out-of-town applicants should not make special trips to Washington unless they are specifically requested to do so by the Library.

Types of Positions and Their Requirements

The Library needs qualified personnel in many hundreds of different jobs at all levels of education from high school and above. Some samples of the most frequent openings may be useful.

Librarians

The usual entrance grade for this position is GS-9 (paying $11,046 in 1972), and specialists in processing skills, reference work, or administration are used in large numbers. The basic requirements are graduation from a college or university of recognized standing plus a graduate degree from an accredited library school. Most librarian positions need a degree of specialization in an appropriate subject field, and in many cases the ability to use a foreign language is essential. Under certain circumstances, some special language or subject competence or appropriate experience in a reference or research library may be substituted for formal training in library science.

Subject Specialists

The Library needs many subject specialists (who need not be librarians) in such areas as economics, military affairs, the environment, technology, and engineering. Depending upon the job and the applicant's qualifications, a position of this nature may start at the GS-5 or 7 level ($7,319 to $9,053), or if a graduate degree is requested, at a GS-9 ($11,046).

Law

The Library requires many lawyers in such departments as the Law Library, the Copyright Office, and the Congressional Research Service. The usual entrance grade in these positions is the GS-9 or 11 ($11,046 to $13,309). The requirement for attorneys is graduation from a law school of recognized standing with either an LL.B. or J.D. The ability to write effectively is important for most positions of this nature, and membership in a bar is usually required for positions GS-11 or above.

Administrative Officers and Personnel Specialists

The entrance grade for these specialties is GS-5 or 7, or if a graduate degree is required, GS-9. These require graduation from a college or university of recognized standing, preferably with a degree in public or business administration.

Data Processing

The Library employs many programers and systems analysts whose positions fall within the GS-7, 9, or 11 entrance grades. Requirements include responsible experience in third-generation computer equipment and experience in assembly language or higher-level programing languages. There are also numerous positions of information systems specialists, which combine librarianship and the design of information systems as they relate to library processes.

Library Aides

The Library employs many arrangers, card drawers, and deck attendants at the GS-2 and 3 levels ($5,166 and $5,828). The positions generally require high school graduation as entrance minimums.

Library Technicians

Positions like accessioners, searchers, shelf listers, and filers can fall in the GS-4, 5, 6, or 7 entrance levels. These positions normally require two years of college and some experience appropriate to the entering grade level; a knowledge of a foreign language or some typing ability is often also requested.

Photoduplication Service

Positions in this unit call for such skills as microphotographer, photoduplication assistant, laboratory technician, and electrostatic print operator. Entrance levels here begin at GS-2 through GS-4, and requirements usually involve high school graduation and an interest in learning photographic equipment operation and processes.

Clerical Positions

Like all agencies of the federal government, the Library of Congress has a continuing (and usually unfilled) need for typists, stenographers, and secretaries whose skills fall in all grades from GS-2 through 7, and whose typing skills involve forty words a minute or more. In the case of stenographers, the ability to transcribe dictation given at up to eighty words a minute is also sought.

Appendix B

Librarians of Congress

John James Beckley	1802–1807
Patrick Magruder	1807–1815
George Watterston	1815–1829
John Silva Meehan	1829–1861
John G. Stephenson	1861–1864
Ainsworth Rand Spofford	1864–1897
John Russell Young	1897–1899
Herbert Putnam	1899–1939
Archibald MacLeish	1939–1944
Luther Harris Evans	1945–1953
Lawrence Quincy Mumford	1954–

A List for Further Reading

Selected by John Y. Cole

GENERAL

The Library of Congress has thoroughly documented its own activities in *Annual Reports* (1866–), *Quarterly Journal of the Library of Congress* (1943–), and the weekly *Information Bulletin* (1942–). The Library's publications, which frequently describe specific functions, collections, and services, are listed in the annual compilation, *Library of Congress Publications in Print*.

HAMER, ELIZABETH E. "Everybody's Library." *Library Journal,* v. 90, January 1, 1965, pp. 49–55.

"The Library of Congress in 1971." In *The Bowker Annual of Library and Book Trade Information, 1972*. New York: Bowker, 1972, pp. 25–30.

LORENZ, JOHN G., et al. "The Library of Congress Abroad." *Library Trends*, v. 20, January, 1972, pp. 548–76.

MEARNS, DAVID C. "A Fog-Laden Panorama of LC's Collections." *Library Journal*, v. 90, April 1, 1965, pp. 1600–07, and April 15, 1965, pp. 1834–40.

MUMFORD, L. QUINCY. "Two Decisive Decades: The Library of Congress— Twice as Fast." *American Libraries*, v. 3, July–August, 1972, pp. 769–73.

HISTORICAL DEVELOPMENT

COLE, JOHN Y. "Of Copyright, Men, and a National Library." *Quarterly Journal of the Library of Congress*, v. 28, April, 1971, pp. 114–36.

JOHNSTON, WILLIAM D. *History of the Library of Congress, 1800–1864*. Washington: Government Printing Office, 1904.

LACY, DAN. "The Library of Congress: A Sesquicentennial Review." *Library Quarterly*, v. 20, July, 1950, pp. 157–79; October, 1950, pp. 235–58.

MEARNS, DAVID C. *The Story Up to Now: The Library of Congress, 1800–1946*. Washington: Government Printing Office, 1947. (Also in the Library's 1946 *Annual Report*, pp. 13–227.)

SMALL, HERBERT, comp. *Handbook of the New Library of Congress*. Boston: Curtis & Cameron, 1899.

THE LIBRARY OF CONGRESS AS A NATIONAL LIBRARY

"The Bryant Memorandum on 'The Library of Congress' and the Report of the Librarian of Congress on the Bryant Memorandum." In the *Annual Report of the Librarian of Congress for 1962*, Washington: Government Printing Office, 1963, pp. 89–111.

CLAPP, VERNER W. "The Library of Congress and the Other Scholarly Libraries of the Nation." *College and Research Libraries,* v. 9, April, 1948, pp. 116–25.

EVANS, LUTHER H. "The Strength by Which We Live." *ALA Bulletin*, v. 44, October, 1950, pp. 339–45.

"The Library of Congress as the National Library: Potentialities for Service," in *Libraries at Large: Tradition, Innovation and the National Interest*, ed. by Douglas M. Knight and E. Shepley Nourse. New York: Bowker, 1969, pp. 435–65. (A statement prepared by the staff of the Library for the National Advisory Commission on Libraries.)

PUTNAM, HERBERT. "The Library of Congress as a National Library." *Library Journal*, v. 30, September, 1905, pp. C27–C34.

RANGANATHAN, S. R. "The Library of Congress Among National Libraries." *ALA Bulletin*, v. 44, October, 1950, pp. 355–57.

"Report of the Library of Congress Planning Committee." In the *Annual Report of the Librarian of Congress for 1947*, Washington: Government Printing Office, 1948, pp. 102–08.

SPOFFORD, AINSWORTH R. "The Function of a National Library." In *Handbook of the New Library of Congress*, comp. by Herbert Small. Boston: Curtis & Cameron, 1899, pp. 123–28.

ORGANIZATION AND ADMINISTRATION

BERRY, PAUL L. "The Space Race at LC." *Library Journal*, v. 90, August, 1965, pp. 3179–83.

EDLUND, PAUL, "The Continuing Quest: Care of LC's Collections." *Library Journal*, v. 90, September 1, 1965, pp. 3397–3402.

GOODRUM, CHARLES A. "Librarians to the Congress." *Library Journal*, v. 90, February 1, 1965, pp. 572–77. (The Congressional Research Service.)

MCFARLAND, MARVIN W. "Service to an Infinite Public." *Library Journal*, v. 90, March 1, 1965, pp. 1053–57. (The Reference Department.)

MACLEISH, ARCHIBALD. "The Reorganization of the Library of Congress, 1939–1944." *Library Quarterly*, October, 1944, pp. 277–315.

RINGER, BARBARA A. "No Place for Poetic License: The Copyright Office at LC." *Library Journal*, v. 90, July, 1965, pp. 2958–63.

ROGERS, RUTHERFORD D. "Administering a Giant: An Intimate View." *Library Journal*, v. 90, October 15, 1965, pp. 4303–10.

STRAUSS, WILLIAM S. "Laboratory for the World's Laws." *Library Journal*, v. 90, June 1, 1965, pp. 2504–08. (The Law Library.)

WALLACE, SARAH L. "Windows on the World: LC's Processing Department." *Library Journal*, v. 90, October 1, 1965, pp. 4005–12.

AUTOMATION AND PROCESSING ACTIVITIES

AVRAM, HENRIETTE D., LENORE S. MARUYAMA, and JOHN S. RATHER. "Automation in the Processing Department of the Library of Congress." *Library Resources & Technical Services*, v. 16, Spring 1972, pp. 195–239.

CLAPP, VERNER W. "The Greatest Invention Since the Title Page? Autobibliography from Incipit to Cataloging-in-Publication." *Wilson Library Bulletin*, v. 46, December, 1971, pp. 348–59.

CLAPP, VERNER W., and WILLIAM J. WELSH, eds. "The Age of Cronin: Aspects of the Accomplishments of John W. Cronin, Library of Congress, 1925–1968." *Library Resources & Technical Services*, v. 12, Fall 1968, pp. 385–405. (A symposium.)

LIEBAERS, HERMAN. "Shared Cataloging." *UNESCO Bulletin for Libraries*, v. 24, March–April, 1970, pp. 62–72; May–June, 1970, pp. 126–38.

REIMERS, PAUL R., and HENRIETTE D. AVRAM. "Automation and the Library of Congress, 1970." *Datamation*, v. 16, June, 1970, pp. 138–43.

SNYDER, SAMUEL S. "Automation at LC: Philosophy, Plans, Progress." *Library Journal*, v. 90, November 1, 1965, pp. 4709–14.

REFERENCE, RESEARCH, AND BIBLIOGRAPHIC SERVICES

BREITENBACH, EDGAR. "Picture Research at the Library of Congress." *Special Libraries*, v. 51, July, 1960, pp. 281–87.

BUTTERFIELD, LYMAN H. "An African Game Preserve: A Scholar's View of LC." *Library Journal*, v. 90, December 15, 1965, pp. 5333–40.

GABRIEL, RALPH H. "The Library of Congress and American Scholarship." *ALA Bulletin*, v. 44, October, 1950, pp. 349–51.

GOODRUM, CHARLES A. "The Reference Factory Revisited." *Library Journal*, v. 93, April 15, 1968, pp. 1577–80. (The Congressional Research Service.)

HAMER, ELIZABETH E. "The Library of Congress and Enchanced Bibliographical Services to History." In *Bibliography and the Historian*, ed. by DAGMAN H. PERMAN. Santa Barbara: ABC-Clio Press, 1968, pp. 57–67.

HILKER, HELEN-ANNE. "The Quiet Ferment." *Library Journal*, v. 90, May 1, 1965, pp. 2094–2103. (LC's role as a patron of the arts.)

JAYSON, LESTER S. ["The Congressional Research Service."] *Law Library Journal*, v. 63, November, 1970, pp. 542–49.

KUIPER, JOHN B. "Opportunities for Film Study at the Library of Congress." *Film Library Quarterly*, v. 1, Winter 1967–68, pp. 30–32.

LEAVITT, DONALD L. "Recorded Sound in the Library of Congress." *Library Trends*, v. 21, July, 1972, pp. 53–59.

METCALF, KEYES D. "The Library of Congress as a Bibliographic Center." *ALA Bulletin*, v. 44, October, 1950, pp. 352–54.

MUMFORD, L. QUINCY. "The Role of the National Library in Science and Technology, with Special Reference to the U.S. Library of Congress." *UNESCO Bulletin for Libraries*, v. 18, July–August, 1964, pp. 170–77, 192.

ROBERTS, MARTIN A. "The Library of Congress in Relation to Research." In U.S. National Resources Committee, *Research—A National Resource*, v. 1. Washington: Government Printing Office, 1938, pp. 233–55.

WITHERELL, JULIAN W. "Africana in the Library of Congress: The Role of the African Section." *Quarterly Journal of the Library of Congress*, v. 27, July, 1970, pp. 184–96.

Index